Growing Up Girls

AC / SS
Adolescent Cultures, School & Society

Joseph L. DeVitis & Linda Irwin-DeVitis
General Editors

Vol. 9

PETER LANG
New York ◦ Washington, D.C./Baltimore ◦ Boston ◦ Bern
Frankfurt am Main ◦ Berlin ◦ Brussels ◦ Vienna ◦ Canterbury

GROWING UP GIRLS

Popular Culture
and the Construction of Identity

EDITED BY
Sharon R. Mazzarella
and Norma Odom Pecora

PETER LANG
New York ◇ Washington, D.C./Baltimore ◇ Boston ◇ Bern
Frankfurt am Main ◇ Berlin ◇ Brussels ◇ Vienna ◇ Canterbury

Library of Congress Cataloging-in-Publication Data

Growing up girls: popular culture and the construction
of identity / [edited by] Sharon R. Mazzarella and Norma Odom Pecora.
p. cm. — (Adolescent cultures, school, and society; vol. 9)
Includes bibliographical references.
1. Teenage girls—Psychology. 2. Teenage girls—Attitudes. 3. Teenage girls
in popular culture. 4. Adolescent psychology. 5. Identity (Psychology).
6. Stereotype (Psychology) in mass media. I. Mazzarella, Sharon R. II. Pecora, Norma
Odom. III. Series: Adolescent cultures, school, and society; v. 9.
HQ798.G76   305.235—dc21   98-9272
ISBN 0-8204-4021-3
ISSN 1091-1464

Die Deutsche Bibliothek-CIP-Einheitsaufnahme

Growing up girls: popular culture and the construction
of identity / ed. by: Sharon R. Mazzarella and Norma Odom Pecora.
–New York; Washington, D.C./Baltimore; Boston; Bern;
Frankfurt am Main; Berlin; Brussels; Vienna; Canterbury: Lang.
(Adolescent cultures, school, and society; Vol. 9)
ISBN 0-8204-4021-3

Cover design by Lisa Dillon
Cover art consists of childhood photos of this book's contributors

The paper in this book meets the guidelines for permanence and durability
of the Committee on Production Guidelines for Book Longevity
of the Council of Library Resources.

Printed in the United States of America

Acknowledgments

We would like to acknowledge the support, both personal and professional, of many people. To begin, we thank those who have contributed essays to this book. Without their contributions and enthusiasm this book simply wouldn't be. They were patient with our requests for revisions, understanding about the inevitable delays, and unwavering in their support for this project. We also appreciate the support of the series editors, Joseph L. DeVitis and Linda Irwin-DeVitis, who recognized the value in our idea. In addition, we wish to acknowledge the hard work and guidance of our agent, Gordon Massman, who saw potential in a book prospectus sent to him so many years ago. And we thank Ellen Wartella who sent us down this road, and who continues to serve as a source of inspiration and support.

To my daughter who has taught me the meaning of girl power and who is my inspiration and ideal. And to Sharon, who gives my writing value and keeps me to a schedule.

Norma Pecora

To my mother who has taught me what it means to be a strong woman and who always supports me in my endeavors. And to Norma, who gives my writing value and who helps me to see that sometimes it's Okay *not* to keep to a schedule.

Sharon R. Mazzarella

Contents

Introduction

Norma Pecora and Sharon R. Mazzarella

In the late 1970s, feminist cultural studies scholar Angela McRobbie first observed how little of the scholarship on youth culture in Britain focused on teenage girls. In particular, she singled out seminal works on youth subcultures, Paul Willis's *Learning to Labour* and Dick Hebdige's *Subculture*, both of which virtually ignored teenage girls in the subcultures they studied. McRobbie's work, which brings together feminist and cultural theories, attempts to transcend this omission, and has paved the way for a growing cadre of feminist cultural studies scholars focusing on the culture of girls.

Cultural studies scholars are not the only ones who originally ignored adolescent females. The history of child and adolescent development research and theory in the United States is also a history of the development of boys. In her ground-breaking work, *In a Different Voice*, Carol Gilligan begins by acknowledging that influential theories of child and adolescent development—those advanced by Jean Piaget and Lawrence Kohlberg, for example—are based on male scholars studying male youth. It is problematic, she argues, to apply such theories to both male and female youth, since they often develop and mature in different ways.

With the publication of *In a Different Voice* in 1982, scholars in psychology and education began to focus on the distinctive development of adolescent girls. The work of Gilligan and her colleagues has been instrumental in shifting the focus away from adolescent development in general (as defined by boys) and onto the unique experience of adolescent girl development. Thanks to the work of both Gilligan and McRobbie, scholarly analysis of girls and girl culture has increased dramatically in the past two decades. This book seeks to contribute to the dialogue.

Throughout the 1990s, a growing and compelling body of research has documented the dramatic decline in self-esteem, body image, and academic performance experienced by girls at what Brown and Gilligan call "the crossroads," that point in time when girls are poised to enter adulthood. Girls who once had a strong sense of self turn their attention to peer acceptance and worries about body image (see American Association of University Women; Brown and Gilligan; Brumberg; Orenstein; Pipher; Sadker and Sadker). Their once-strong voices become silenced as they begin to recognize that our culture values conciliation over competition in women.

The popularity of Mary Pipher's 1994 best seller, *Reviving Ophelia* demonstrates that the general public as well as educators, public health professionals, and academics share these concerns about growing up girls. Pipher asserts that we have perpetuated a "girl poisoning culture" (12) which "smack(s) girls on the head in early adolescence" (23). She contends that girls today "are coming of age in a more dangerous, sexualized and media-saturated culture. They face incredible pressures to be beautiful and sophisticated, which in junior high means using chemicals and being sexual" (12).

Pipher's concerns are echoed by Joan Brumberg who asserts in the introduction to her 1997 thought-provoking history of American girlhood, *The Body Project: An Intimate History of American Girls*: "At the close of the twentieth century, the female body poses an enormous problem for American girls, and it does so because of the culture in which we live" (xvii). Brumberg documents the evolution of adolescent girls' concerns with their bodies such that girls currently make their bodies an all-consuming focus and, as a result, engage in numerous "body projects" in an attempt to both fit some culturally imposed beauty ideal and to communicate their identities to others. She argues that although girls no longer are literally restrained by corsets, as were their Victorian-era great-grandmothers, they are, however, figuratively restrained by social and cultural norms dictating an excessive emphasis on the female body.

While one could make the argument that in today's culture girls are socialized to believe it is more important to have a "perfect" body than a voice, it may be more appropriate to argue that our culture inundates girls with messages that their bodies are their voices—their identities. Many academics and child advocates, including Pipher and Brumberg, implicate popular culture in the crisis facing adolescent girls. For example, the children's advocacy organization Children Now sponsored a three-day conference in May, 1997, titled "Reflections of Girls in the Media." The event, attended by media industry executives, parents, educators, and teenagers, was organized to discuss how to better portray girls in a variety of media (Gardner 10–11).

When examining the messages presented to girls through various forms of popular culture, it becomes evident that issues of identity and body image are foregrounded in such a way that a girl's identity is intricately linked to her physical appearance.[1] From Barbie to *Cosmopolitan*, girls today grow up in a culture that places extreme emphasis on the female body—a body ideal that is unattainable for the majority of girls and women. This beauty/body obsession, according to Brumberg, starts at a younger and younger age with each succeeding generation. (Will any of us soon forget the sexualized pageant and publicity photos of six-year-old JonBenét Ramsey plastered across the front pages of numerous tabloids and mainstream publications following her murder in December, 1996?) In fact, according to Ingeborg O'Sickey, the products of popular culture targeted at very young girls have already begun to socialize them into an obsession with physical beauty and their bodies.

The intent of this book is to help us better understand the complex relationship between girls and these products of popular culture. Informed by a broad range of theoretical perspectives and employing a variety of methodologies, the essays in this collection address the ways in which mainstream culture "instructs" girls on how to become women—the ways in which the culture approves of growing up girls—and the ways some girls negotiate those messages. Specifically, these essays examine the messages mainstream culture gives girls about how to make sense of romance, sexuality, life experiences, body image, as well as gender and cultural identity, and the ways girls themselves negotiate these messages. In addition, these essays reflect our desire to strike a balance between studies of content, studies of audience, and personal reflections, and our desire to give often silenced voices the opportunity to be heard. All of the contributors are female, and several are young, emerging feminist scholars. Three are preadolescent/adolescent girls who have had conversations about these issues with their feminist scholar mothers. We believe this opportunity to hear the voices of preadolescent and adolescent girls, something that is unusual in academic literature, is important to our understanding. We let the girls and their mothers speak for themselves without imposing our own interpretations or analyses on their dialogue. Al-

though analysis of the lives of girls is valuable (Brown and Gilligan)
our goal for these conversations is to provide an opportunity for mothers and daughters to speak on their own terms.

The book opens as we eavesdrop on the first of these conversations. Feminist scholar Lana F. Rakow and her ten-year-old daughter,
Caitlin S. Rakow, discuss Caitlin's experiences with and feelings about
Barbie. This conversation provides us with our first indication that
girls might actively be resisting popular culture messages that they
find offensive and even dangerous.

In the second essay, Amy Bowles-Reyer takes an in-depth look at
coming-of-age teen romance novels published between 1963 and
1979—a period of rebirth for the feminist movement and a time when
feminist themes dominated much of the popular literature produced
for girls. Focusing on such themes as biological rights, sexual behavior
and rights, and sexual orientation, Bowles-Reyer shows how these
books (many of which are still popular today) "challenged the dominant cultural representations of femininity" and "offered their adolescent readers a language with which to articulate a new sexual identity."

While novels have long been popular with adolescent girls, perhaps
the best known series of books for girls has been Nancy Drew. Although, as Norma Pecora notes in her essay, Nancy Drew books have
been around for more than fifty years, her character changed little
until the mid-1980s, at which time the publisher introduced a new
Nancy Drew series focused not on solving mysteries but rather on
romance. In this essay, Pecora examines these new books as both the
results of industry trends—that is, a boom in teen romance novels—
and as a potential backlash—the rewriting of a previously strong character to reinforce an ideology of femininity that includes "romance
. . . glamour, and soap opera-like adventures but, most important, the
idea of woman-as-couple." The early Nancy Drews offered girls an
identity based on adventure and strength. The more recent series presents a character concerned with appearance and romance. This is
reinforced in yet another new series introduced in the early 1990s in
which Nancy Drew goes off to college. The setting changes, but these
are simply romance novels set on a college campus, reinforcing, yet
again, an identity bound by sex and sexuality.

In the second mother-daughter conversation, Sarah Eisenstein
Stumbar and her mother, Zillah Eisenstein, explore the experiences of
being a twelve-year-old girl and a feminist scholar mother in a male-
dominated culture. Specifically, mother and daughter reflect on the

American Girls Collection—a collection of dolls, books, clothes, and the like representing girls of various historical periods. While both agree the collection has its strengths and weaknesses, its contradictions keep mother and daughter talking about issues related to growing up a girl in a boy's culture.

Moving to a different form of print media targeted to adolescent girls, Sharon R. Mazzarella deconstructs the once-a-year prom issues of several teen magazines—YM, *Seventeen*, *'Teen* and *Your Prom*—to ascertain how these magazines define and commodify "the perfect prom." The overwhelming message of these magazines is that the prom is a life-defining experience for a young woman and that she must take every precaution necessary to make it all that it should be. Of course, the magazines and their advertisers are only too happy to suggest numerous commodity solutions to ensure she can "achieve her ultimate goal—the perfect prom."

Advertising in these teen girl magazines typically features beauty and health care products targeted to teenage girls. In her essay, Debra L. Merskin examines *Seventeen* to determine whether modern advertising messages about menstruation and feminine hygiene products perpetuate long-held myths of shame, secrecy, and uncleanliness. Merskin documents the continued prevalence of themes of "social humiliation," "impending discovery," and "secrecy" in advertising messages, and concludes that "modern advertisements for feminine hygiene products are compilations of centuries-old myths and taboos associated with controlling women's bodies."

While generally considered a "kid" movie, Disney's *Pocahontas* features an adolescent female heroine who may be a role model for girls, particularly Native American girls. In her essay, Amy Aidman conducts a critical reading of the film in an attempt to deconstruct its messages about race and gender. In addition, through group viewings and interviews with Native American and Euro-American preadolescent girls, she attempts to understand how they relate to the character. Based on her finding that *Pocahontas* is "prosocial yet problematic," Aidman concludes with a reaffirmation of the "importance of continuing to deconstruct the texts and subtexts of children's popular culture particularly as they relate to gender and race," and of "the necessity of talking with girls about their understanding of popular culture."

The final mother-daughter conversation finds Angharad N. Valdivia and her daughter, Rhiannon S. Bettivia, discussing "the place and role of popular culture in [the] everyday lived experience" of a twelve-year-old and her feminist mother. Specifically, Valdivia and Bettivia examine girl culture in schools, the types of popular culture products available to girls, and the differences between what kind of cultural products appeal to girls and what is available to them. While a major focus of this essay is mass-produced cultural products for girls, the authors conclude with a discussion of a growing trend among girls, creating their own cultural artifacts, a phenomenon in which girls are taking back their "voice."

The music industry has long been notorious for ignoring women at best, and for perpetuating blatantly misogynistic messages and images at worst. One response in recent years has been the "riot grrrl" movement, a major component of which is the proliferation of teenage girls forming their own bands and singing strong feminist lyrics. In addition, the success of 1997's Lilith Fair—a traveling music festival featuring female performers—evidences the commercial viability of female musical acts. But the importance of women/girls in music transcends feminist politics and commerce. In her essay, Carol Jennings shows how teenage girls use their music (in particular their ability to play traditionally "masculine" musical instruments) to create and communicate their identities. Despite the obstacles they face, the act of making music provides them with a form of personal resistance and a wealth of "pleasure and self-confidence"—a voice.

In her theoretically grounded, personal reflection on her youth spent moving between Canada, India, and the United States, Meenakshi Gigi Durham examines the role of media mythologies in constructing her own racial and gender identity. Durham recalls how she was both affected by, and resistant to, often paradoxical mediated and cultural messages prescribing appropriate behavior and appearance for women. She concludes with a call for "developing a new and radical politics of identity that would give adolescents some way to understand themselves and to frame their experiences between cultures."

Mary K. Bentley, in an attempt to understand the increased incidence of such high-risk health behaviors as those associated with eating disorders among adolescent girls, argues that contemporary culture presents girls with a narrowly defined ideal of physical attractiveness. Further, she proposes that this ideal is often in conflict with the physical changes girls undergo during puberty and adolescence, resulting in girls' attempts to regain "control" over their bodies, in part by attempting to control what and how they eat. Bentley argues that we need to offer girls alternative ways of relating to culture and to their bodies. Specifically, she advocates providing girls with "a critical lens" through which to deconstruct cultural myths, "safe spaces" to be, and "voice lessons" to assist them in expressing themselves.

There can be no denying that the mass media in the late 1990s have rediscovered the adolescent girl market. Magazines as diverse as *TV Guide* and *Spin* have devoted recent issues to "girl culture." Spurred by the popularity of the CD-ROM "Barbie Fashion Designer," more and more CD-ROMs are being produced for girls (Krantz 48). Although many tend to focus on stereotypically "feminine" pursuits such as fashion and beauty, more are beginning to incorporate less stereotypical content (Krantz 48–49). The new magazines *Jump* and *Jane* have joined the already-crowded teen girl magazine market. These two new magazines have promised content that differs from the traditional emphasis on dating, fashion, and beauty, although their early issues nonetheless still appear to focus on these topics. Even network television has begun to program more for adolescent girls and to show girls as strong and independent, unfortunately with TV girls who still meet narrowly defined standards of female beauty. Some examples are *Buffy the Vampire Slayer*, *Sabrina the Teenage Witch*, and *Clueless*, all of which were introduced during the 1996–97 television season. Perhaps the most interesting trend in popular culture is that of girls themselves getting into the act by designing their own Web sites, creating their own rock bands, and publishing their own zines. Clearly, in the late 1990s, there are more forms of mass media and popular culture content being produced for, about, and by pre-adolescent and adolescent girls than ever before.

As a whole, these essays indicate that popular culture—given certain exceptions, such as the 1970s coming-of-age novels studied by Bowles-Reyer—continues to present to girls stereotyped and potentially dangerous messages about a femaleness we hope to move beyond. Fortunately, though, several essays in this collection offer evidence that some girls may be actively resisting and deconstructing these messages and have begun to create their own alternative messages. Given the current content of popular culture, we take up Mary Bentley's call for providing girls with a "critical lens." We need to encourage and educate girls to resist, deconstruct, and negotiate these messages and in the process create a sense of self that speaks in a loud voice, much as Caitlin Rakow does when her mother encourages her to summarize her feelings about Barbie. "Ok. Barbie sucks. There we go."

Notes

1. Numerous studies have provided evidence that teen girl culture, particularly magazines and romance novels, present stereotypical notions of femininity— beauty, fashion, and romance (Christian-Smith, *Becoming a Woman*; Christian-Smith, "Romancing the Girl"; Duffy and Gotcher; Durham; Evans, Rutberg, Sather and Turner; Guillen and Barr; Mazzarella; McRobbie; Peirce, "A Feminist Theoretical Perspective"; Peirce, "Socialization of Teenage Girls"). There is also evidence that girls rely somewhat on this content (Duke and Kreshel) and that girls and young women are often negatively affected by such content (Levine, Smolak and Hayden; Martin and Gentry; Martin and Kennedy; Turner, Hamiliton, Jacobs, Angood, and Dwyer).

Works Cited

American Association of University Women. *Shortchanging Girls, Shortchanging America: A Nationwide Poll to Assess Self-Esteem, Educational Experiences, Interest in Math and Science, and Career Aspirations of Girls and Boys Aged 9–15.* Washington, D.C.: Author. ED 340–657. 1991.

Brown, Lyn Mikel, and Carol Gilligan. *Meeting at the Crossroads: Women's Psychology and Girls' Development.* Cambridge, MA: Harvard University Press, 1992.

Brumberg, Joan Jacobs. *The Body Project: An Intimate History of American Girls.* New York: Random House. 1997.

Christian-Smith, Linda K. *Becoming a Woman through Romance.* New York: Routledge, 1990.

———. "Romancing the Girl: Adolescent Romance Novels and the Construction of Femininity." *Becoming Feminine: The Politics of Popular Culture.* Eds. Linda G. Roman, Linda K. Christian-Smith, and Elizabeth Ellsworth. London: Falmer Press, 1988. 76–101.

Duffy, Margaret, and J. Micheal Gotcher. "Crucial Advice on How to Get the Guy: The Rhetorical Vision of Power and Seduction in the Teen Magazine *YM.*" *Journal of Communication Inquiry* 20 (1996): 32–48.

Duke, Lisa L., and Peggy J. Kreshel. "Negotiating Femininity: Girls in Early Adolescence Read Teen Magazines." *Journal of Communication Inquiry* 22 (1998): 48–71.

Durham, Meenakshi G. "Dilemmas of Desire: Representations of Adolescent Sexuality in Two Teen Magazines." *Youth and Society* 29 (1998): 369–389.

Evans, Ellis D., Judith Rutberg, Carmela Sather, and Charlie Turner. "Content Analysis of Contemporary Teen Magazines for Adolescent Females." *Youth and Society* 23 (1991): 99–120.

Gardner, Marilyn. "Role Models in Media: Girls Go on Dates, Boys Go to Work." *Christian Science Monitor* 2 May 1997: 12.

Gilligan, Carol. *In a Different Voice: Psychological Theory and Women's Development.* Cambridge, MA: Harvard University Press, 1982.

Guillen, Eileen O., and Susan I. Barr. "Nutrition, Dieting, and Fitness Messages in a Magazine for Adolescent Women, 1970–1990." *Journal of Adolescent Health* 15 (1994): 464–472.

Krantz, Michael. "A ROM of Their Own." *Time* 9 June 1997: 48–49.

Levine, Michael P., Linda Smolak, and Helen Hayden. "The Relation of Sociocultural Factors to Eating Attitudes and Behaviors among Middle School Girls." *Journal of Early Adolescence* 14 (1994): 471–490.

Martin, Mary C., and James W. Gentry. "Stuck in the Model Trap: The Effects of Beautiful Models in Ads on Female Pre-Adolescents and Adolescents." *Journal of Advertising* 26 (1997): 19–33.

Martin, Mary C., and Patricia F. Kennedy. "Advertising and Social Comparison: Consequences for Female Preadolescents and Adolescents." *Psychology and Marketing* 10 (1993): 513–530.

Mazzarella, Sharon R. "The 'Perfect' Prom: Teenage Girl Magazines and the Selling of the Prom." Paper presented to the annual meeting of the International Communication Association, Albuquerque, NM, May 1995.

McRobbie, Angela. *Feminism and Youth Culture: From Jackie to Just Seventeen.* Boston: Unwin Hyman, 1991.

Orenstein, Peggy. *Schoolgirls: Young Women, Self-Esteem, and the Confidence Gap.* New York: Doubleday, 1994.

O'Sickey, Ingeborg M. *"Barbie Magazine* and the Aesthetic Commodification of Girls' Bodies." *On Fashion.* Eds. S. Benstock and S. Ferriss. New Brunswick, NJ: Rutgers University Press, 1994. 21–40.

Peirce, Kate. "A Feminist Theoretical Perspective on the Socialization of Teenage Girls through *Seventeen* Magazine." *Sex Roles* 23 (1990): 491–500.

———. "Socialization of Teenage Girls through Teen-Magazine Fiction: The Making of a New Woman or an Old Lady?" *Sex Roles* 29 (1993): 59–68.

Pipher, Mary. *Reviving Ophelia: Saving the Selves of Adolescent Girls.* New York: Ballantine Books, 1994.

Sadker, Myra, and David Sadker. *Failing at Fairness: How America's Schools Cheat Girls.* New York: Scribner's, 1994.

Spin. Nov. 1997.

Turner, Sherry, L., Heather Hamilton, Meija Jacobs, Laurie M. Angood, and Deanne Hovde Dwyer. "The Influence of Fashion Magazines on the Body Image Satisfaction of College Women: An Exploratory Analysis." *Adolescence* 32 (1997): 603–614.

TV Guide. 25–31 Oct 1997.

Chapter 1

Educating Barbie

Lana F. Rakow and Caitlin S. Rakow

The following is a conversation between us, Lana Rakow, forty-five, and daughter Caitlin Rakow, ten, about "Barbie Culture" and how girls feel about Barbie. Not all girls want Barbies or think they are good for girls to play with.

LANA: Do you remember when you got your first Barbie? What do you remember about Barbies that you had?

CAITLIN: They were always dressed in stupid pink, short miniskirts stuff. Dumb things.

LANA: Do you remember having a lot of them?

CAITLIN: No. I always had like maybe four.

LANA: Do you know that I didn't want to buy you a Barbie ever? Do you know how you got your first Barbie?

CAITLIN: I think the first Barbie was Gymnast Barbie.

LANA: Yeah, and do you know who gave it to you?

CAITLIN: Dad. It was when we were moving. There was nothing left at home to play with so we went out to Toys R Us, and I wanted to buy a Barbie because I never had one before.

LANA: You had a Barbie before that.

CAITLIN: I did?

LANA: You got your first Barbie for your third birthday.

CAITLIN: From Grandma.

LANA: Well, it could've been Grandma. I can't remember, or it was, maybe Patrick, one of your friends from preschool. Somebody gave it to you and how do you think I felt?

CAITLIN: Like looooook . . . we'll just be throwing this in the trash now. (*laughs*)

LANA: *(laughs)* But I didn't.
CAITLIN: Oh, I had no idea.
LANA: It was hard for me because I didn't want you to have one. Why do you think I didn't want you to have one?
CAITLIN: Because it's stupid and sexist and has no point, it's not, I repeat, NOT the American dream. *(laughs)*
LANA: *(laughs)* But that's not what you thought at the time. You kinda wanted one, I think.
CAITLIN: Well, of course I did. I never had one before.
LANA: Yeah, but why would girls want one if it's stupid and pointless and not, you repeat, NOT the American dream?
CAITLIN: They don't want one. Their curiosity gets the better of them, and so they buy one. And they look at it, and they just kind of da da da da da da, and so all these other girls are getting Barbie's, so they think it's cool, and they keep on buying Barbie's, and pretty soon they're Barbie freaks.
LANA: How come you never became a Barbie freak?
CAITLIN: Because I'm not a little kid that's brainwashed and stupid.
LANA: Oh, you mean this is for an age group?
CAITLIN: Ah, yeah.
LANA: How old would you say girls are who like Barbie? If they like Barbies, when are they over it?
CAITLIN: Four through six.
LANA: Ages four through six? After that it's not cool any more, or what?
CAITLIN: It was never cool. *(laughs)*
LANA: Do you remember what you used to do with your Barbies?
CAITLIN: *(laughs)* No. What did I used to do with my Barbies?
LANA: You never played with them very much. And they never had clothes on. You always took their clothes off.
CAITLIN: *(laughs)* Why did I do that?
LANA: *(laughs)* I don't know. You never had clothes on any of your dolls.
CAITLIN: I think it was because I took them off and I started putting on my T-shirts and stuff on them and I couldn't ever find their clothes again.
LANA: That could be. You used to take their heads off, too. Do you remember that?
CAITLIN: *(laughs)* Yeah.
LANA: Why did you do that?

CAITLIN: It looks better without a head. (*laughs*)

LANA: (*laughs*) Just the body?

CAITLIN: (*laughs*) Well, no. The arms and maybe the legs are okay. No, just the arms.

LANA: Arms?

CAITLIN: I remember when me and my friend Carla took a Barbie head, like, off, and spent all night trying to split the body in half, as a friendship thing. (*laughs*)

LANA: (*laughs*) Like a wishbone?

CAITLIN: (*laughs*) Yeah.

LANA: (*laughs*) How awful. Well, what do you think of Barbie's body? Is it realistic?

CAITLIN: (*laughs*) Why are you asking me this?

LANA: Well, why do you think I didn't want you to have a Barbie?

CAITLIN: Because, it's sexist, it has no point, and I repeat, I repeat is NOT the American dream.

LANA: Well, why isn't it the American dream? What is the Amerian dream?

CAITLIN: To be highly respected? I don't know. . . . There is no American dream.

LANA: Oh.

CAITLIN: Everybody has their own dream.

LANA: Well, what about all the girls who dream that they want to be Barbie? Would that be a good thing?

CAITLIN: I wouldn't be surprised if they committed suicide when they were about fifty.

LANA: Really? Why?

CAITLIN: Because people don't want to see them anymore. They have nothing else to live on, because that was their career, that's what they chose to do (*laughs*), and now people don't want that any more. And so she's stuck broke, probably, and never heard of again.

LANA: Wow. So what is Barbie's career? What do you mean?

CAITLIN: Baking cookies and going shopping.

LANA: Does she even bake cookies? I don't remember.

CAITLIN: Yeah, there's this talking Barbie: "Let's bake cookies for the boys. Let's go shopping at the mall."

LANA: Oh dear. What about her body?

CAITLIN: What about it?

LANA: Do you think she has a normal body size?

CAITLIN: No, it's disgusting and humiliating.

LANA: That's why I didn't want you to have one.

CAITLIN: She has no body. It's too small. Her head is so big and her body is so small.

LANA: And look at how thin she is.

CAITLIN: She doesn't have a stomach.

LANA: She doesn't have a stomach, that's for sure. She doesn't have any flesh and bones, and she wears those high heels. Her feet are always up in the air, her heels are up in the air.

CAITLIN: Barbie learned how to fly early.

LANA: What do you mean?

CAITLIN: She hasn't had her foot on the ground since she was a little kid. (*laughs*)

LANA: (*laughs*) And her breasts, do you think they are proportional?

CAITLIN: (*laughs*) I think her breasts are preposterous.

LANA: Preposterous?

CAITLIN: They're almost as big as balloons.

LANA: When did you notice this about her? When you were really little did you think that?

CAITLIN: Yeah. And I think that the commercials are really stupid. "Let's go ride with Stacy on her bike." Wow. "Her legs can really move." Woo, woo, woo!

LANA: Well, why do you think Mattel makes Barbie?

CAITLIN: Because lots of little girls buy them.

LANA: It's a lot of stuff to buy, isn't it? So tell me about this Barbie song. Who does the song? And it's called the what?

CAITLIN: (*laughs*) Aqua. It's called the Barbie Girl Song. I like the song because it makes her look stupid.

LANA: Do you think that's why it's so popular—because it makes fun of her?

CAITLIN: I don't know. (*laughs*)

LANA: So little girls like to play with Barbie, but bigger girls like you like the song because it makes fun of Barbie?

CAITLIN: Yeah.

LANA: So what do you think boys think about Barbie?

CAITLIN: They don't think about Barbie.

LANA: They don't? Don't you think girls who think about Barbie are thinking about boys thinking about them?

CAITLIN: Girls that age don't think about that.
LANA: Well, but don't you think girls over six years old play with Barbie?
CAITLIN: Well, yeah. A couple of airhead girls, maybe.
LANA: So, Barbie is not a big deal anymore. Are there some girls in your class yet who still like Barbie?
CAITLIN: No.
LANA: By your age it's all over?
CAITLIN: I hope so.
LANA: And you think that a lot of girls your age think that Barbie is sexist?
CAITLIN: Yeah. Like kids our age. If anybody knew they had a Barbie they would be outcasts for the rest of their life.
LANA: Really?
CAITLIN: I'm just exaggerating. (laughs)
LANA: But, yes? And that's not just because it's not cool, but because girls your age know better about women?
CAITLIN: It's like saying, "Like, play with Barbie, and Sesame Street, and like, Barney."
LANA: Oh, so it's little kids' stuff. It's not 'cause they think it's sexist.
CAITLIN: Well, yeah, that too.
LANA: Well, what do girls your age like? Do they like things that are, what? For girls? Good for girls?
CAITLIN: What do you mean good for girls?
LANA: That aren't sexist?
CAITLIN: Well, we like Nintendo, Sega, I don't know . . . boys. (laughs)
LANA: Boys? (laughs)
CAITLIN: Well, we certainly don't like Barbie.
LANA: Yeah, but. What about liking boys? Do you think you learn that from liking Barbie?
CAITLIN: No. It comes natural. Puberty. I don't know.
LANA: What about boys? What do they like?
CAITLIN: I don't know. Little kids like Batman and Superman and stuff. But certainly the kids on the commercials our age don't play with them at all.
LANA: Do you think parents should not get their little girls Barbies?
CAITLIN: I think they should not get the Barbies.
LANA: You don't? What would that do to help anything?

CAITLIN: They would probably become president of the United States. Maybe. Probably not. But probably.

LANA: You think it has any effect on girls?

CAITLIN: Well, yeah. It's not like girls are going to go, "Hey, we don't have Barbie. Let's go become homemakers."

LANA: They're not going to do that, or they are?

CAITLIN: No. They aren't going to do that.

LANA: So they might do something instead like, let's become president. But you had Barbies, and you might become president.

CAITLIN: That's because I took off their heads.

LANA: (*laughs*) And why did you do that and the other girls didn't?

CAITLIN: Umm . . . because she has been my sworn enemy, ever since, umm, I don't know. Ever since . . . I don't know. But I just always hated her.

LANA: Are you different from most other girls. Or were you different then?

CAITLIN: No, not really.

LANA: Do you think that I had any effect on that?

CAITLIN: No, not really.

LANA: Do you think that I had any effect on whether you think she's sexist or not?

CAITLIN: No, not really. (*laughs*)

LANA: Do you think that my being a feminist had any effect on that?

CAITLIN: No, not really. (*laughs*)

LANA: Well, are you a feminist?

CAITLIN: Yeah. Really. (*laughs*)

LANA: Well, how did you become a feminist then?

CAITLIN: I don't know. Just cause.

LANA: But you're the kind of girl that likes to wear a T-shirt that says, "Girls Rule."

CAITLIN: Yeah.

LANA: Yeah. Do you think girls are different now than they used to be? More assertive?

CAITLIN: Yeah, they aren't that much of an airhead now. Even though there are some girls who are airheads.

LANA: How many different kinds of girls are there? About your age.

CAITLIN: Airheads. Athletic braggy girls. There are girls that hate stuff. (*laughs*)

LANA: Hate stuff? Like what stuff?

CAITLIN: Like always depressed. They like playing depressed or
          something, I don't know. They just have a low self-esteem.
          Well, it's not that bad as you think. It's like Daria.

LANA: I don't know who Daria is. Is Daria a singer or something?

CAITLIN: No, Daria is a cartoon character on MTV. She's depressed
          all the time, but she likes it.

LANA: Are there boys who are depressed all the time?

CAITLIN: No. They go around bragging about how athletic they
          are.

LANA: Are you one of these groups?

CAITLIN: You can just put down, "other."

LANA: And they're the kind that wears the "Girls Rule" T-shirts?

CAITLIN: Umm . . . I guess.

LANA: You know, just recently you had a Barbie doll that was
          given to you and you did something to it. What did you do
          to it?

CAITLIN: (laughs) I almost cut off a collector Barbie's hair and hog
          tied her and slapped a paper face on her with a frown and
          X for eyes, and blood trickling out of her mouth and hung
          her from my cabinet knob. (laughs)

LANA: And how did I feel about that? Do you think it made me a
          little worried about you?

CAITLIN: I don't know. (laughs)

LANA: Should I be worried that you are going to become a vio-
          lent person?

CAITLIN: I'm not going to become a violent person. It's just ex-
          pressing my feelings for Barbie because you can't talk to
          her.

LANA: Really. That she . . . what? This is symbolic murder? You
          know there is a lot of violence against women. This con-
          cerns me.

CAITLIN: That's not what this is. She's NOT a woman. You can't
          hurt a toy.

LANA: You really hate Barbie that much?

CAITLIN: Well, it's just fun to do to her.

LANA: Because she's what?

CAITLIN: Because she gives us girls a bad name.

LANA: You don't like having Barbie out there standing for girls?

CAITLIN: I mean, if there were no Barbie, boys would probably be
          going, "Oh yeah, good job. Way to, like, smash down that

guy or run to home base" or something. We wouldn't need girls' special rules when we play boys against girls in basketball.

LANA: You have special rules in gym? Why do they do that?

CAITLIN: I don't know.

LANA: So you think there's some link between this Barbie out there and girls? What other things affect . . .

CAITLIN: Well, no, it just affects them the way men think about women. About airheads and bimbos, "Oh, I broke a nail!" and stuff. You know there are some people out there like that.

LANA: Then the question is how did they get like that? Why are they like that?

CAITLIN: They're just natural snobs.

LANA: Well, I don't know if it's natural. They learn it somewhere, don't they?

CAITLIN: Barbie's very rare, I'll tell you that. Even though I saw these two sisters that called themselves the Barbie twins. They liked Barbie and dressed up like Barbie and they dyed their hair blond and stuff.

LANA: So, I shouldn't worry about you anymore?

CAITLIN: Anymore? What do you mean?

LANA: Well, I used to worry that if you had Barbies . . . that . . . you know . . . here I am a feminist and my daughter had Barbies?

CAITLIN: Mom, I had four Barbies. Wow.

LANA: And you took their heads off. (*laughs*)

CAITLIN: (*laughs*)

LANA: OK. So here's a question. Do we get your little brother guns, or do we get him Barbies?

CAITLIN: Neither.

LANA: Neither one? So what if someone gives him a gun for his birthday?

CAITLIN: Oh, brother. Throw it in the trash.

LANA: So I should've thrown that Barbie in the trash, too, maybe, instead of letting you have it?

CAITLIN: Well, not really. If you didn't let me have it I would probably be going, "What's this? Ooh! Barbie!"

LANA: So what's the solution? How do we get rid of Barbie?

CAITLIN: I'm afraid it's too late. She's already taken over the world.

LANA: (*laughs*) She took over our world. And that's why you did what you did to her? Trying to get rid of her symbolically?

CAITLIN: Yeah. (*laughs*)

LANA: What if girls all got together and said, "No more Barbie. It's not good for girls?"

CAITLIN: We could put on a strike, like, if you buy Barbie, we know where you live. (*laughs*)

LANA: (*laughs*) Well, that will inspire everyone. Is there any way to break this cycle?

CAITLIN: No. Probably not. Of course, little kids are pretty easy to persuade. You know, if you want a swing and they're on a swing you just say, "Get off!" and they get off. (*laughs*)

LANA: (*laughs*) But is there anything you can do? Can you convince them—nicely—"You know, have you ever thought about Barbies and what they stand for?" Maybe parents should do something. Should they get together and try to stop Barbie?

CAITLIN: Mom, I do not know what parents need to do, or what they should do. I'm just here because you asked me to do this, okay?

LANA: Well, sometimes kids have good answers to things and maybe a good solution. Do you think there are other things in popular culture that are as bad as Barbie?

CAITLIN: Yeah. But what do you mean, like what?

LANA: Oh, stuff on TV and commercials and stuff for sale and music and games and clothes . . .

CAITLIN: Well, what's wrong with fun games and awesome toys? It's not popular culture. Mom, kids buy things and they get popular because they're awesome, they're cool. (*laughs*)

LANA: Well, couldn't you say that about Barbie? You buy them, and it's awesome and cool, and all those girls go, "It's awesome and cool!"

CAITLIN: They don't have a life. Let's put it that way. They probably just switched on the TV for the first time in their life and they saw Barbie and they say, like, "Yeah! I guess if the TV says so I can go and buy one. That's really cool." And when they get older they find out they have a mental problem.

LANA: Do you really think that girls who think a lot about Barbie end up having problems later?

CAITLIN: They're definitely, one, very insecure or, two, paranoid. I have no idea which one.

LANA: Well, is there anything else you'd like to say about Barbie?

CAITLIN: No. I know everything there is to know about Barbie.

LANA: And your conclusion is?

CAITLIN: What? Haven't I like made that clear?

LANA: Maybe you'd just like to summarize it.

CAITLIN: OK. Barbie sucks. There we go.

LANA: That would say it all, wouldn't it? And here we are, signing off, September 28, 1997, at 9:05 p.m.

Chapter 2

Becoming a Woman in the 1970s: Female Adolescent Sexual Identity and Popular Literature

Amy Bowles-Reyer

This essay focuses on a new type of literature aimed at girls that emerged in the 1970s. This coming-of-age genre in Young Adult Literature presents a vision of womanhood that encourages a new kind of female identity, emphasizing sexual knowledge and sexual expression. I investigate how female sexuality is expressed and articulated in seven young adult texts. The theme threading its way throughout this popular literature is that female adolescents should have more power and control over their bodies and more authority to make choices about them. In all seven books, the female protagonist learns to assert her identity by gaining confidence in her sexual knowledge and understanding.

Influencing these young adult books was a plethora of adult literature, both fiction and nonfiction, produced in the 1970s that encouraged women to explore their sexual feelings and to demand sexual pleasure from their partners. For example, the feminist messages in the first publication of *Our Bodies, Ourselves* (1970) by the Boston Women's Health Book Collective, Erica Jong's *Fear of Flying* (1973), Nancy Friday's *My Secret Garden* (1973), and Germaine Greer's *The Female Eunuch* (1970), among others, encouraged women's sexual subjectivity and exploration and provided a language for female sexual maturation and physiology. The messages in this adult popular literature appeared in some of the adolescent popular fiction produced during this period, such as Judy Blume's *Are You There God? It's Me, Margaret* (1970) and *Forever* (1975), Norma Klein's *It's Not*

What You Expect (1973), and Bette Greene's *Summer of My German Soldier* (1973) and *Morning Is a Long Time Coming* (1978). These young adult books promote sexual exploration and pleasure and provide a language for female sexual maturation.

My argument is that the feminist adolescent fiction produced during the early years of the contemporary women's movement offers the possibility of a new sexual identity for adolescent readers. Popular adolescent fiction informed by the women's movement empowers girls by validating that they can and should have sexual feelings and by providing them with a language to express their sexuality. These viewpoints emerged from and complemented feminist rhetoric, though the adolescent fiction writers did not identify the viewpoints as feminist. The authors present a sexually informed viewpoint as the "norm" in these novels.

The books I have chosen to analyze share the following characteristics: (1) they were published between 1963 and 1979 (Christian-Smith 4); (2) they encourage female readers to consider the pros and cons of sexual exploration while acknowledging that girls have sexual feelings; (3) they provide a language for sexual maturation; and (4) they attempt to articulate a sexual identity for their female character. The seven popular books are Judy Blume, *Are You There God? It's Me, Margaret* (1970); Norma Klein, *It's Not What You Expect* (1973); Bette Greene, *The Summer of My German Soldier* (1973); Judy Blume, *Forever* (1975); Rosa Guy, *Ruby* (1976); Richard Peck, *Are You in the House Alone?* (1976); and Bette Greene, *Morning Is a Long Time Coming* (1978).

Feminist writer Kate Millet argues in *Sexual Politics* (1970) that the way women are represented in literature has an impact on the way they define themselves as subjects in their own lives. The young adult books analyzed in this essay present adolescent girls and young women at different stages of becoming women. Each of these protagonists defines for herself how she will negotiate this process in the face of new options available to women. These "new options" however, are overstated in many of these books underscoring a utopian style of writing common to these texts.

The young adult texts also follow the historical patterns of the popular literature of the women's movement. The first phase of feminist fiction, developed around the late 1960s and early 1970s, is characterized by its presentation of events that epitomize what feminism is fighting against: prohibitive notions of sex, unplanned pregnancy, lim-

ited access to abortion, and premature marriage. This type of literature usually relies on a first-person linear narrative and emphasizes
literary realism. These are novels of awakening where the heroines
learn about their bodies and their sexuality. This includes from this
sample *Are You There God? It's Me, Margaret* and *Summer of My
German Soldier*. The second phase of feminist fiction, starting roughly
from the mid-1970s, offers what Maria Lauret describes in *Liberating
Literature* as a feminist subject that is already "fully constituted." This
permits feminism to be directly investigated in these texts and the
feminist subject to become an agent of change in her life and in others'.

Prevalent in both the Young Adult Literature and the feminist adult
literature is what Lauret describes as the trope of "what if." Texts
common to literature of the women's movement often present utopian
feminist scenarios as if the battles of the women's movement had already been won. In contrast with these idealistic settings, these young
adult books also feature a realist style of writing. These texts are written in a plain language utilizing the slang and colloquial style familiar
to adolescent girls, making them believable and identifiable to adolescent readers. While sexual awakening is featured in this second phase,
the heroine is farther along in the process of sexual awareness. For
example, she may not have had sex at the beginning of the novel but
she already knows a lot about it. This includes *It's Not What You
Expect* and *Forever*. A third type of feminist literature most common
in the second phase differs from the other two in its presentation of a
feminist subjectivity in transition and explores the emotional ramifica-
tions of living a feminist lifestyle. These include *Ruby, Are You in the
House Alone?*, and *Morning Is a Long Time Coming*.

The feminist assertion that the "personal is political" encouraged
both the popular writers of the women's movement and the feminist
young adult authors to combine female concerns and genres with a
feminist aesthetic of counterculture writing. A significant similarity
between the adult and the young adult mode of writing was the new
open ending. The male-coming-of-age novel usually traces a physical
journey during which the male protagonist sets out to find himself and
his calling in life. He is usually successful in his endeavors. The female
protagonists are in a state of confusion and entrenched in a complicated process of self-awareness that is not yet resolved by the end of
the novel. This dramatic change in popular writing for women and
girls eschewed the closure so common to the male-coming-of-age genre
and emphasized a psychic journey instead of a physical one. The femi-

nist protagonist may never physically leave her familiar surroundings, but instead pursues a psychological journey that requires intimate connections with other characters.

As my argument focuses on female sexuality in these texts, I will first explain the dominant cultural values about adolescent female sexuality to establish what these books are refuting. The code of sexuality in traditional romance fiction is described by Linda Christian-Smith in *Becoming a Woman through Romance* as limiting the heroine's behavior. She finds that "for heroines, sexuality involves a great deal of repression, very little pleasure, and considerable danger" (31). These female limitations are either not as extreme or overtly challenged in the feminist adolescent popular literature that I will examine.

Christian-Smith describes how the code of sexuality is constructed in teen romance novels: "In the context of the novels, sexuality refers to girls' acquisition of knowledge about their bodies as well as about their relation to them. Closely connected to this relation are the rules surrounding the use of the body, rules that involve not only prohibitions and constraints, but also pleasure and desire. Power enters the picture in the form of girls' struggles to control their bodies and define what sexuality means to them" (31). In the more traditional young adult popular literature analyzed by Christian-Smith, the teen protagonists are prevented from learning about their bodies and defining their own sexuality by their parents, boyfriends and male friends, teachers, and other authority figures. By being denied education about their bodies, girls learn to feel shame and to remain silent about them. These female characters are also taught to depend on others, usually authority figures like parents or doctors, to make decisions for them about how to use their bodies.

There are two general formulas by which the female characters challenge the pervasive constraints found in traditional texts to achieve sexual knowledge and liberation. One is the relationship between the protagonist and a more precocious and sexually informed "other girl" or best friend who provides information and guidance about her sexually developing body and desires. The second formula gives us a liberated protagonist who lives in a world that either is already liberated or is on a mission to change the world to fit her liberated ideas. These types of coming-of-age formulas rely more on the mentor/student relationship between girls of the same age rather than the more standard older mentor who educates his or her younger student about the ways of the world. In this sense, these young adult feminist novels challenge male canonical texts by questioning the necessity of an es-

tablished hierarchy in the learning process. The sexually ignorant protagonist versus the sexually informed and confident "other girl" is
emblematic of the relationship between the feminist authors of the
1970s such as Erica Jong, and their female readers. What is created in
these texts, however, is an informal social hierarchy of those female
adolescents with sexual knowledge and confidence over those who
lack it.

While the intentionality of these young adult authors is beyond the
scope of this essay, it didn't take them long to write books that addressed the concerns being generated by feminists. As feminists debated the validity of women's sexual liberation and the possibility of a
heterosexually liberated woman, some very astute young adult authors
set out to educate adolescent girls about how to become sexually liberated. In these books the adolescent heroines learn to feel more confident about their bodies and their sexuality and to understand and
assert their rights as young women. By providing information about
female sexual development, sexual expression and, rarely, sexual orientation, these authors offered their adolescent readers a language
with which to articulate a new sexual identity.

Messages about Girls' Biological Rights

The young adult books analyzed in this section share many of the
same conceptions about the importance of female body awareness
and education: girls have the right to demystify their bodies, to learn
about their anatomy, to choose to use birth control, and to choose to
have an abortion. The authors unveil the emotional and physical process of puberty and sexual maturation by articulating the kinds of
reactions teens can expect from themselves, their friends, parents,
and members of the opposite sex. The authors of *Our Bodies, Ourselves* describe a similar kind of philosophy: "This is an exciting kind
of learning, where information and feelings are allowed to interact. It
has made the difference between rote memorization and relevant learning, between fragmented pieces of a puzzle and the integrated picture,
between abstractions and real knowledge" (2–3). Young adult authors
of the 1960s and 1970s brought the empowering sexual ideologies of
the women's movement to teen and preteen girls.

Puberty Rights: Breast Development and Menstruation
Judy Blume, the most widely read author in this study, explores breast
development and menstruation in *Are You There God? It's Me, Mar-*

garet by discussing what girls can expect physically as well as emotionally. She is one of the few best-selling young adult authors, along with Paula Danziger and Norma Klein, to write stories about puberty. By encouraging female sexual independence at a young age, Blume directly challenges generational gender roles and rules about female sexuality. Blume raises issues of sexual knowledge, power, and hierarchy between preteen girls that your standard medical text book or science class does not address. She reinscribes a feminist agenda of body image and sex education for women into a comprehensible language for adolescent readers. In Blume's novels, girls have a right to privacy about their bodies and deserve to have their decisions respected. For example, girls have the right to decide when they want to start wearing a bra or learning about menstruation. If girls are educated about both the medical facts and the emotional experiences, then they are able to have confidence in themselves and their bodies.

Are You There God? It's Me, Margaret is a story about Margaret Simon, who moves to a new town in New Jersey just before her twelfth birthday. She quickly makes new friends who introduce her to a social world focused on puberty and boys. These female characters seek companionship in negotiating the difficulties of adolescent development. Margaret forms a club with Nancy and two other girls from school called the Pre-Teen Sensations. They have to wear bras to the meetings and tell each other when they start menstruating. Gretchen, one of the club members, adds the rule that each girl has to say what her first period "feels like." The girls have an understanding of menstruation from science class but still don't know what to expect. Underneath, each girl wants to feel a part of a group: "Are you there God It's me, Margaret. I just told my mother I want a bra. Please help me grow God. You know where. I want to be like everyone else" (37). Blume demonstrates that these gatherings provide an opportunity for girls to share their feelings and experiences about their sexuality and to begin to form a language with which to express who they are as a sexual person. This ritual of gathering as a group to discuss issues relevant to their preteen lives, namely sexual development and boys, signifies the necessity of female camaraderie in negotiating the information and messages available to them about becoming women. This type of gathering also mirrors the consciousness-raising groups of the women's movement in its agenda of female bonding against an oppressive force: for adult feminists, the patriarchal social structure; and for teen girls, the adult world.

While these girls do want to develop sexually into women, they do not want the objectification that accompanies this process. Their relationship with the character Laura Danker underscores this female sexual predicament. Laura, a girl in Margaret's class, is more physically developed than the others. The rumors about her sexual activities are integrally related to her advanced breast development. In the novel, the sexual stigma of having big breasts at a young age involves the suspicion among her schoolmates that she is having sexual relations with boys. In this novel, while adolescent girls covet physical development, they do not want to appear more developed than anyone else. To be more physically mature makes you sexually suspect and to be less means that you are still a child. The pressure to conform is very strong. The girls' attentiveness to Laura's behavior reveals their fascination with her sexuality: "Laura Danker wore a sweater to school for the first time. Mr. Benedict's eyes almost popped out of his head. Freddy the Lobster noticed too. He asked me, 'How come you don't look like that in a sweater, Margaret?' . . . Very funny, I thought. I wore sweaters every day . . . Even if I stuffed my bra with socks I still wouldn't look like Laura Danker. I wondered if it was true that she went behind the A&P with Evan and Moose. Why would she do a stupid thing like that?" (62). The association with Laura's body and a mythic "advanced sexuality" reveals that her body has become contested terrain for the girls over their own apprehension about their developing bodies and subsequent sexual responsibilities.

Blume critiques this conformity by giving Laura a voice in the text. In an argument between Laura and Margaret, Laura expresses the harm her false reputation has caused her: "Do you think it's any fun to be the biggest kid in the class? . . . Think about how you'd feel if you had to wear a bra in fourth grade and how everybody laughed and how you always had to cross your arms in front of you. And about how the boys called you dirty names just because of how you looked" (117). Margaret discovers that Laura is a devout Catholic with strong religious values, the antithesis of her reputation at school. Margaret realizes the destructiveness of her judgments against Laura and understands that Laura's body does not represent who she is as a person.

In the following scene, Margaret is role playing about her future mature body. In this intensely personal scene, Margaret tries on her new bras without the limiting presence of her mother in the fitting room. She stuffs the bra with socks to see what she will look like when she develops breasts: "I took off my dress and put on the bra. I fastened it first around my waist, then wiggled it up to where it belonged. I threw my shoulders back and stood sideways. I didn't look any different. I took out a pair of socks and stuffed one sock into each side of the bra, to see if it really grew with me. It was too tight that way, but I liked the way it looked. Like Laura Danker" (44). By referencing Laura Danker, Blume's symbol for a prematurely sexualized and stigmatized female adolescent, Blume articulates the fractured adolescent female sexual identity. This fractured identity contains the desire to physically develop more quickly but also the fear of the consequences of inheriting a woman's body too soon.

Playing roles to unearth the unknown about sexual maturation is an empowering practice in Blume's novel, not unlike the gesture of role playing in carnival described by Mary Russo when she argues that carnival practices both reinforce and challenge gender roles at the same time (215). Carnival offers the possibility of role playing and identification with behavior that opposes the rigid gender roles of the current status quo. In the novels, role playing validates the practice of self-examination for female readers who may not know that this is "normal." Along with Russo, I believe that activities like carnival (or "bra stuffing") where lasting social change is usually not the outcome, can provide a type of social transformation. If change is only defined by a drastic shift in the status quo, then much of the transformative potential for the practice of carnival is eluded. In her self-examination and speculation about what is happening to her maturing body, Margaret actively involves herself as an agent in this process rather than a passive spectator. She wants to control the psychological aspects of her breast development and to prepare herself for the physical transformation before it occurs.

When one of the girls in the group gets her period, the opportunity arises for "real" and relevant information on menstruation. This information comes not from medical authorities or psychiatrists but from girls themselves. This feminist privileging of "real" information is well established in women's popular literature and in consciousness-raising groups. When Gretchen recounts her story to the other girls they are disappointed by its lack of drama. Blume demystifies and naturalizes menstruation by situating it as an anticlimactic event in the story. When Margaret finally gets her period at the end of the book, she knows what to expect. She concludes the story by saying, "How about that! Now I am growing for sure. Now I am almost a woman!" (148). She does not yet call herself a woman but considers this the beginning of the process.

This notion of process is further reinforced through the character Nancy, who functions as the more sexually informed "other girl" in the book. She is the organizer and leader of the Pre-Teen Sensations. She teaches the girls exercises to speed up their breast development and is the most physically developed of the group. She instigates group discussions about female anatomy and encourages the group to tell each other "everything." She is also highly competitive and angry that she is not the one to menstruate first. In an interesting turn of events, Nancy lies to the other girls about getting her period. Since it is her role to lead the way in these matters, she feels that it is imperative as group leader to also menstruate. Margaret is stunned to discover Nancy's secret and begins to realize that this competition over menstruation is ridiculous. Menstruation is revealed to be only the beginning of a long process of womanhood, not an end in itself.

Are You There God? It's Me, Margaret is typical of the first phase of feminist literature that came out around the late 1960s and early 1970s in that it presents a string of events that feminism is fighting against: lack of relevant information on menstruation, patronizing adults removed from girls' need for sexual knowledge, representations of women as sexual objects, and prohibitive notions of sex. Margaret goes through the process of sexual awakening by learning about her developing body before and during its transformation. This book is written in a first person linear narrative and emphasizes literary realism. Also typical of this kind of feminist writing is the open ending where Margaret recognizes that she is only beginning to achieve the womanhood that she thought would accompany menstruation.

Reproductive Rights: Birth Control and Abortion

Two novels, Judy Blume's *Forever* and Norma Klein's *It's Not What You Expect*, reveal the informative and utopian style of feminist writing so common in adult feminist fiction in the mid-1970s. These books explore birth control and abortion as legitimate options for adolescent females.

Blume's novel *Forever* stands out because of its explicit education about birth control and gynecology and how young women can make informed decisions about their bodies. Katherine, the protagonist of the novel, becomes sexually active in her relationship with Michael, her first love. After they start dating, Katherine's grandmother, a feminist activist with NOW and Planned Parenthood, sends her some brochures on birth control and abortion. Blume clearly sends the message that girls need to be informed about birth control: "When I'd finished I thought, well, I can start a service in school I know so much, which might not be a bad idea, considering there is a girl in my gym class who, until this year, never knew that intercourse was how you got pregnant, and she's already done it!" (Blume 129). The next morning Katherine makes an appointment to go to Planned Parenthood.

Blume does not just convey the importance of being informed, she actually provides a lot of birth control information in the book. When Katherine goes to Planned Parenthood, the reader moves through the birth control interview and gynecological exam with her, overhearing the information and viewing the procedure. Katherine's clinic interview at Planned Parenthood called "personal counseling" consists of questions posed by a social worker about how often Katherine plans to have sex, whether she will know in advance, and information about her medical history:

> "Have you already had sexual intercourse?" "Yes." "Have you been using a birth control device? . . ." "A rubber . . . that is, a condom." . . . "But you plan to have intercourse regularly?" "Yes." "Do you think you'll know in advance or will it be a spontaneous decision?" "I guess I'll know in advance." ". . . How old were you when you began to menstruate?" "Almost fourteen" "And are your periods regular?" "Sort of . . . I get it every four to five weeks. . . ." "How about your mother . . . is she in good health?" "Yes, she's fine." "Does she take birth control pills?" "No . . . she uses a diaphragm . . . I'd rather take the Pill. . . ." "The whole idea of coming here is to find the birth control device that best suits the individual" (136–37).

The reader learns about what she can expect from a trip to this kind of clinic and what information she needs to know about herself. She understands the decisions she will be facing when considering birth control. The reader is also exposed to some of the relevant medical terminology and birth control methods.

Just as informative is Blume's description of Katherine's first gynecological exam. The details are explicit and clear:

> My physical exam consisted of weight and blood pressure, a routine breast exam, with the doctor explaining how I should check my breasts each month, then my first pelvic examination. "Try to relax, Katherine. This isn't going to hurt." And it didn't either, but it was uncomfortable for a minute, like when he pushed with one hand from inside and with the other from the outside. Then he slipped this cold thing into my vagina and explained, "This is a vaginal speculum. It holds the walls of the vagina open so that the inside is easily seen. Would you like to see your cervix?"
>
> "I don't know . . ."
>
> "I think it's a good idea to become familiar with your body" (138–39).

The overall message is that teenage girls deserve to be educated and informed about their bodies so that they can care for their bodies and make responsible choices about birth control. Girls learn words to describe female anatomy and to see their use as ordinary and not embarrassing. This scene also establishes a set of expectations about quality health care for adolescent girls. Katherine's doctor is comfortable with her anatomy and encourages her sexual independence by suggesting that she become "familiar" with her body. The clinic emphasizes her right to choose a method of birth control that meets her medical needs and sexual lifestyle. Katherine is treated with respect and dignity as she learns to become an agent in meeting her biological needs.

It's Not What You Expect (1973) presents a utopian feminist world where abortion is legal and safe and socially acceptable. More typical of feminist novels written in the mid-1970s, the story offers a female protagonist with a solid sexual identity. Like the first and second phase writing, the story is told in the first person from Carla's point of view. Carla's older brother, Ralph, has a steady girlfriend, Sara Lee, who gets pregnant over the summer and chooses to have an abortion. Carla and her brother Oliver offer to help pay for the abortion with a portion of their summer wages.

Carla's sexual identity as a girl who expects protected sex from her peers is expressed in a conversation she has with Oliver when she finds out about Sara Lee's pregnancy:

> "How can she be pregnant?"
> "How? What do you mean how?"
> "I mean, like, isn't she on the pill or something. . . . What's going to happen?
> . . ."
> "She'll have an abortion, I guess."
> "Done by who?"
> ". . . there's this article in *Consumer Reports* I read a couple of months ago that . . . tells the whole spiel and it's not that expensive—safe, recommended doctors, etc." (86–87).

Carla is surprised that Sara Lee would get pregnant because she assumed that Sara Lee is on a viable type of birth control. Carla and her brother never question the legitimacy of abortion as a solution to the problem and are already fully informed about the procedure. What's more the procedure is so socially acceptable that *Consumer Reports* is covering it as a topic!

Abortion is dealt with as what one of the chapter titles calls "A Perfectly Simple Operation." Sara Lee does not get sick or permanently disfigured but instead seems fine. When Carla and Oliver go to see Sara Lee the day after, they find her in the kitchen with her mother: "I kept looking at Sara Lee. She looked so calm and composed. Of course, why shouldn't she? It's only in old-time movies that people lie around pale and fainting after abortions . . . I wonder how mom would take it if such a thing happened to me. Would I tell her or what?. . . it seems like these events you expect to be so melodramatic never are" (111–12).

The abortion raises questions for Carla about women's sexual responsibilities. Her desire to clarify this slips out when she tells her mother about the abortion. Her mother responds: "I'm glad she's okay . . . Poor thing, though . . . You know, your generation is lucky, Car, really, they really are. Things are so much more open now. I remember when I had an abortion, the doctor was so nasty and cold. He made me feel so rotten, like I'd committed some heinous act. It was so humiliating! That was worse than the pain of it really" (115). Carla is shocked by her mother's confession but concludes: "On the other hand, I was really glad Mom was telling me all this . . . She must think I'm fairly mature to tell me this" (115).

In the next quotation, Carla's mother further discusses her experience with having an abortion in a different era. Without making reference to the women's movement, she talks about the generational progress in women's health care. In many of these novels, the mothers and grandmothers are the spokespersons for the feminist agenda on women's sexuality and biology. Her mother explains, "You know, it's not easy to have an abortion, Car. I mean, even for me, believing in it, still I think there are always some mixed feelings. . . . Maybe if my mother had talked to me about those things, but she just never did. I mean I hope if something like this ever happens to you, you'd feel you could come to me. . . . I felt so lonely when it happened" (116). As Carla and her mother talk, it comes out that her aborted pregnancy did not occur with Carla's father but another man that she had been in love with. Carla is not only learning about her mother's biological history but also her sexual history. She assumed that her mother had slept only with her father. As Carla learns about her mother's sexuality, she is able to envision her own. She particularly savors her mother's confidence in her about these womanly issues. She ponders on the situation and thinks:

The other funny part, though is to think of Mom having these love affairs or whatever before she met Dad. It certainly sounded like she was in love with

Leonard Weisberg. I mean, I may not be objective but I think most people would agree Mom isn't exactly the sexy type. Even if you thought she was pretty or you liked her face, I don't think you'd say it was sexy. Of course, maybe that just doesn't matter all that much. I wonder if Leonard Weisberg was the only one. Of course, she did meet Dad when she was twenty. (120)

This makes Carla look forward to a more independent and mature stage in her life when she can keep things private, even from her brother. Carla thinks to herself: "Just wait. When I'm having a hot, rousing affair, I'll come in smiling enigmatically and won't tell him a darn thing" (120).

This novel is more typical of the second phase of popular novels with its already fully constituted feminist subject. Rather than having the story revolve around the process of becoming self-aware or sexually educated, as in Blume's early novel *Are You There God? It's Me, Margaret*, the female character is already a whole and empowered being who becomes an agent of change in her attempt to support Sara Lee's abortion. This novel is utopian in that it presents a world where women are no longer oppressed.

This new social acceptance of abortion and birth control as a solution to young pregnancy by the early 1970s reflects a definitive change in attitude regarding not only women's biology but also women's social status. As the women's movement promoted a broader life for women outside of marriage and motherhood, women's control over their reproductive rights became crucial to that progress. Regardless of the way in which girls' biological rights are represented in the young adult texts, the fact that they were being addressed at all signified a dramatic shift in popular consciousness.

Messages About Girls' Sexual Behavior and Rights

The seven texts analyzed in this essay do not reflect one type of feminism but rather they represent feminist debates: feminist messages about biological rights were more clear than those about sexual behavior and rights. Nonetheless there were three distinctive types of messages about appropriate behavior in five of the novels. The first type of message emphasizes sex as pleasurable and fulfilling and can be found in *Forever, Summer of My German Soldier*, and *Morning Is a Long Time Coming*. The second type of message criticizes the heterosexual imperative in both romance novels and feminist novels and can be found in the novel *Ruby*. The last type of message is that sex can be dangerous, and this is explored in *Are You in the House Alone?*

Sexual Pleasure

Blume participates in a feminist redefinition in public discourse of heterosexuality with an emphasis on female sexual pleasure. In *Forever*, when Katherine has her first sexual encounter with Michael, she says, "When we kissed again, Michael used his tongue. I wanted him to" (27). This overt declaration of desire expresses Katherine's sexual subjectivity and identity. Katherine defines her sexual identity throughout the story, including many feelings of doubt: "It occurred to me in the middle of the night that Michael asked if I was a virgin to find out what I expected of him. If I hadn't been one then he probably would have made love to me. What scares me is I'm not sure how I feel about that" (28). But these feelings of doubt are juxtaposed with other viewpoints from female characters in the story. Katherine's friend Erica articulates a different sexual identity in the following discussion between the two of them about the purpose of sexual intercourse:

> Erica: It might not be a bad idea to get laid before college.
> Katherine: What about love?
> Erica: You don't need love to have sex.
> Katherine: But it means more that way.
> Erica: Oh, I don't know. They say the first time's never any good anyway
> . . . I'm always thinking about it . . . wondering who's going to be
> the one . . . like tonight, I kept picturing myself with Artie . . . and
> in school I sit in class thinking how it would be with every guy . . .
> even the teachers . . . I wonder about them too . . . especially Mr.
> Frazier, since he never zips his fly all the way . . . You're a roman-
> tic . . . I'm a realist . . . we look at sex differently . . . I see it as a
> physical thing and you see it as a way of expressing love. (37)

This presents two distinctive female voices with diverging sexual perspectives. Just as feminists were debating differing sexual viewpoints and their viability, so are they debated in these popular texts for adolescent girls. As a "romantic," Katherine is repelled by the notion of meaningless sex. As she is trying to figure out who she is sexually, she rejects the option of an overly sexualized identity.

Erica's sexual identity serves as a less appealing contrast to the more identifiable Katherine. Katherine reflects the "good girl" of the 1970s in that she is open to exploring her sexuality but does not want to lose control of it. In a moment of passion with Michael she tells him, "I have to control my body with my mind," and "A person has to think . . . a person has to be sure" (57). The biggest barrier to Katherine's decision to have sex with Michael turns out to be her fear that she won't know what to do. She is embarrassed by her lack of experience and knowledge.

Forever contains some soft erotica that offers the adolescent reader fodder for fantasy, as does the erotic literature written for women at this time. The following scene from *Forever* is remarkable for Young Adult Literature in its explicit expression of Katherine's sexual desire. The reference to Katherine's orgasm and to Michael's penis and its nickname, "Ralph," is extraordinary, even in this time period: "We got into his bed and fell asleep for an hour and when we woke up Ralph was hard again. This time Michael made it last much, much longer and I got so carried away I grabbed his backside with both hands, trying to push him deeper and deeper into me—and I spread my legs as far apart as I could—and I raised my hips off the bed—and I moved with him, again and again and again—and at last, I came" (150). This articulation of female sexual pleasure is the most outspoken in the entire sample. Katherine disapprovingly makes reference to a previous encounter in which she was not sexually gratified. In this instance she expects to have an orgasm and does. Finally, her sexual desire for Michael is a vital part of who she is becoming as a woman, and this process is validated in the novel.

Blume defies the traditional heterosexual romance formula by breaking up Katherine and Michael when she is attracted to another boy. Her sexual exploration does not have to result in marriage for it to be authenticated as a positive part of Katherine's development into womanhood. By the end of the novel Katherine has reconciled the dichotomy between the good girl of the 1970s and the sexual exploiter represented by Erica by finding a middle ground. Blume implicitly suggests that one of the best things about female sexual liberation is that it enables young women to have multiple sexual partners and relationships.

Forever offers an important vehicle for the articulation of female adolescent sexual identity: sexual slang. This "slang" reflects the private language used by female adolescents to describe their sexual experiences. Words like "laid," "fuck," and "cherry" serve to set aside a creative and malleable vocabulary in which teens can talk about sex. The slang used to describe one's sexuality reflects the nature of that type of sexual identity. For example, Katherine uses the word "laid" to describe her friend Sybil having casual sex but would not use such a crass word to describe "making love" to Michael. The first sentence of the novel reads: "Sybil Davison has a genius IQ and has been laid by at least six different guys" (9). Katherine becomes angry and is insulted by her younger sister when she asks "Were you fucking?" When Erica refers to Katherine's father's reluctance to let her go on a ski trip with Michael she says "It has nothing to do with breaking your leg . . . it has to do with breaking your cherry" referring to Katherine's loss of virginity.

Bette Greene's *Summer of My German Soldier* (1973) and its sequel, *Morning Is a Long Time Coming* (1978), together tell the tale of the coming of age of its protagonist, Patty Bergen. Patty comes from a horrible family with an unspeakably evil father who emotionally and physically abuses her. The first part of the story takes place during World War II, where Patty befriends a German POW named Anton. She falls in love with Anton and tries to help him escape. The Bergens are Jewish, and the conflict within the small town about the relationship between Anton and Patty is catastrophic. She is sent away to a reform school after Anton is killed trying to escape and her complicity is revealed.

While the relationship between Patty and Anton is mostly platonic, he does give her a romantic kiss goodbye. It is not until the second part of the story that Patty builds on her sexual feelings for Anton with other men. She describes the kiss by saying, "I saw or felt it coming—my chin tilted up as my eyes closed. Then our lips touched, lingered together briefly before going their own separate ways" (135). This is the last time Patty sees Anton, but he becomes the pivotal force behind Patty's journey abroad seeking sexual awareness.

Patty's sexuality comes up often with her father, who is constantly accusing her of being a "dirty" girl. He is suspicious of her without provocation. After her involvement with Anton is discovered, her father tries to get her to admit to sexual encounters that never took place:

> "And this man, you gave him something too, didn't you?" My father's voice had become calm, almost confidential . . . *"What did he do to you?"*
> "The only thing he did was to thank me. He was very polite."
> "You're lying, you dirty girl."
> "No, sir, I'm telling the truth."
> "Liar! He touched you. You let him put his hands on you, *filthy, fil-thy* girl!"
> (143)

Patty's declaration of independence from her parents in the sequel involves her development into a sexual being despite her father's opinions about female sexual identity in the first novel. Patty denounces her father by embracing her own sexual identity and by seeking love from other men.

In the sequel *Morning Is a Long Time Coming*, Patty informs her family that she is not going to college but is going abroad instead. Patty's problematic relationship with her father and his bizarre preoccupation with her assumed sexual activities continue in the sequel. In the previous novel he assumed that she was having sex with the German soldier. In this novel he assumes that she is going to Europe to hide a pregnancy. The reality is that she has a healthy curiosity about sex but knows nothing about it.

Patty and her father represent clashing sexual discourses that were present in 1970s American popular culture. Her father articulates a patriarchal, misogynistic, and oppressive sexual ideology that attempts to limit women's sexual freedom and knowledge. He presents a simple notion of the virgin/whore dichotomy and casts Patty as the latter. Patty articulates a more contemporary female sexual ideology that assumes a healthy sexual curiosity in adolescent girls. She wants to learn about sex and to feel sexual arousal. Despite her father's accusations, she somehow has the conviction that he is wrong.

Another layer to the novel is its historical setting. The sequel takes place right after World War II when women were encouraged to "give back" their jobs to the men who had been fighting the war. The ideal woman was supposed to go back to her role as wife and mother in the home: repressive ideologies of womanhood that feminists were challenging in the 1970s. By situating Patty's sexual awakening amidst the postwar context, Greene is able to interrogate these fundamentally repressive ideologies of womanhood: "Somehow" says Patty "my father and maybe my mother too, got this notion that I'm oversexed and that any moment now I'm going to present them with a bastard grandchild. . . . Why me? Me, of all people! And yet I wouldn't even give them the satisfaction of telling them just how pure—speak about your Ivory soap—I am. Where, I'd really like to know, did my father get the idea that I was sexually voracious?" (72). The only clue that Greene gives us is that Patty is an assertive, opinionated, and independent girl—which means, according to her father that she must also be sexual. And this enrages her father.

After Patty informs her parents that she is leaving for Europe instead of college, she embarks on a symbolic journey of becoming a woman by acquiring sexual knowledge. In a conversation with her friend Edna Louise, they discuss the sexual mores of French culture. Edna Louise says that Frenchmen engage in "unnatural sex." Patty asks her to define "unnatural sex": "For someone who had gained a reputation for having succulent nipples, Edna Louise began to look surprisingly uncomfortable. Finally her gaze seemed to refocus as she said, 'About the same thing, I reckon, that other people mean when they say . . . unnatural sex'" (109). Patty finds that her small town friends are not sources of "real" information. Her trip to Europe is an attempt to learn about herself beyond the constraints of her hometown: "People say that Frenchmen have sex almost at the drop of a hat and even if it's in the daytime! 'Really,' I answered, never before having realized that the Baptists placed a greater penalty on daytime sex. To some extent, I agree. I mean, who in their right mind would want to have sex in the daylight when your body can be looked at like just so much meat?" (110). Greene appears to present Patty's bashful attitudes about nudity to demonstrate the status of her unformed sexual identity before her trip to Europe.

For Patty, becoming a woman is intimately connected with feeling sexual desire for a man. When she arrives in France, she meets Roger. While this novel is not as sexually explicit or provocative as *Forever*, it does have some of the most overt articulations of female sexual desire. Patty talks about her desire in the following erotic quotation:

> With his finger, he leisurely traced the outline of my lips. I don't remember ever before wanting to be kissed. But I wanted it now. . . . As his lips moved in maddening slow motion toward mine, my eyes again closed. This time, I thought, I'm going to get something that I want. And when at last his lips touched mine, they moved me so deeply that for this moment, there was nothing else. . . . Then Roger's hand circled my breast. . . . Then our bodies began responding to a rhythm that was never scored by Mendelssohn. Something I want. Something I need. Just this once, by God, I deserve to get something I need! And it would be . . . and it would happen. And then no more alien and adrift . . . but connected and complete. (177–78)

While they are making love, explicit details are left to the imagination. But her expression of female desire is almost as strong as those in Blume's books and is significant because it offers a language that teen readers can use to begin to articulate a sexual subjectivity that they are denied by the dominant popular culture.

Challenging the Heterosexual Imperative

Rosa Guy's *Ruby* (1976) is the only novel in the sample to explore homosexuality and the first young adult novel to question the hetero-sexual imperative in teen fiction for girls. The story features two Black heroines who fall in love within a homophobic community committed to keeping them separate. Ruby Cathy and Daphne Duprey also fall in love despite their insurmountable differences. The former is shy, plain, unassertive, and dominated by her father, Calvin, who keeps a tight watch on her as she develops into a young woman. Daphne is bril-liant, intellectual, beautiful, and ambitious. She is also extremely as-sertive about her political convictions as a Black nationalist. She takes Ruby under her wing and attempts to educate her about love, politics, and female confidence.

Linda Christian-Smith dismisses this novel as heterosexist in its emphasis on the hostility experienced by the girls as they fall more deeply in love. One of the boys in their class says to Ruby, "I knew something was wrong with you. Dykes is your thing. He put his hand to his forever swollen crotch. You want to feel the real thing? Here, I'll let you feel it" (50). Christian-Smith argues, the penis represents the "normal" sexuality that these girls seem to be eschewing. Christian-Smith also argues that with the omnipresence of these kinds of hos-tile attitudes by parents, teachers, and male suitors, Guy highlights the abnormality of the relationship between Ruby and Daphne. She also supports this argument by pointing to the fact that Daphne de-cides to go straight at the end. She concludes that Guy represents this adolescent lesbian relationship as a temporary developmental phase.

Another reading of this text is offered by Nancy Tillman Romalov in her essay "Spirals of Consciousness: Rosa Guy's 'Friends' Trilogy." According to Romalov, Guy demonstrates a full grasp of the complex-ity and convergence of the themes of adolescence, lesbianism, and womanhood. Romalov contends that regardless of whether we agree with Daphne's decision to go straight, she exercises her right to make choices. She is the epitome of female agency, which has even further significance for her as a young Black woman. She states that what is rare and commendable about Daphne is that she chooses not to ac-cept limitations on her life. When Daphne takes her destiny into her own hands, she becomes, in Alice Walker's words, "master of her own history" (30). Guy seems to imply that there is a strong connection between Daphne's choice to love women and her ability to challenge life's limitations.

Daphne calls herself a lover and refuses to specify this as particular to either sex. She puts herself first and is clearly college bound from the beginning of the story. She is comfortable playing different roles and exudes a sort of androgynous style. Ruby describes her lovingly, "Feminine Daphne with her thick, crisply curly, black shoulder-length hair. Boyish Daphne with her thick neck, her colorful silk skirts, her tweeds" (15). She is always deliberate about her choices and assertive with her desires. And she is very comfortable with her sexuality. Her decision at the end seems more calculated than simply an abandonment of her sexuality. She always has a strategy in mind and never acts passively. Daphne is not "straight" at the end of story but has decided to live a straight lifestyle at college.

This novel, unlike the others in the sample, is not written in the first person. It does, however, parallel the second wave of feminist novels by presenting the reader with an already fully constituted feminist (Daphne) and by exploring feminism. This novel simultaneously indicts feminism for its exclusion of Black women and lesbians. Daphne's mother, a "women's libber" as Daphne calls her, feels rejected by the women's movement as a Black woman. Throughout the novel her mother pressures her to "go straight," indicating that even feminists do not condone this kind of relationship.

In this novel female sexuality involves a lesbian consciousness that enables both of the lesbian heroines to enjoy women on many different intimate levels. Ruby has an intimate moment with her teacher that a homophobic mentality might have prevented: "The teacher pulled her aside as she was leaving. Gently massaging the back of Ruby's neck, her shoulders, she drew her close. 'Is there anything you want to tell me?. . .' The soothing hand touching, caring, feeling deeply down into where some pain, some unknown bruise waited for the balm of concern" (30). These kinds of interactions between women in the novel are not unusual. Psychic healing between women, especially between Daphne and Ruby, is featured as necessary to combat the misogyny around them. This "healing" is not usually overtly sexual but is acceptable within a female sphere.

Guy does not write sexually explicit scenes but instead provides a metaphorical representation of sex. For example, one description of a sexual encounter is the following: "Holding, touching, fondling, body intertwined with body, racing around the world on rays of brilliant color, roaring into eternity on cresting waves of violence, returning to tenderness, a gentle, lapping tenderness" (49). This reference to violence and tenderness mirrors the relationship between the two girls.

The "violence" and "tenderness" of their physical encounters underscore the social context for their relationship. It is forbidden, dangerous, and arousing. Their sexual encounters are not treated as separate from their psychological ones. Daphne is often angry with Ruby for being an "Uncle Tom" and acting without self-respect. In these moments, Ruby finds a way to reach a "tender" side of Daphne and to teach her compassion for others. Their sexual encounters reflect this dynamic in their relationship.

This novel does not seem to suffer from the pitfalls of the other novels in that it represents the obstacles facing female adolescents. It does not glaze over feminist battles by presenting a utopian lesbian environment where their relationship is given validity and dignity. It does not, however, represent lesbian relationship as doomed from the start. Instead it provides a balanced account of the hostility and difficulties faced by those who choose to love someone of the same sex as well as the strength that can come from a lesbian consciousness. It does not mislead the reader about feminist battles that have yet to be won. And, finally, it teaches adolescent readers that heterosexual expression is not the only legitimate form of sexual expression.

Sexual Danger

Some of the messages about sexuality in these novels provide a constructive social critique of girls' lack of sexual rights. In Richard Peck's *Are You in the House Alone?* rape is presented as one of the biggest threats to a girl's liberation and underscores a radical feminist antiviolence sentiment. Sexual danger pervades the novel as the heroine, Gail, is anonymously threatened and then raped by her best friend's boyfriend Phil. After Gail is raped, she wants to take legal action. She reports the attack to the police and finds their reaction to be suspicious, accusatory and hostile. When she recounts this to her attorney, he responds:

> Attorney: That's the official posture. . . . And if he hadn't had the medical report, he'd have been convinced nothing happened at all.
>
> Gail: Isn't the medical report a point in our favor?
>
> Attorney: It would be if . . . the assailant had forced his way in—picked a lock or broken a window. . . . If he'd been a stranger . . . If you'd been a virgin . . . If you hadn't been on birth control pills, because that's part of the medical report.
>
> Gail: Why does the law protect the rapist instead of the victim?
>
> Attorney: Because the law is wrong. (135–37)

This passage functions as a feminist critique of the legal system by exposing the sexist practices of silencing young women. In this instance, the legal system works against a women's rights, as the victim of a violent sexual crime is left without legal recourse. This rape case serves as a warning to young women about their lack of legal and sexual rights.

Peck provides a harsh critique of the popular representation of women and its relationship to sexual crimes like rape. In the school assembly, Gail and her classmates watch an old movie featuring their acting teacher, Madam Malevich. In the movie she plays a "maiden being ravished. Terror gradually replaced by passion" (89). While these kinds of assemblies are usually lost on the students, this movie captivates them. After Gail is raped, Madam Malevich comes to visit her and says, "I was ravished myself many times in those primitive films I made. You saw one yourself. The old, old stories of the maiden who resists man's desire and her own, only to be liberated by what she cannot forestall. Harmless myths, I thought when I was young and dazed with dreaming. But not harmless when the myth fixes itself into a sick mind" (143).

Phil's threatening notes to Gail include "pornographic" descriptions of what he plans to do to her. Gail describes one of the notes, "All the things someone thought I was. And all the things someone planned to do to me, to make me do. Every perverted, sadistic, sick, and sickening ugly act. A twisted porno movie playing in somebody's brain" (49). Clearly, Peck is implying that cultural images of women "wanting it" when they say they don't is evidence that women are to be preyed upon and used for men's desires.

The language that Phil uses in the rape scene reveals the devastating effects of the "myths" that Madam Malevich refers to. He addresses Gail as a girl who wants it:

> "I've been keeping tabs on you. Checking you out pretty close. The phone calls just to keep in touch. And the notes. It was a lot of trouble, actually, for a cheap little—but then I guess you know what I think about you. . . . Something ought to be done about girls like you, Gail. As my mother would say, you tend to lower the tone."
>
> "Phil, look, I think you've got a problem, and—"
>
> "Don't use the psychological approach with me, Gail. You're more the physical type anyway, aren't you?. . . I'm in very good shape Gail. It comes from clean living, which you wouldn't know anything about. So if you struggle much, you might wish you hadn't. Of course, if struggling turns you on, go right ahead. But I can't be responsible. I can't be responsible for anything.

. . . And don't worry. I don't want you to do anything you haven't already done. Just look at it this way, Gail. You've had more experience in certain matters than I have. And this is your chance to share it." (107)

When Gail does struggle he knocks her out with one of the fireplace tools. His language implies that his concocted fantasy included the assumption that Gail desired him sexually because she was sexually active. He assumed that all girls who would have sex before marriage would want sex with anybody.

Gail is not devastated by the rape. As she demonstrated in the conversation with her attorney, she wants to fight back. She does not internalize Phil's perception of her but sees him as a sick person in need of help. She demonstrates a new attitude as a result of her experience when she is hassled by a man on the street:

"Hey, momma, whatcher hurry? Want a little action? Wanna get it on? Wanna . . ."
I walked around him in the flow of pedestrians. He should have scared me out of my wits. But I nearly went blind with hatred instead. If he had something to prove about himself, what made him think he could use me? Did I owe him something because I was female and he was male?
It was the first time I'd thought anything like that. I wished I'd had something very sharp and very lethal in my hand. I was ready to use it on anybody. (69)

Gail is expressing not only her anger but her desire to take control of her body. She wants to be able to physically protect herself and to maintain her dignity as a woman. This assertion of power comes about as a result of her fury about male aggression and intimidation.

Conclusion

The young adult novels analyzed in this essay were written in a time when the cultural representations of women were being renegotiated. Many feminists in the 1970s believed that if women were to gain power, confidence in themselves, and the ability to play a wider role in the public domain, they would have to fundamentally change their relationship with their bodies. The way that women perceived their bodies had everything to do with how they perceived themselves. This essay has traced how seven young adult novels written in the 1970s challenged the dominant cultural representations of femininity by drawing on feminist discourse to teach female readers about their bodies, to encourage readers to rebel against oppressive rules surrounding the use of the female body, and to exercise power and control over their bodies by consciously making informed decisions about them.

These novels attempted to reclaim female sexual power by providing a language for adolescent female sexual identity, particularly female sexual anxiety. Female sexuality became a hotly contested issue amidst feminists, and the nature of this new and burgeoning female sexuality was unclear. But what the feminist debates helped to clarify was the complexity involved in the assertion of female sexual identity. These young adult novels introduced female characters who were struggling to define who they were becoming as sexual beings in a world of conflicting cultural messages. While these novels did not resolve female sexual confusion, they did attempt to articulate the trepidation felt by female adolescents as they negotiated the obstacle course of sexual development, sexual expression, and sexual orientation.

The limitations of these novels reflect the shortcomings of feminist messages about sexuality in the 1970s. By emphasizing feminist utopias, most of the novels in this sample do not address the kind of social realities examined by Rosa Guy or Richard Peck. These authors, in attempting to instill confidence in readers, often neglected to address certain issues considered unworthy by the women's movement such as dreading your first menstruation, not feeling ready to learn about your body, not being interested in sex, or having lesbian tendencies. By presenting a sexually informed and often utopian feminist viewpoint as the norm, these authors imply that feminism has achieved its goals and won its battles.

Female sexuality becomes contested terrain in these novels as the protagonist explores her relationship with her body, its needs, and her role in society. It is covertly implied in these texts of "what if" and the "personal is political" that a liberated female identity is an end in itself rather than a means to a more liberated world. In other words, few of the novels advocate social change but rather offer a map for how girls can learn to liberate themselves within the system. The heroine's personal sexual liberation is usually the goal, not social change.

Social change requires more than merely an empowered gender perspective or established sexual identity. As Karen DeCrow writes in *The Young Woman's Guide to Liberation* (1971): "The women of today are more ambitious: we want as much pleasure out in the city as we have been granted in the bedroom" (xxv). Women's liberation from a patriarchal social structure requires more than female confidence and conviction about sexuality. Teaching adolescent girls in the 1970s to be assertive and confident about themselves and their bodies was not enough to prepare them for the oppressive counter messages generated by the dominant culture that feminists had yet to defeat. Feminist and young adult authors would have better served their audience by using Richard Peck's approach in *Are You in the House Alone?* Rather than implying a false utopia and gender equity, he tells the story of a young woman who is raped and how the legal system denies her voice and her version of the story. The reader is left with a clearer and more accurate story about how far the American legal system needs to go in honoring and respecting the viewpoints of rape victims. Peck's message is that women's sexual rights are not yet protected under the current legislation.

This weakness has to do with the feminist dictum that the personal is political. This often meant that the personal became a substitute for the political. These books were not encouraging girls to enter the public sphere and protest for women's rights but rather to learn to see themselves as already empowered young women, despite the political realities. The feminist battle is subtly characterized as one's individual empowerment and confidence via learning about how to have power and control over one's body. This battle is presented as waged in the private sphere of relationships and family life, not in the public sphere of working for social change.

Regardless of the fact that these books could have gone farther in preparing girls for the sexist realities of society, they must be recognized for what they did accomplish. These books were trailblazers within Young Adult Literature, which had not previously dealt with issues of female sexual liberation or conviction. Not only did these young adult authors teach female sexual liberation, they emphasized to female adolescent readers that they had the same rights as adult women. The strict line that had existed between adults and children in Young Adult Literature written before the 1970s was now blurred. As feminists were examining the detrimental influence of sexism in female adolescence, these young adult authors set out to educate their female readers about their rights as young women.

The popularity of these books suggests that female adolescent readers found them to be both pleasurable to read and relevant to their lives. They offered the reader a raised consciousness about the female body and its relationship with the social construction of gender. The reader could learn from and live vicariously through these female characters who were "trying on" different sexual identities as they moved toward sexual determination. They learned through role playing to take risks, make mistakes, and, most important to find confidence and pleasure in learning about and using their bodies. In addition, these heroines learn how to find safety in romantic relationships that allow them to express this burgeoning sexual identity without physical or emotional repercussions.

Blume, Klein, Greene, Guy, and Peck began to reconfigure the romantic novel and to offer possible solutions to the problem of clarifying a new feminist sexual identity for adolescent readers. While these young adult authors were in the minority, they began to envision what female sexual empowerment might entail and to pass this on to their readers. While many feminists were skeptical about the role of sexual empowerment in women's political empowerment, these authors seemed convinced that their adolescent readers needed to be sexually educated and encouraged in order to become confident and healthy women. Central to this redefinition of teen romance was the implicit message that mature young men and women did not have different romantic and sexual needs. As Klein said in writing about Blume's book: "[Forever] showed that boys are often as vulnerable and sensitive as girls when it comes to their first sexual experience. It showed that there are no rules about what will cause pleasure or pain, that each person, as he or she emerges into the adult world, must find a way to live and love that makes sense to him or her, even if that way is at odds with the beliefs of parents or community" (Klein, "Thoughts" 22).

Works Cited

Blume, Judy. *Are You There God? It's Me, Margaret.* New York: Dell Publishing, 1970.

———. *Forever.* New York: Pocket Books, 1975.

Boston Women's Health Book Collective. *Our Bodies, Ourselves.* New York: Simon and Schuster, 1971.

Christian-Smith, Linda. *Becoming a Woman through Romance.* New York: Routledge, 1990.

DeCrow, Karen. *The Young Woman's Guide to Liberation.* New York: Pegasus, 1971.

Friday, Nancy. *My Secret Garden: Women's Sexual Fantasies.* New York: Pocket Books, 1973.

Greene, Bette. *Morning Is a Long Time Coming.* New York: Dell Publishing, 1978.

———. *Summer of My German Soldier.* New York: Dell Publishing, 1973.

Greer, Germaine. *The Female Eunuch.* New York: McGraw-Hill, 1970.

Guy, Rosa. *Ruby.* New York: Dell Publishing, 1976.

Jong, Erica. *Fear of Flying.* London: Granada, 1973.

Klein, Norma. *It's Not What You Expect.* New York: Pantheon Books, 1973.

———. "Thoughts on the Adolescent Novel." *Writing on Writing for Young Adults.* Eds. Patricia Feehan and Pamela Barron. Detroit: Omnigraphics, 1991. 21–31.

Lauret, Maria. *Liberating Literature: Feminist Fiction in America.* London: Routledge, 1994.

Millet, Kate. *Sexual Politics.* New York: Doubleday, 1970.

Peck, Richard. *Are You in the House Alone?* New York: Laurel-Leaf Books, 1976.

Romalov, Nancy Tillman. "Spirals of Consciousness: Rosa Guy's "Friends' Trilogy." *Children's Literature Association Quarter* 1.16 (1991): 27–32.

Russo, Mary. "Female Grotesques: Carnival and Theory." *Feminist Studies/Critical Studies.* Ed. Teresa de Lauretis. Bloomington: Indiana University Press, 1986. 215.

Chapter 3

Identity by Design: The Corporate Construction of Teen Romance Novels

Norma Pecora

The contribution of teen novels to the construction of young girls' identity has been well-established. In casual conversation women will often reveal stories about growing up with Nancy or Jessica and Elizabeth—the characters from the Nancy Drew and Sweet Valley High young adult series books. In the past, these extraordinarily popular novels have represented intrigue and romance portrayed by characters who are themselves teenagers. Now Nancy and her pals and Jessica and Elizabeth are growing up and going off to college, adding yet another dimension to the characters as well as twenty more books to buy each year. Using Janice Radway's analysis of romance novels as a model, this essay will explore the ideological consequences of "an event that is affected and at least partially controlled by the material nature of book publishing" (20). Building on Radway's work, I will examine, first, the industry trends that have led to new versions of the Nancy Drew and Sweet Valley Twins series novels. Second, I will explore how the shift from mystery genre to romance genre in the early 1980s redefined the character of the Nancy Drew novels. And, finally, I will compare the representation of college life in the newest in the series, Nancy Drew on Campus and Sweet Valley University, with the experience of real young women finishing their first year of college. These books suggest that dating and social alienation are the central plot in the day-to-day lives of college women, while interviews with freshmen girls at a midwestern state college indicate that their experiences are much more complex and multidimensional.[1]

Nancy Drew started life in the 1930s as a "spunky" young girl clever at solving mysteries. Jessica and Elizabeth began life in the early 1980s as twin sisters living in Sweet Valley, California. Responding to marketplace changes, publishing houses have extended the initial market for these books to stories that combine romance and mystery or variations on the characters' lives. In the 1980s the traditional Nancy Drew series expanded to include a romance series, a preteen version, and a series of stories set in her hometown. Now, in the Nancy Drew on Campus series, they have sent her off to Wilder University, establishing yet another market niche. Meanwhile, stories about Jessica and Elizabeth have also been developed as a preteen series and a mystery series. They are now attending Sweet Valley University.

Girls of twelve or so, the primary audience for these books, are in transition from child to adult. They are learning who they are, what they want to be, the rules of growing up—constructing their adult identity. It is a time for them to learn what can be accomplished. Unfortunately for many preadolescent girls, it is also a time when they lose a sense of themselves. According to Carol Gilligan and others (see for example Brown and Gilligan; Gilligan; Mann; Pipher; Stern; Taylor, Gilligan, and Sullivan), they learn to speak in a voice not their own, a voice that is modified by the preferential treatment of boys and a socialization process based on observations of women's place (see for example Rothenberg). Because the books under consideration are targeted to young girls between the ages of ten and fourteen, they serve as one part of this socialization process. For girls learning about themselves and their place in the world, these books offer a view of the future. Consequently, it is important that we look to see what future the books present.

Although these teen novels are purveyors of a particular ideological positioning—a white, middle-class, heterosexual notion of romance—this does not preclude them from being a site of contestation. Elisabeth Frazer points out that readers are not necessarily "'in the grip' of ideology" (423) and disputes the notion of a single reading of the text (411). Addressing the slippery concept of ideology in her work on readers of *Jackie,* a British teen magazine, she found that the girls in her study appeared to have different "'discourse registers' . . . an institutionalized, situationally specific, culturally familiar, public, way of talking" (420). That is, her interviews with the readers of *Jackie* challenged the notion of a single reading available to all. In addition, Joyce Litton found that the readers of the Sweet Valley High series were "well aware that they were not dealing with reality" (23). At issue here is not the interpretation of these texts but rather the apparent story lines and the economic motivation behind the proliferation of teen novels: if one Nancy Drew or Sweet Valley is successful—four Nancy Drew and Sweet Valley series are more successful. The "reading" of these stories cannot be guaranteed but we can speculate on the intent of the publisher and the way life is represented.

Very little of the research on these novels examines the role of the publishing industry and the expedience of the marketplace. Radway's work on adult readers was one of the first and has become a model for a few others. For example, one review of the research on young girls' literature found that studies generally examine the work of an individual writer, the themes and characters of the books, the images of adults, the representation of social issues, or the selection made by readers (Poe, Samuels, and Carter). Although, as they report, more recent research, such as reader-response analysis, draws our attention "not to the characteristics of a book in a vacuum but to how individuals respond to a book" (48). Not surprisingly, given the focus of the romance genre, the primary concern of reader-response analysis is often the "construction of femininity" (see for example Christian-Smith's work) or what Christine Bachen and Eva Illouz have called the "romantic imagination" (279). Attention is on the way girls learn about their social roles and identities: adolescent, female, daughter, student, girlfriend (Moffitt 238). Little has been written on the construction of identity beyond traditional or normative roles of daughter, wife, mother.

An Academic Look at Teen Romances

The work of Angela McRobbie was perhaps the first to consider both girls' culture and the role of romance in their popular reading. She and Jenny Garber argued that girls' culture unfolded in the "'culture of the bedroom'—experimenting with makeup, listening to records, reading the mags, sizing up the boyfriends, chatting, jiving" (213). Unlike boys, who were perceived to be "active participants," girls were the fans of music and "collectors and readers of the 'teenage-hero' magazines and love comics" (213–14). In her analysis of *Jackie*, McRobbie found that "romance pervades every story" ("*Jackie*" 271) presenting a "romantic individualism" as the teenage girl is "alone in her quest for love" (282). According to McRobbie, this popular British teen magazine extended a "system of messages, a signifying system and a bearer of a certain ideology; an ideology which deals with the construction of teenage 'femininity'" ("*Jackie*" 263).

In a more recent work, "Shut Up and Dance," McRobbie claimed that the love comics of the 1960s and 1970s have been replaced by magazines like *Just Seventeen,* where "the experience of teenage femininity, i.e., romance, have disappeared and have been replaced by a more diffuse femininity" (422) embracing autonomy and consumption (416). On the other hand, it may be that love comics like *Jackie* have simply been replaced or supplemented by the new genre of teen romance novels (Moss). Frazer claimed that the picture strips of *Jackie* magazines are "organised, produced and consumed according to different rules from those governing the production and consumption of teenage romance books such as the SVH [Sweet Valley High] series" (122).

Gemma Moss builds on the reading histories of four teenage girls who are clearly aware of the fictional nature of the books, but nonetheless major fans of the Sweet Valley High series (126). Although they defined the series as "soppy" and rejected the books in the context of a group interview, they identified themselves as readers of Sweet Valley High or other teen romance fiction (125, 127, 131).

Mary Anne Moffitt's analysis of a community of teen girls who read adult romance novels examined the "social and discursive pressures that lead members of this particular gender/social/age group to pursue romance reading and help articulate certain meanings to them" (238). She argued that "The unique textual features of the romance novel serve as a cultural, ideological terrain where the reader struggles to work out her felt social and identity pressures. In other words, the text *has* meaning and *articulates* meaning because events and characters portrayed in the text speak to the reader's lived experiences and felt social expectations" (239, emphasis in original).

Moffitt found that the eighteen girls she interviewed "overwhelmingly" identified with the story's heroine (240) and took pleasure in reading about the "physical beauty, independent spirit, and wealth of the heroine" (240). Additionally, negotiations between hero and heroine (240), the happy ending (241), and the "rules" of heterosexual relationships (242–43) played a part in the girls' reading experience. Moffitt stated that "reading a romance novel served as a vicarious, pseudo real experience of expected adult behaviors and identities and as momentarily empowering act that confirmed for the reader an identity to match discursive ideals of adult, wife, girlfriend, women, or worker" (247).

Gilbert and Taylor's work on the Australian teen romance series Dolly, modeled on the Sweet Valley High books, points to the universality of these books. An analysis of the texts demonstrated the predictable formula of a romance novel (86) with themes of love/sex, jealousy, and altruism. As in the Sweet Valley High series, the families in the Dolly books follow traditional roles of the nuclear family. Important to this essay: in only two of the eighteen Dolly stories did girls appear to have life plans "beyond the kiss" (91). In one, the heroine plans to play in a band (albeit with her boyfriend) and in another, the girl likes her job in a city boutique (91). On the other hand, the boys in the books strive to be or are in a wide range of professions, from athletes to aeronautical engineers. Contradicting the work of Frazer, Gilbert and Taylor point out that unlike many texts, romance novels and their formulaic structure and textual conventions leave little room for polysemic readings. They state: "Readers are actively discouraged from making idiosyncratic meaning from the text" (93). Using a community of readers who were *not* romance readers, Gilbert and Taylor asked the girls to read as many books in the series as they liked and to keep reading journals. These girls selected stories that were not typical of the romance genre (97); rejected the "unreality" of the books (99); and often devalued the reading. One girl wrote in her journal: "I thought about this and thought—oh, how embarrassing—I actually got hooked into a romance book" (98). Gilbert and Taylor reinforce the complex nature of the *social* act of reading romance novels, and in one of the few studies that consider the economic motives, argued that: "Formula romance novels should not be protected from scrutiny because they are popular culture, nor because they are fiction, nor because they are specially written for women and give women pleasure. They do not grow out of discourses which serve women well. They grow out of consumer-oriented discourses which have vested interests in constructing groups of women as identifiable and therefore commercially marketable; and they grow out of patriarchal discourses which depend upon the continuation of unequal heterosexual couplings and domestic labor" (103).

Two other studies that contribute to an understanding of teen romance novels and the construction of gender are the work of Linda Christian-Smith and Meredith Rogers Cherland. Perhaps the most comprehensive study of teen romance reading in the construction of femininity is reflected in the work of Christian-Smith. Recognizing that changes within the book publishing industry and the book-buying public account for the increasing availability of these books, her work focuses on the way reader and text come together to negotiate meaning. In her analysis of young reader fiction published from 1942–1982, she found that adolescent romance novels offer the reader a way of exploring relationships though never challenge them. Romance shapes femininity, an inevitable experience ("Romancing the Girl" 96). In her survey of seventy-nine girls who read romance fiction, four reasons for reading these books emerged: (1) escape, a way to get away from problems at home and school; (2) better reading than dreary text-books; (3) enjoyment and pleasure; (4) to learn what romance and dating are about (*Becoming a Woman* 105). According to Christian-Smith, romance reading occurs at a time when young women begin to consider their place in the world. Interviews with teen girls who iden-tified themselves as "heavy readers" revealed a "tug of war" between the girls' pleasure in identifying with the conventional femininity of the heroine and their preference for assertive heroines (*Becoming a Woman* 112–13). Christian-Smith found that the books "influence young women's self-conception through complex and often contradic-tory processes" (*Becoming a Woman* 115). They are "a vehicle for making sense of their sexuality [but] deeply implicated in reconciling young women to traditional places in the world ("Young Women" 223).

However, Cherland argues that Christian-Smith "sees language and literacy as the place where a sense of self, a subjectivity, is constructed" (14) while Cherland, on the other hand, sees the practice of reading in a social context: "living things negotiate the world's meaning *together* . . . *negotiating* meaning, and in that process constructing their shared social and cultural reality" (3; emphasis in original). She points out that "because gender is a cultural construction and reading is a social practice, gender is also unavoidably present in reading" (13). The girls of Cherland's reading community were fans of both the Sweet Valley High series and the Nancy Drew books. One girl said about the Sweet Valley series: "It is interesting to see what other girls do. Even if it's not true, it's so close to life" (97). *Agency* was central to the girls' reading experience according to Cherland: the girls used fiction like the teen romances to "explore" the various possibilities in their world (166), to negotiate the cultural messages from the texts (167), and anticipate their future roles (169).

All would agree there is no one reading—this is not a generation of young girls in the "grip of ideology" (Frazer 423). However, there is a "preferred reading" that offers the girls a particular view of what life "ought to be." Based on the teen literature reviewed here, it "ought to be" a romantic world (Gilbert and Taylor; McRobbie; Moffitt; Moss). And while most would agree with Cherland that the girls use romance novels to "explore" and "negotiate the world" (see also Christian-Smith and Moffitt), this genre of teen reading offers a somewhat limited world to explore. Because they are romance novels, it is a world of relationships and romances, accomplishments are defined as getting a guy and living happily ever after.

The Corporate Evolution of Nancy Drew[2]

Both the Nancy Drew and the Sweet Valley series are well-established teen reading (Motes 40; Huntwork 137–38; see also Dyer and Romalov). The Nancy Drew books began as a mystery series in the early 1930s and now are available in several adaptations: Nancy Drew Cases (mystery books), Nancy Drew Files (romances), River Heights (set in her hometown), Nancy Drew Notebooks (for preteens), and Nancy Drew on Campus. The Sweet Valley High series began as teen romances in the early 1980s and now include Sweet Valley Kids (for preteens), Sweet Valley Twins (the original series), The Unicorn Club (set in their hometown), Sweet Valley Team (about athletic events), and Sweet Valley University. In addition, there are books in the mystery, historical saga, and horror genres. All the books in the Sweet Valley series are unrepentant romance novels. Each new series is simply an overlay onto the original teen romance genre, consequently, all the Sweet Valley books are romance novels first, building on all the conventions of a romance novel (see for example Moffitt; Christian-Smith, *Becoming a Woman*; Christian-Smith, "Romancing the Girl"). Nancy Drew, however, began as a mystery series and only recently came to the romance genre after years as a well-established young adult mystery series.

The Nancy Drew of the mystery series showed us that spunkiness is good and that we could survive, quite well thank you, without a man. But, as we will see, this message changed with the Nancy Drew of the romance series. Until the mid-1980s the books had changed little. In the late 1950s they were revised to reflect social change. The age requirement for driving (at sixteen Nancy would not have been allowed to drive in most states) was brought in line with those in society and many of the overt stereotypes were eliminated (Billman 114). These changes reflected changes in society. However, in 1986 the plot and characters were revised in response to changes in the marketplace. There was a perceived, growing market for teen romance novels, a market defined by and for the twelve to fifteen-year-old girl. This created two separate series:

The Nancy Drew *Cases*, mystery novels, were introduced in 1930 and published by Grossett & Dunlap. In 1979 Simon and Schuster negotiated the rights to the series and publication of future books. The Nancy Drew *Files*, romance/mystery novels, were introduced in September 1986 and are published by Simon and Schuster.

With the introduction of the romance novels, Nancy again underwent cosmetic changes to make her more contemporary. She was issued a credit card and designer jeans. In addition, fundamental changes were made to the character and stories that reflect the differences between mystery novels and romance stories. Also, where once there was only one Nancy Drew, there were now two—the Nancy of the mystery Nancy Drew Series (mystery novels) and Nancy Drew Files. Industry trends led to the publication of this new genre and, it is argued here, this has had consequences for the characterization of Nancy Drew and her friends that brings into question her role as a model of independence and "spunkiness."

A 1986 survey indicated that teenagers had become an important market for books, as they were buying proportionately the same number of books as adults (Wood, "How Teenage Book"; Wood, "Teenage Book Buying"). According to the survey, 79 percent of the books bought by teens were paperback novels (the format of choice for romance novels) and 44 percent of the female respondents reported buying romance novels (Wood, "How Teenage Book"). In addition, a decline in educational book sales, because of decreased federal funding to schools and libraries, encouraged publishers to further develop markets for young adult books.

Building on the growing interest in teen romances, Simon and Schuster used the name recognition and marketability of the Nancy Drew character to establish a successful line of romances—the Nancy Drew Files. At least two national bookstore chains, B. Dalton and Waldenbooks, shelved these books among the racks featuring other teen romance series such as Wildfire Romances, Sweet Dreams, and Sweet Valley High. By marketing the Nancy Drew Files alongside these other teen romances, and pricing the books competitively, Simon and Schuster made obvious their intentions to expand Nancy into the romance market.

Clearly, this marketing trend and the history of the Nancy Drew novels support the notion of the reader/book relationship as affected by what Radway called, the "material nature of the book publishing industry" (20). When the series was introduced in 1930 it was as a part of a new genre of books called the junior novel. These books were immensely popular because of their low cost, bright jackets, and "snappy" dialog (Yost). Like the new romances available today at book stores in shopping malls, the junior novels were available in the natural habitat of the teens—department stores, toy shops, and drugstores (Yost).

However, Nancy Drew is more than just a part of an economic trend. She is a tradition. The books have been passed down from mother to daughter or aunt to niece with each generation introducing the stories to the next. The formulaic structure of the plot brings to the reader guaranteed entertainment, but more than that, the novels bring to the reader the comfort of familiarity: "Like the vacationer who returns to a beloved summer house year after year, the addicted reader opens book three or four or eleven . . . and is thoroughly at home in the locale—its by now familiar native characters, the verbal shrubbery and the narrative floorboards that occasionally creak" (Selma Lanes in Billman 13). And the publisher is offered a guaranteed seller.

But what did the marketing as a "romance" mean for the representation of Nancy Drew? In the mysteries she is independent and spunky and relies on her own resourcefulness. These are not the characteristics of the heroine in romance novels (see Radway 79–81).

From Mystery to Romance
The formula of the Nancy Drew mystery novels—the familiar characters and creaky floorboards—has not changed since their introduction more than seventy years ago. When picking up a Nancy Drew mystery, a reader can be assured that certain conventions will be followed and repeated in each novel and that Nancy will be spunky. Nancy Drew mysteries always establish an element of danger, mystery, and excitement on page one. And soon a mystery appears → Nancy is warned → Nancy is pursued → villains attack → Nancy triumphs → deserving people benefit (Jones 710). Trivialities such as geographic location may change, but the reader *knows* that within the first pages a mystery will appear and soon Nancy will be warned to "stay away." This warning never weakens Nancy's resolve and the formula plays itself out as Nancy befriends an innocent victim, discovers a secret in a prominent family, and encounters a sinister villain (Mason 56). And all ends well.

These are the conventions of the mystery novels. But how does this formula change as the novels make the transition from mystery to romance? More important, do these changes affect Nancy Drew's character and her relationship with others? In this section we will explore some of the differences between the two genres as represented in the Nancy Drew Cases (the mysteries) and the Nancy Drew Files (the romances).

In mystery novels, the plot revolves around the adventures associated with solving the dilemma. In romance novels, plot lines generally revolve around the problems of "relationships" and the traumas of love. According to John Cawelti the romance novel is the female equivalent of the adventure story, however, the stories are organized around love and relationships and adventure is only to challenge and then "cement" a relationship (41). The plots build on the relationship between the heroine and hero. The heroine is usually pretty and blond, the setting is small-town America, and the ending is happy (Smith). The problems she faces are personal and emotional and concern family and friends, whatever the problem, the most important element is her experience with romantic love ("Teen Romances").

Nancy Drew Series—The Mystery Novels
Because a love story is never primary (or even secondary) in the mystery genre, the plots of the Nancy Drew mysteries clearly do not follow the conventions of a romance novel. Nancy's relationships with others, romantic or social, are never integral to the plot. A review of the novels demonstrates the routine of the plots over time. (See Appendix A for a list of titles reviewed.) In each story the six conventions (mystery/warning/pursuit/attack/triumph/gain) are clearly identifiable as demonstrated in *The Hidden Staircase*. A mystery is established in the opening pages:

> Nancy receives a telephone call from her friend Helen asking Nancy to investigate some "mysterious" things that have been happening at her Aunt Rosemary's house. (2)

And soon there is a warning

> "I've come out of the goodness of my heart to warn you and your father," he said pompously. "Warn us? About what?" Nancy asked quickly. (3)

She is pursued

> Turning she was horrified to see that the truck was moving toward them. Nancy and her father, hemmed in by the concrete piers, had no way to escape being run down. (18)

And attacked

> They stared in horror at the scene before them [a ceiling has fallen]. Nancy
> lay unconscious and Helen seemed too dazed to move. (114)

But she triumphs

> "It's a real victory for you!" Nancy's father praised his daughter proudly. (181)

And deserving people gain

> Mr. Drew's kidnappers were caught, the "loot" was returned, and Miss Flora
> did not have to sell her house. (181)

And so it goes in other mysteries with variations only in location,
victim, secret, or villains.

The location is generic; the victim is sympathetic; the secret is the
stuff of mysteries—secret societies, treasure maps, and stolen jewels;
and the villains are scoundrels (Pecora). A representative list of plot
characteristics from the books reveals some of these characteristics.
(See Table 1.)

Of the forty-one mystery novels reviewed here for location, only four
are set in foreign lands (10 percent); three are set in cities (New Or-
leans, San Francisco, Tucson) and 10 in various states like Montana
or upstate New York (31 percent); while over half are placed in River
Heights or generic small towns or locations like the fictional Emerson

Table 1
Nancy Drew Mysteries
(1930–1994)

Case	Date	Place	Victim	Crime
2	1930	Twin Lakes	widow	jewel theft
8	1932	River Heights	missing heiress	swindling/inheritance
16	1938	Berryville	retired actress	jewel theft
22	1945	River Heights	professional dancer	swindling/inheritance
32	1955	River Heights	refugees	jewel/art theft
42	1965	Emerson College	old man	stolen treasure
51	1974	Emerson College	Ned (her boyfriend)	kidnapping
64	1981	Europe	orphans	espionage
86	1988	Montana	ranch owner	kidnapping
96	1990	River Heights	foreign athlete	sabotage
117	1994	New York state	chef/cooking school	attempted murder

College, a ranch, or an ocean liner (58 percent). Victims are most often orphans or widows or friends of Nancy and her pals or professionals like a track star, dancer, or photojournalist. The crimes are overwhelmingly burglaries, jewel theft, or attempts to steal inheritances or treasures (53 percent) or kidnappings (20 percent); occasionally there is a touch of poaching (one), blackmail (one), espionage or sabotage (five). In only one of the mystery novels is the crime murder. The mysteries offer formulaic plots set in generic places, about ordinary victims suffering crimes against property.

Expectations of the reader are confirmed—the floorboard always creaks in the same place and the locales and the victims are those of our imagination while the crime is never "really" threatening.

Nancy Drew Files—The Romance Novels

An analysis of the Nancy Drew romance novels illustrates that the conventions of the mysteries still hold in the story. (See Appendix B for a list of titles reviewed.) *Buried Secrets* offers an example of this as a mystery is established in the opening pages:

> While running for governor of the state, an election everyone was sure he'd win, John Harrington had died. His body was found at the bottom of the cliffs . . . No one was ever sure how or why he'd died . . . He was young, he was successful, and he was close to being elected governor of the State of Illinois. (6)

And soon there is a warning

> "Stay away from that case!" she said in a shaky voice. "I beg you, Nancy, don't have anything to do with it!" (23)

In fact twice in this story

> "I came to warn you, Miss Drew." The whisper was deep and harsh, and it made Nancy shiver. (64)

She is pursued

> Nancy checked the mirror again. The black car was still behind her, inches from her car. And now there was another car behind it—a tomato red model that was staying very close to the black one. (41)

And attacked

> It was a column of stone—a decorative element. As Nancy watched, it continued to wobble and then it started to fall—straight at her head. (107)

But she triumphs

"Well, congratulations, Nancy," Brenda Carlton [her rival] said over the phone a couple of days later. "You won." (149)

And deserving people gain

The hardest part had been telling Hannah [housekeeper for Nancy and her father] about Charles Ogden. Nancy had dreaded it, but when she finally told her, Hannah was very calm. "I'm lucky, in a way," she said. "If things had worked out and I'd married Charlie, I probably would have had a miserable life. I would never have met my husband—or come to work for your family." She smiled at Nancy. "And look at the wonderful life I've had." (151)

As in the Nancy Drew mystery books, variations in the romance novel narratives are minor. However, there are some interesting differences between the mysteries and the romances as revealed in the representative list in Table 2.

Table 2
Nancy Drew Romances
(1986 –1994)

Files	Date	Place	Victim	Crime
1	August 1986	River Heights	students	murder/ espionage
5	December 1986	Ft. Lauderdale	immigrants	attempted murder
11	August 1987	Texas	retired rancher	kidnapping
22	April 1988	Washington D.C.	chef/cooking school	blackmail
36	June 1989	Washington State	corporate takeover	murder
48–50	June–August 1990 (Trilogy)	The Hamptons	Russian ballet troupe	espionage
54	December 1990	Emerson College	Ned's friend	jewel theft
68	February 1992	Baltimore	The National Aquarium	illegal dumping
72–74	June–August 1992 (Trilogy)	Greek Isles	Nancy's friend	terrorism/ espionage
81	March 1993	Annapolis	boat owner	murder
92	February 1994	Emerson College	sorority house	stalking

In the forty-six romance novels reviewed, it is evident things changed. Although Nancy's hometown of River Heights still figures in more than a third of the books reviewed and Emerson College (the fictitious school Ned attends) in three, none of the other stories are set in generic locations. The stories are much more likely to take place in a major city or state. Settings like Los Angeles and Chicago and adventures like white water rafting in Colorado and skiing in Vermont account for almost half (41 percent) of the locales. Widows and orphans no longer appear, as the victim is more frequently a friend of Nancy or her boyfriend Ned or a public figure like a politician, athlete, or entertainer. There are still the jewel thefts, burglaries, and smuggling rings (eight) and sabotage/espionage (seven) but the crimes are as likely to be corporate fraud (six). Threats against people (kidnapping, stalking, blackmail, or murder) account for 52 percent of the crimes in the romance novels.

The locale in the romances is much more likely to be an identifiable place such as New York, Ft. Lauderdale, or Chicago; as compared with the generic old mansions and small towns of the mystery novels; none of these books are set in a small town like Berryville or Twin Lakes. And victims in the romances are generally young professionals; where death or its threat was a rare occurrence in the original mystery series in the romance novels it is more likely to be central to the theme. Still, the conventions of the mysteries are a part of the romances—a mystery appears, Nancy is warned, Nancy is pursued, Nancy is attacked, Nancy triumphs, and deserving people win—but now there are also romantic interludes.

Analysis of the plots in the Nancy Drew romance novels reveals other, more subtle, changes. One example is the recurring theme of corporate crime, in the romance novels the crime is often directed toward some form of corporate or organizational takeover. In *Deadly Intent*, the case involves "a conspiracy that could blow the lid off the music industry." The secondary plot in *Smile and Say Murder* is the corporate takeover of the "hottest new teen magazine." In addition to kidnappers in *Heart of Danger*, Nancy must thwart a young man's plans to take over his elderly stepfather's ranch. Never do we see orphans or old ladies about to lose their home as in the mystery books (though the old rancher comes close in *Heart of Danger*) and only in *Buried Secrets* does the plot revolve around past misdeeds as in the mysteries series.

The Consequences

The shift from mystery to romance has several implications—first for teen reading, in general, and second for the alternative identity offered young girls. By looking at the way the Nancy Drew novels change in the shift from mystery to romance genre it becomes evident that the imaginative energy the books begin with—helping old ladies, generic small town America, crimes against property—is recast. Girls are now offered an imaginative, more glamorous, world not unlike that of the soap opera.[3] Plots set in exciting and exotic places (to some Chicago is exotic) with attractive people doing interesting things. They have a soap-opera-like quality and change the nature of the fiction: marine biologists saving the planet or rock stars in danger or corporate fraud in the fashion world. In the romance novels reviewed here there were two instances where the plot continued for more than three books in a trilogy, none of the mystery novels have ever been presented in that way. The reader is enticed with glamour and danger, not the ordinariness and clever plot developments of the mysteries. One can only be concerned when teen reading shifts from jewel thefts to murder and stalking.

As could be predicted, the most significant changes between Nancy Drew mysteries and romances lie in the characterization of Nancy Drew herself and the emphasis on her relationship with Ned. In the mystery books he is her long-standing boyfriend, in the romance novels he often is a central figure. The opening paragraph of the first romance book establishes other changes to her character:

> "Something weird's going on here." Bess Marvin smiled and then glanced at her friend Nancy Drew. "Can you figure out what it is, famous detective?"
>
> Eighteen-year-old Nancy Drew stuck her credit card back in her wallet, shook her reddish blond hair back out of her blue eyes, and looked around the River Heights shopping mall. Nancy *was* famous for her detective work, but at the moment she was more interested in new clothes than a new case. (*Buried Secrets* 1)

The first two paragraphs establish a new Nancy—she is still the eighteen-year-old, blond, blue-eyed famous detective. But now she has a credit card and goes to shopping malls—the ideal of a teenager (in the eyes of a publishing house). Nancy Drew's character of the mystery novels was based on a formula established in the 1930s: "a personal involvement with the hero who overcomes some opposition using vivid but realistic action with the American virtues of hard work, honesty, clean living and wholesomeness encouraged and rewarded" (Dizer 58). Following in that tradition, over the years she has been portrayed as "clever, capable, popular, athletic, unusually pretty, friendly, attractive, skillful, kind, modest, good, brave, poised, keen-minded, plucky, self-reliant, unforgettable, distinctive, forceful, wise, splendid, observant, healthy, responsible, remarkable, and amazingly 'normal'" (Jones 707).

In addition, she has always been the central, dominant character in the mystery books. Other supporting characters have been her best friends, Bess and George (Bess is concerned with boys and her weight; George is a "tomboy"); the nurturing housekeeper, Hannah; and Nancy's adoring and adored father, Carson Drew: Lawyer. Ned, Nancy's boyfriend, has played a relatively minor role since his introduction in 1932. In almost all the mystery books he appears in, he does no more than hold Nancy's hand. Sexuality is never an issue, as the closest Nancy gets to "admiring" him is in a 1933 novel (Jones 713):

> As Nancy regarded his splendid physique, she mentally pitied anyone who challenged him to a fight. (*The Secret of Larkspur Lane*)

Clearly this was a rash moment of emotionality on her part but one not soon repeated.

Changes to other characters have been relatively minor in the Nancy Drew romances: Bess now eats yogurt and George has "the beautifully toned body of an athlete" (*Secrets Can Kill* 3). However, changes to Nancy and Ned have been more fundamental and reflect elements typical of the romance genre. Ned now appears in each of the stories, usually as a major figure and always as a love interest as others compete for Nancy's affection. In the first Nancy Drew romance story, *Secrets Can Kill*, Nancy is attracted to Daryl Gray, a gorgeous high school senior with blueberry eyes and a Porsche. Unfortunately, he turns out to be part of the blackmail ring and so, although Daryl's actions were pivotal to the romance novel, it's back to Ned:

> Nancy turned and caught Ned's eye. He was smiling at her and she felt a sudden urge to run her fingers through his hair. She also felt relieved that she's told him the truth about Daryl. She didn't want any secrets between her and Ned. (*Secrets Can Kill* 152)

The two are always kissing and hugging; Nancy has urges "to run her fingers through his hair," and she "tingles to his touch" (*Cold as*

Ice 3). They plan weekends away together (though, as always, chaper-oned—*Smile and Say Murder*) and he is always in her thoughts.

> After dinner that evening, Nancy went to her room to make her own phone call—to Ned. It was something she'd been looking forward to all day, and the familiar sound of Ned's voice warmed her. (*Heart of Danger* 30)

Nancy Drew romance novels still maintain her image as "girl detective," able to break up blackmail rings and solve mysteries. But now, as stated earlier, Nancy's relationship with Ned is much more fundamental to the story line. He has become her support.

> All at once the tension and terror of the past few hours hit Nancy. She felt weak. All she wanted was a pair of strong arms around her, holding her. The anger and pain she'd been holding inside for the last few days dissolved into nothing. She sank gratefully against Ned's chest. "It's over," she said at last. (*Smile and Say Murder* 143)

The old Nancy would never have "sank," gratefully or otherwise.

There have been other significant changes made to the earlier Nancy Drew. While in the mystery series Nancy spent little time with clothes,

> She hurried upstairs to her bedroom and packed some summer knits. When the suitcase was filled, she went to the kitchen. (*The Crooked Bannister* 2)

the new Nancy is often found preening,

> Nancy studied herself in the mirror. She liked what she saw. The tight jeans looked great on her long, slim legs and the green sweater complimented her strawberry-blond hair . . . "Right now," she said to her two friends, "the hardest part of this case is deciding what to wear." (*Secrets Can Kill* 3)

Where once Nancy was imperturbable, taking on any situation with little fear and/or emotion, she now demonstrates emotions not unlike those of most teenage girls. Her sense of self appears to be unwavering, as one would expect from an internationally known detective, but she is subject to tears and many of the same emotions we all felt as teenagers—guilt, shyness, and fear.

One reader described the new Nancy as a "1980s materialist, a narcissist, a yuppie" (Knepper in Sunstein 98). She has become a "workaholic" (*Smile and Say Murder* 145) who cries (*Heart of Danger* 89). The old Nancy would have never cried, nor would she have been nervous (*Secrets Can Kill* 12), guilty (*Secrets Can Kill* 54), shy

(*Buried Secrets* 15), shocked (*Secrets Can Kill* 83), and she didn't scream (*Deadly Doubles* 69). Though she still manages to bring home the pizza (*Buried Secrets* 63).

Clearly the people at Simon and Schuster have made changes to the character of Nancy Drew in the romance novels. At one level she remains the Nancy of old as she takes on mysterious adventures. But at another level she has become a romance heroine. She has become the victim of Ned's manliness as she "tingles to his touch" and worries about losing him to other girls.

An important contemporary issue has also become a concern of Nancy's, namely, the balance between boyfriend and "career." Often Ned complains about the time she spends away from him and the fact that her career is dangerous (Pecora). As one would expect in a shift from the mystery to romance genre, major changes to the text have been in the relationship between Nancy and Ned. No longer is Ned forgotten as he becomes an integral part of the stories. His relationship with Nancy more closely conforms to the fantasies of romance. And both Nancy and Ned encounter romantic rivals, the foundation of romance novels.

Although Nancy retains much of her autonomy in the romances, going off to exotic places to solve mysteries, she is now far more dependent on male affirmation and support. In the Nancy Drew mysteries she worries about treasures and scoundrels, in the romance novels she worries about relationships.

So It's Off to College . . .

Expanding the market even further, in the early 1990s a new series of teen novels entered the marketplace, telling stories of life on the college campus. Sweet Valley University was issued in 1993 and Nancy Drew on Campus was released in 1995. These tell stories of life after high school without parental supervision and guidance. In this section the books published in the first year of both series will be reviewed. (See Appendix C for a list of titles reviewed.)

Given the series' theme—life on a college campus—one would wish to find the books a model for planning the future, a primer for college life. More than 80 percent of high school girls expect to attend college (Karraker) and many college women aspire to successful careers (Pecora and Mazzarella). These are not unreasonable expectations for the Nancy Drew books because one of the characteristics of the mystery books was the lecture. The action of the story often stopped while Nancy explained, generally in a very pedantic manner, some esoteric issue. In the college series, the questions become: What information do these books offer? What advice do they confer?

As the Nancy Drew on Campus series begins, the primary characters are the people we know from the other Nancy Drew series: her boyfriend Ned, as before a student at nearby Emerson College; her best friends George, an athlete, and Bess, who still worries about her weight; and on very rare occasions her father, Carson Drew, who now has a new, younger wife. At Wilder University, new characters and a diversity lacking in the earlier books are introduced such as George's roommate Pam, an African-American woman who also happens to be an athlete; George's boyfriend, Will Blackfeather, a Native American and environmental activist; Jamal, Pam's boyfriend also African-American; and Bess' friend from the drama group, Brian, and his partner, Chris, both gay. Diversity and stereotypes. Then there are Paul, Dave, Harry, Bill, Dan, Tim, Ray, Scooter, and Charley and numerous other male characters (*New Lives, New Loves*).

As they begin college, the three girls—Nancy, Bess, and George—split up to begin new lives after having been friends since the 1930s, evident in the title of the first series book, *New Lives, New Loves*. Published once a month, these books chronicle life at Wilder University described by Nancy Drew as in a town where, "The streets were clean and wide, and the houses were a jumbled collection of old Victorians. . . . [with] a small organic food co-op, a diner, a used bookstore, and a Laundromat" (*New Lives, New Loves* 3).

The stories of Sweet Valley University revolve around Elizabeth and Jessica Wakefield, the twins of the Sweet Valley series, and their friends. Elizabeth is studious and responsible, while Jessica loves to date and party. Like Nancy Drew, they start college with many of their chums from earlier series. As they arrive on campus, Jessica and Elizabeth see "sun-dappled tree-lined streets . . . beautiful red-tiled buildings . . . groups of students laughing and talking as they strolled across the lawns, everything about the campus seemed to say, 'Welcome to college. Welcome to freedom.'" (*College Girls* 19).

In her analysis of the first year of the *Sweet Valley University* books, Joyce Litton found the books paid "little serious attention to what college life is like . . . trivial plots dominate . . . young women are silly, conniving and weak" (21). There are very few intellectual pursuits—studying takes place in response to parental pressure or boredom (21). According to Litton, "the view of college life is distorted because the series almost instantly plunges readers into the problems of Jessica's relationship and eventual marriage to Mike McAllery" (22), giving the books a soap-opera-like quality that is best illustrated by the story of Jessica's marriage presented over more than four novels. As Litton describes it,

> Mike drinks excessively and becomes abusive . . . Jessica becomes both fright-
> ened and fed up. Mike goes after her and pulls out a gun . . . Mike and Steven
> [their friend] struggle with each other, the gun goes off . . . Mike is paralyzed
> . . . Jessica has the marriage annulled, Mike regains use of his legs. (22)

Because these books are still in the genre of teen romance novels, one would expect issues of relationship to be foregrounded. However, Jessica's abusive marriage is certainly beyond the innocent relationships of most teen romance novels where love and sex are often discussed but seldom consummated.

The Real Challenges of College Life

To understand what image of college life is being presented to these girls and how representative this is of actual college experiences, this section will compare story lines in the first year of the books with issues identified as important by college students at Ohio University, a midwestern state school. In discussion, these students talked about problems of college life they encountered but were not prepared for— some as mundane as doing the laundry, others more serious even including issues such as date rape. Interviews and focus groups were held with students who were asked to talk about their experience at college and to explain what they had felt prepared to face during their first year and what came as a surprise. The students identified a number of issues that can be categorized into three broad areas: *Life Skills*, those situations that arise in day-to-day living such as doing laundry, shopping for food, getting cars repaired, earning money and paying bills, and taking care of health issues; *Academic Skills* including information about major areas of study, courses and grades, professors, and the intellectual experience; and *Social Skills*, the experience of dating, making friends, learning to live with a roommate, and joining extracurricular activities.

Life Skills: Several of the students interviewed for this project expressed the problems they had when faced with tasks that had always been done for them—clean clothes that magically appeared, food in the refrigerator, and an allowance that was generally adequate. When they arrived at school they were surprised that these things now needed their attention. Other students said they had been doing these things all along during high school so it was "no big thing" to continue when in college. Some of the first-year students talked about the problems of being sick and away from home for the first time. They weren't used to taking responsibility for going to the doctor or treating a cold. All agreed that it was a nuisance to have to deal with the everyday tasks of life.

Although college offers "new responsibilities and new freedoms" in the two series of novels, the characters in these books do not appear to be accountable for their own care. Nancy noted the food co-op and the Laundromat her first day on campus and that was one of the rare mentions of these institutions associated with tasks such as cooking dinner or doing laundry. While it is true that most colleges and universities require students to live on campus the first year, thus freeing students from many responsibilities, the students in these novels do not seem to be responsible for even the most basic tasks. Even if a student lives in the dorm, there is laundry to do and shopping for the essentials. Shopping for Nancy and her friends and for Jessica and Elizabeth is most often for clothes, though in one book problems arise when sorority pledges must do the shopping for party snacks (ND: *New Lives, New Loves*). No one has to get a car repaired, earn money, pay bills, or balance a checkbook. Housekeeping is limited to descriptions of messy rooms, generally in the context of the tensions between roommates. One of the rare home-cooked meals to appear in the books is an exotic affair cooked for Jessica by Mike—but they are "distracted" and never get to have the meal (SVU: *Love, Lies, and Jessica Wakefield*). Mostly, like the students interviewed, the characters eat pizza.

When fiction does confront life in the form of responsibility for a car accident, Jessica gives the other driver involved her phone number, not because of a sense of responsibility but in the hope he will telephone her. While he is railing about the damage to his car, she is recounting his physical appearance in her mind (SVU: *College Girls* 71).

None of the major characters appear to have part-time jobs, though a few minor characters wait tables or dispense coffee to pay their way through college. One exception is a suitemate of Nancy Drew who, with a male friend, starts a consulting firm to earn money for more expensive computer equipment. They eventually—in the euphemism of the books—become more than friends (ND: *New Lives, New Loves*).

And the bureaucracies of financial assistance, the bane of most students' lives, does not seem to exist. George is the only student who is having problems with Financial Aid. Her loan is denied because she is mistaken for a man who had not registered for Selective Service (thus denying access to federal support). Problems with the Federal Government are straightened out by her new friend Will Blackfeather, who is knowledgeable about problems with the government because of his experiences as a Native American. Go figure.

It would appear that very little attention is paid to the problems of daily life throughout these books. Students at Wilder University and Sweet Valley University, unlike the students at Ohio University, do not worry about the mundane tasks of life.

Academic Skills: Here the "real" students talked about the differences between high school and college, the different expectations and the difficulty in learning the process. At college, they claimed, learning to understand classroom expectations and the grading process was a challenge, as was making decisions about a major area of study that they perceived would be a commitment to a particular future. Several also lamented the fact that they had not yet had an "intellectual experience," that all night session discussing the meaning of life and the universe, and they felt they would not really feel like they had been in college until they had that experience.

One would expect (hope) that, in novels about college life, the reader could be offered some wisdom about the intellectual experience. The books could almost be seen as "how to manuals" and, indeed, in the first Sweet Valley University book Jessica explains how to cope with large lecture classes.

> Jessica headed for a seat in the middle of the large, crowded classrooms. Experience had taught her that if you sat in the front, teachers would notice when you weren't paying attention, but that if you sat at the back, they expected you not to be paying attention and would always ask you questions to make sure you were still awake. If you sat in the center, they hardly knew you were there. (SVU: *College Girls* 114)

Unfortunately for Jessica, the technique is not entirely successful and she is called on; however, she relies on her backup technique:

> She gave [the professor] one of her three-hundred-watt smiles and looked at him expectantly. It was a technique that used to work in high school. . . . he stared back at her like a rabbit in the headlights of an oncoming car. (SVU: *College Girls* 115–116)

Beyond that, little is to be learned about academics from these novels. Studying is something done only under duress. Too often the sentiment is that expressed by Casey in the Nancy Drew novel, *Party Weekend*: "Just a couple of hours in a study carrel can feel like *forever*" (25).

Interestingly, Nancy Drew and Elizabeth, one of the Sweet Valley twins, are enrolled in journalism programs. According to Nancy Drew on Campus, Nancy selected Wilder University, not only to be "out of Ned's shadow" but also because it has "one of the best journalism programs in the country" (ND: *New Lives, New Loves* 6). Elizabeth Wakefield is enrolled in the broadcast journalism program at Sweet Valley University and works for the campus station as an investigative reporter (SVU: *College Girls*). Bess majors in theater and her "cold-fish" roommate is a pre-med major (ND: *New Lives, New Loves*) and Liz's is an architecture major (ND: *Secret Rules*). Of course Ginny and Ray are "majoring in" romance (ND: *Broken Promises*) which appears to be the most popular area of study.

Based on the rare mention of courses, students appear to have interesting options. During her first year, Elizabeth takes a creative writing workshop, a literature course on the roots of feminism, a foundation course in classical thought and culture, the social history of the twentieth century, and an introductory journalism course (SVU: *College Girls* 54). No mention is made of those college or university-wide required courses that are often the curse of the freshmen student. Jessica takes the courses her adviser suggests because she thinks he's cute (SVU: *College Girls* 114).

College professors are a diverse group based on the descriptions in these books. Young readers can anticipate philosophy professors who are "balding, middle-aged [men] with glasses and a slight stoop" (SVU: *College Girls* 114) or loveable [male] journalism professors (SVU: *College Girls* 160). Nancy's journalism professor, a "retired war correspondent who'd defied everyone from presidents to generals to get the 'untold story'" inspires her so "her blood was pumping so hard she thought her veins would burst" (ND: *New Lives, New Loves* 156)—would that we all should inspire so. The only female professor encountered is a dynamic lecturer who turns out to be a blackmailer (ND: *It's Your Move* 6). The occasional teaching assistant is always male and hunk-like.

Grades are rarely an issue except in one novel where the murder of a math professor is the mystery plot when Bess's roommate is accused of the murder, he had been making sexual demands from her in exchange for a much needed high grade.

As Litton noted, studying is done under duress and pressure from parents or boredom (22). In one novel, Liz, an architecture student, spends much of her time in the studio (ND: *Secret Rules*) but places like the library are used only by those who are avoiding roommates or committing fraternity pranks (ND: *Secret Rules* 54). Bess groans at one point that she has to resort to studying to avoid guys (ND: *On Her Own* 151). She is also frustrated by how complicated her first year at college is but not because of any academic challenge but rather because of problems with relationships (ND: *Don't Look Back* 72). And Nancy laments on her first days on campus: "There's so much to do! . . . When is there time for class?" (ND: *New Lives, New Loves* 11).

Any sense of intellectual community or experience is strangely missing as the defining experience is not "college" but rather "romance." *Social Skills*: But these are, after all, romance novels. Consequently, relationships are first and foremost. Dating, making friends, living with a roommate, and extracurricular activities—the interest of the Ohio University students—are also the interest of the fictional college students. Many of the stories revolve around fraternity and sorority events, football games, school dances and dates, and the tensions in a relationship. In each series one character has a difficult time adjusting to college life: Elizabeth in Sweet Valley University and Bess in Nancy Drew on Campus. Also, in each the ugly duckling from high school becomes the swan. George, always considered "the tomboy," is the first to get a man, and Winthrop is put in the school system as Winnie and is placed in an all-female dorm too late to make a room change. He becomes a hero to the other guys (SVU: *College Girls* 228).

One of the "new freedoms" the characters of Nancy Drew on Campus and Sweet Valley University must face is premarital sex. Elizabeth and Todd, her high-school sweetheart, break up because she is not ready to spend the night (SVU: *College Girls* 90); George and Will take the big step (ND: *Secret Rules* 7); and even Nancy Drew begins to wonder about her "first time" (ND: *Secret Rules* 30).

Often these situations are frightening. During the first few days on campus, Bess is confronted with the potential of date rape at a campus party (ND: *New Lives, New Loves* 50) and George is stranded on a deserted road by a date (ND: *On Her Own*). A stalker follows Casey (ND: *Party Weekend*) and Jessica is saved from attackers twice by the end of the first Sweet Valley University novel (SVU: *College Girls*).

She is raped in a later novel (SVU: *Take Back the Night*). Rape, sexual harassment, and intimidation are themes in many of the stories. Overwhelmingly though these stories are about romantic love and here George and Will set a standard:

> The moon was streaking through the clouds, showering their campsite with white moonlight. The night air was surprisingly warm, and the only sounds were the crickets chirping softly in the trees and the nearby brook gurgling against the rocks. Will had held her gently as they stretched out side by side in their tent, which they'd set up on a springy bed of pine needles.
>
> Surprisingly, George hadn't felt uncomfortable. Will was gentle and loving—and he'd thought of everything. She didn't even have to bring up the subject of protection. They'd talked it all out before. (ND: *Secret Rules* 7)

This, and a conversation between Jessica and her roommate (SVU: *Loves, Lies, and Jessica Wakefield*), is one of the rare mentions of safe sex.

Because the market for these books is primarily young girls, one would like to see gender issues play a more central role in the stories. Strong friendships do form among the women in the books, with Nancy and Elizabeth often counseling, advising, and nurturing their friends. Unfortunately "girl talk" is limited to clothes and boys. Conversations about bras, waxing, and tampons only take place around Winnie when his dorm mates seek to embarrass him (SVU: *College Girls* 48). Issues of rape, substance abuse, and eating disorders for example, are present but the message is ambivalent and they are rarely confronted. In the Sweet Valley books, *Take Back the Night* and *No Means No*, a central plot is the issue of rape and credibility. Jessica is raped by a popular campus athlete and when she reports the crime, the authorities do not believe her story. Only after her sister Elizabeth organizes a "Take Back the Night" rally and the rape becomes public knowledge, does she receive support. Later in the series, when Jessica leaves her husband because he had been "womanizing" and assaulting her, one woman sees Jessica at fault.

> You know, she was his wife. He was wrong to threaten her, but she did her best to drive him nuts. She married him, then ran away from him every chance she got. (SVU: *Good-bye to Love* 17)

From volume four through twelve, a subtext in the Sweet Valley series is the stalking of Elizabeth by a psychopath she had thought to be the man of her dreams. The issue of "woman as victim" is ambivalent

though too often reinforcing traditional notions of secrecy and women
as tease.

Alcohol abuse and its consequences are in some way a part of each
book. For example, throughout the early Sweet Valley University series Jessica's husband beats her because he is an alcoholic and Bess is
almost raped because of having too much to drink at a fraternity party
(ND: *New Lives, New Loves*). Many schools and universities face campus disturbances based on alcohol abuse, and while this is a theme
returned to often in the books, few alternatives are offered. People go
to bars on dates, fraternities have beer parties, and athletes are portrayed as drinking frequently. Drug abuse is very rarely mentioned.

Another major contemporary problem on college campuses is eating disorders. However, the women in these books are always thin
and mostly blond perpetuating an idealized image of femaleness. When
Elizabeth gains "a little" weight in the first book she spends much of
the rest of the time thinking about the food she is or isn't eating (SVU:
College Girls). In one of the few scenes where the women are having
lunch together, the menu is lite (SVU: *No Means No* 162).

Finally, though this was not a part of the student discussions and
interviews, college is a time when we have the opportunity to meet
people from diverse backgrounds and become involved in political
causes. Yet, in these books, characters are often portrayed as stereotypes and only rarely involved in political action. In the Nancy Drew
on Campus series, characters fit the stereotypes assigned to them
elsewhere. Brian is the gay man in theater; Will Blackfeather, a Native
American, is a leader in the environmental movement, camper, and
familiar with the bureaucracies of government; Jamal and Pamela are
African-American athletes, at one point Jamal is accused of gambling;
and the two from New York, Liz and Danny, dress in black. The characters of Sweet Valley University appear to be less tied to stereotypes:
Jessica dates Danny who, though African-American, is neither an athlete nor a musician; Tom, an athlete, is the only one, male or female,
who appears to use an iron and ironing board.

Colleges are traditionally the site of political action movements and
many, though by no means all, students are first introduced to politics
while in college. Indeed, both series do address political action at
some level. Throughout the first year of the Nancy Drew series, Will
and George are active members of an environmental group and the
problem of fraternity hazing is the central plot in one book where
punishment for those involved included expulsion from school (ND:

Secret Rules). At Sweet Valley University, there is a political sorority but the message about political activism is clear. This is not the sorority of the "right" people: "They [weren't] the most popular and wealthiest girls. None of them were models or daughters of film stars" (SVU: *College Girls* 67–68). Pi Beta Phi was the sorority of "eccentrics and activists" (SVU: *College Girls* 68). Issues of racism and gay rights are present in both series but themes of political activism are subtle at best.

Overall, these books focus on relationships that just happen to be in a college environment. The books construct an image of "college life," the future of many of the readers, as one centered on the frustrations and joys of relationships—primarily heterosexual. Girls compete with each other for dates, they party often, and they worry about the weekend and their appearance. The Nancy Drew and Sweet Valley series offer myths about college life—a new guy every Friday—and ignore the realities of waking up with a cold and not having Mom, or Dad, there to make it better.

Conclusions

I set out to examine the way decisions in the publishing industry change the genre of teen novels—the ideological consequences of economic decisions. What happens when Simon and Schuster, in order to expand the market, transforms the Nancy Drew character from an independent and spirited detective in mystery novels to conform to the attributes of a romance heroine in the teen romance series? She becomes a vamp detective and a valuable commodity. As the publishing industry expands the market for teen novels Simon and Schuster (the publishing house for the Nancy Drew series) and Bantam Books (the publishing house for the Sweet Valley series) capitalize on the tradition and success of known characters and the formula genre. From 1930 to 1980 a young girl could look forward to a new Nancy Drew mystery each Christmas or birthday because only one or two books were published a year.[4] In 1997 more than forty new books in the Nancy Drew series were published. The same strategy is used by Bantam Books with the Sweet Valley series. When first introduced in 1983, Sweet Valley High books were published monthly. Added to those twelve books a year are now the series, Sweet Valley Kids, Sweet Valley Twins, The Unicorn, and Sweet Valley University accounting for more than sixty books a year with an occasional historical saga book or a cookbook or thriller. From Nancy Drew mysteries at less than $5.00 a year per book before the Simon and Schuster increase in market share to the multiple volumes of the series now available that can total almost $300 a year, it is easy to see why publishers keep extending the shelf space of these books. And the trend continues: Simon and Schuster has recently introduced a new series, *@Chat*, based on the growing popularity of (1) computers and (2) coffee houses. The books were first introduced and promoted as a new series in the Nancy Drew Files book, *Crime at the Ch@t Cafe*.

Each of these books is targeted to the preteen or teen market and offers a reality of life that is, at best, a soap opera and, at worst deceptive. As demonstrated in the Nancy Drew series, when the character shifts from the mystery genre to the romance genre, significant changes occur both in character and plot. The heroine, once spunky and independent, preens in front of mirrors and tingles to the touch of a male while the focus on romantic relationships moves to the foreground. In addition, the ambiance of the books changes. Generic victims in need of protection—widows, old men, orphans—are replaced by more glamorous characters like rock stars and tennis players. Meanwhile the action no longer takes place in the small towns of our imagination but is now placed in the big city. Perhaps most disturbing is the shift from crimes against property to crimes against people, from jewel thefts to murder.

If, as Gilbert and Taylor argue, the formal nature of these books discourages readers from making their own interpretations, interpretations that are not "idiosyncratic," and if the girls use the books to explore possibilities (Cherland) or "overwhelmingly identify with the story's heroine" as did those in Moffitt's study, then these young readers will come to understand college life as one long party (though there are those who would see this as a truth). The representation of college life and its incumbent responsibilities are not presented in the context of "real" problems—balancing checkbooks, stretching intellectually, functioning as an adult—but college is seen as a series of parties, dates, and emotional disasters. It is a place where there is no need to worry about the everyday and mundane. These books do, on the other hand, play out much of the sexual ambivalence of our current culture. As in the Sweet Valley High series, often the experience of a rape victim or abused partner is not validated and, as in many of the books' themes, premarital sex is an issue of confusion to many young girls. One would just like the books to offer more.

The young women I spoke with talked of being unprepared for the pressures of college, not only in terms of social life but also life skills and academic skills. They expressed a naivete about the pressures and demands of the college experience. Too often in college, women need the spunkiness of a Nancy Drew to survive. Yet the image of college life offered in the Nancy Drew novels is that of one long romance novel or soap opera, not the serious business of learning to be an adult.

The young readers of these books will learn of an academic life that reflects the 1950s when a woman's college career goal was an MRS. not a B.A. or B.S. degree. Girls were encouraged to attend college to find a "good" husband not a professional career. The young women of Wilder University and Sweet Valley University who go to class or the library to meet guys are perpetuating these outdated roles and not encouraging girls to think about their intellectual and professional potential.[5] Though Nancy and Elizabeth work as student journalists, none of the girls talk of future possibilities. For example, none strive for or make the Dean's list.

In the romance novels the previously strong and spunky character of Nancy Drew has been rewritten to reinforce an ideology of femininity that includes romance and glamor, and soap-opera-like adventures but, most important, the idea of woman-as-couple. There is little opportunity to see the women in these novels as strong and independent. In both the romance and college series, authority figures are rare, the few adults are fathers who pay the bills, or an occasional professor with problems. The formula of romance requires that a central element of the plot—obviously—revolves around romance. However for these books, set on a college campus, there is no reason the stories can't offer girls a more empowering and realistic understanding of their potential and the possibilities of life on a college campus. One wonders what would have happened if Nancy or Elizabeth went to Smith.

Appendix A
Nancy Drew Mystery Books—
Titles Included in Table 1

Case	Year	Title	
2	1930	The Hidden Staircase	—published by Grosset
3	1930	The Bungalow Mystery	and Dunlop
5	1930	The Secret at Shadow Ranch	
6	1931	The Secret of Red Gate Farm	
7	1932	The Clue in the Diary	
8	1932	Nancy's Mysterious Letter	
12	1935	The Message in the Hollow Oak	
14	1937	The Whispering Statue	
16	1938	The Clue of the Tapping Heels	
17	1940	The Mystery of the Brass Bound Trunk	
19	1942	The Quest of the Missing Map	
20	1943	The Clue in the Jewel Box	
21	1944	The Secret in the Old Attic	
22	1945	The Clue in the Crumbling Wall	
25	1948	The Ghost of Blackwood Hall	
29	1952	The Mystery at the Ski Jump	
31	1953	The Ringmaster's Secret	
32	1954	The Scarlet Slipper Mystery	
33	1955	The Witch Tree Symbol	
34	1957	The Hidden Window Mystery	
37	1960	The Clue in the Old Stagecoach	
39	1962	The Clue of the Dancing Puppet	
40	1963	The Moonstone Castle Mystery	
42	1965	The Phantom of Pine Hill	
44	1967	The Clue in the Crossword Cipher	
47	1970	The Mysterious Mannequin	
48	1971	The Crooked Banister	
49	1972	The Secret of Mirror Bay	
51	1974	The Mystery of the Glowing Eye	
52	1975	The Secret of the Forgotten City	
53	1976	The Sky Phantom	
55	1978	The Mystery of Crocodile Island	

58	1980	The Flying Saucer Mystery	—Simon and Schuster
63	1981	The Twin Dilemma	begins publishing the
64	1981	Captive Witness	Nancy Drew Books
71	1983	The Silver Cobweb	
82	1988	The Clue in the Camera	
85	1988	The Secret of Shady Glen	
86	1988	The Mystery of Misty Canyon	
88	1988	The Search for Cindy Austin	
89	1989	The Case of the Disappearing DeeJay	
96	1990	The Case of the Photofinish	
101	1991	The Mystery of the Missing Millionaires	
107	1992	The Legend of Miner's Creek	
108	1992	The Secret of the Tibetan Treasure	
111	1993	The Secret of Solaire	
117	1994	Mystery on the Menu	

Appendix B
Nancy Drew Romance Novels—
Titles Included in Table 2

Case	Year	Title	
1	1986	Secrets Can Kill	—all Nancy Drew Romance
2	1986	Deadly Intent	Novels published by
3	1986	Murder on Ice	Simon and Schuster
4	1986	Smile and Say Murder	
5	1986	Hit and Run Holiday	
6	1986	White River Terror	
7	1987	Deadly Doubles	
9	1987	False Moves	
10	1987	Buried Secrets	
11	1987	Heart of Danger	
16	1987	Never Say Die	
20	1988	Very Deadly Yours	
21	1988	Recipe for Murder	
22	1988	Fatal Attractions	
24	1988	Till Death Do Us Part	
26	1988	Playing With Fire	
34	1989	Vanishing Act	
36	1989	Over the Edge	
41	1989	Something to Hide	
45	1990	Out of Bounds	
48	1990	A Date With Deception	
49	1990	A Portrait in Crime	
50	1990	Deep Secrets	
51	1990	A Model Crime	
52	1990	Danger for Hire	
53	1990	Trail of Lies	
54	1990	Cold As Ice	
57	1991	Into Thin Air	
59	1991	High Risk	
60	1991	Poison Pen	
62	1991	Easy Mark	
66	1991	Tall, Dark and Deadly	
68	1992	Crosscurrents	

71 1992 Hot Tracks
72 1992 Swiss Secrets
74 1992 Greek Odyssey
78 1992 Update on Crime
79 1993 No Laughing Matter
81 1993 Making Waves
83 1993 Diamond Deceit
84 1993 Choosing Sides
89 1993 Designs in Crime
90 1993 Stage Fright
92 1994 My Deadly Valentine
94 1994 Illusions of Evil
95 1994 Instincts of Trouble

Appendix C

Nancy Drew on Campus

Volume	Date	Title
1	1995 July	New Lives, New Loves
2	1995 August	On Her Own
3	1995 November	Don't Look Back
4	1995 December	Tell Me the Truth
5	1996 January	Secret Rules
6	1996 February	It's Your Move
7	1996 March	False Friends
8	1996 April	Getting Closer
9	1996 May	Broke Promises
10	1996 June	Party Weekend
11	1996 July	In the Name of Love
12	1996 August	Just the Two of Us

Sweet Valley University

Volume	Date	Title
1	1993 October	College Girls
2	1993 October	Love, Lies, and Jessica Wakefield
3	1994 February	What Your Parents Don't Know . . .
4	1994 April	Anything for Love
5	1994 June	A Married Woman
6	1994 August	The Love of Her Life
7	1994 October	Goodbye to Love
8	1994 December	Home for Christmas
9	1995 February	Sorority Scandal
10	1995 March	No Means No
11	1995 April	Take Back the Night
12	1995 June	College Cruise

Notes

1. As a part of this project, interviews and focus groups were conducted with students at Ohio University, a large Midwestern state university in Athens Ohio. The students spoke about their experiences at college, the concerns they had as entering freshmen, and the problems they encountered during their college careers. The material here draws on the first-year women who spoke in the focus groups and individual interviews with others students unable to attend the focus group session.

2. There are many histories and commentaries on the Nancy Drew books including the published proceedings from a conference held in Iowa in 1995 (Dyer and Romalov; see also Billman; Inness; and Siegel). However, there are few histories of the Sweet Valley High series (see Christian-Smith, *Becoming a Woman*; and Litton). In part this is because of their relatively recent arrival in young adult reading, but, it is also, one suspects, because of the nature of the books. They are, after all, romance novels and until recently the artifacts of everyday life like soap operas, romance novels, and teen magazines have not been considered worthy of academic study.

3. The author thanks Sharon Mazzarella for pointing out the "glamour factor" and the soap opera-like consequences of the shift from mystery genre to romance genre.

4. This is not to deny the economic nature of the first generation of Nancy Drew books. The series were a part of the Stratemeyer syndication set up in the 1920s and 1930s to mass-produce books for a new market of young readers.

5. On the other hand, these books may reinforce the work of Dorothy Holland and Margaret Eisenhart who claim that the "Academic culture of the university is largely irrelevant to the daily lives of most of the students studied" (Connell in Holland and Eisenhart ix). They also found that "a decreasing investment in school work coincided with an increasing investment in romantic relationships" (220).

Works Cited

Bachen, Christine, and Eva Illouz. "Imagining Romance: Young People's Cultural Models of Romance and Love." *Critical Studies in Mass Communication* 13.4 (1996): 279–308.

Billman, Carol. *The Secret of the Stratemeyer Syndicate.* New York: The Ungar Publishing Company, 1986.

Brown, Lyn Mikel, and Carol Gilligan. *Meeting at the Crossroads: Women's Psychology and Girls' Development.* New York: Ballantine Books, 1993.

Cawelti, John. *Adventure, Mystery, and Romance.* Chicago: University of Chicago Press, 1976.

Cherland, Meredith Rogers. *Private Practices: Girls Reading Fiction and Constructing Identity.* Great Britain: Taylor and Francis, 1994.

Christian-Smith, Linda K. *Becoming a Woman through Romance.* New York: Routledge, 1990.

———. "Romancing the Girl: Adolescent Romance Novels and the Construction of Femininity." *Becoming Feminine: The Politics of Popular Culture.* Eds. Linda Roman, Linda Christian-Smith, and Elizabeth Ellsworth. London: The Falmer Press, 1988. 76–101.

———. "Voices of Resistance: Young Women Readers of Romance Fiction." *Beyond Silenced Voices: Class, Race, and Gender in United States Schools.* Eds. Lois Weis, and Michelle Fine. New York: SUNY Press, 1993. 169–89.

———. "Young Women and Their Dream Lovers: Sexuality in Adolescent Fiction." *Sexual Cultures and the Construction of Adolescent Identities.* Ed. Janice M. Irvine. Philadelphia: Temple University Press, 1994. 206–227.

Dizer, John. *Tom Swift and Company: "Boy's Books" by Stratemeyer and Others.* North Carolina: McFarland and Company, 1982.

Dyer, Carolyn Stewart, and Nancy Tillman Romalov, Ed. *Rediscovering Nancy Drew.* Iowa City: University of Iowa Press, 1995.

Frazer, Elizabeth. "Teenage Girls Reading *Jackie*." *Media, Culture and Society* 9 (1987): 407–425.

Gilbert, Pam, and Sandra Taylor. *Fashioning the Feminine.* North Sydney, Australia: Allen and Unwin, 1991.

Gilligan, Carol. *In a Different Voice.* 2nd ed. Cambridge, MA: Harvard University Press, 1993 (1st ed. 1982).

Holland, Dorothy C., and Margaret A. Eisenhart. *Educated in Romance: Women, Achievement, and College Culture*. Chicago: University of Chicago Press, 1990.

Huntwork, Mary M. "Why Girls Flock to Sweet Valley High." *School Library Journal* 36.3 (1990): 137–140.

Inness, Sherrie A. *Nancy Drew and Company: Culture, Gender, and Girls' Series*. Bowling Green, OH: Bowling Green State University Popular Press, 1997.

Jones, James. "Nancy Drew, WASP Super Girl of the 1930's." *Journal of Popular Culture* 6 (1973): 707–717.

Karraker, Meg Wilkes. "Predicting Adolescent Female's Plans for Higher Education: Race and Socioeconomic Differences." Paper presented at the 16th Annual Meeting of the National Association for Equal Opportunity in Higher Education, Washington D.C. March 1991.

Litton, Joyce A. "The Sweet Valley High Gang Goes to College." *The ALAN Review* (1996): 20–23.

Mann, Judy. *The Difference*. New York: Wagner Books, 1996.

Mason, Bobbie Ann. *The Girl Sleuth*. Old Westway NY: Feminist Press, 1975.

McRobbie, Angela. "*Jackie*: An Ideology of Adolescent Femininity." *Popular Culture: Past and Present*. Eds. Bernard Waites, Tony Bennett, and Graham Martin. London: Croom Helm, 1982. 263–283.

———. "Shut Up and Dance: Youth Culture and Changing Modes of Femininity." *Cultural Studies* 7.3 (1993): 406–426.

———. and Jenny Garber. "Girls and Subcultures." *Resistance through Rituals*. Eds. Stuart Hall, and Tony Jefferson. London: Hutchinson, 1975. 209–229.

Moffitt, Mary Anne. "Articulating Meaning: Reconceptions of the Meaning Process, Fantasy/Reality, and Identity in Leisure Activities." *Communication Theory* 3.3 (1993): 231–251.

Moss, Gemma. "Girls Tell the Teen Romance: Four Reading Histories." *Reading Audiences: Young People and the Media*. Ed. David Buckingham. Manchester U.K.: Manchester University Press, 1993. 116–134.

Motes, Julia J. "Teaching Girls to Be Girls: Young Adult Series Fiction." *The New Advocate* 11.1 (1998): 39–53.

Pecora, Norma. "A Feminist Reading of Nancy Drew." Paper presented at the Association for Education in Journalism and Mass Communication. Minneapolis, Minnesota. Aug. 1989.

———. and Sharon R. Mazzarella. "Kurt Cobain, Generation X, and the Press: College Students Respond." *Popular Music and Society* 19.2 (1995): 3–22.

Pipher, Mary. *Reviving Ophelia: Saving the Selves of Adolescent Girls.* New York: Ballantine Books, 1995.

Poe, Elizabeth, Barbara G. Samuels, and Betty Carter. "Past Perspectives and Future Directions: An Interim Analysis of Twenty-Five Years of Research on Young Adult Literature." *The ALAN Review* (1995): 46–50.

Radway, Janice A. *Reading the Romance.* Chapel Hill: University of North Carolina Press, 1984.

Rothenberg, Dianne. *Supporting Girls in Early Adolescence.* Urbana IL: ERIC Clearinghouse on Elementary and Early Childhood Education, 1995.

Siegel, Deborah L. "Nancy Drew as New Girl Wonder: Solving It All for the 1930s." *Nancy Drew and Company: Culture, Gender, and Girls' Series.* Ed. Sherrie A. Inness. Bowling Green, OH: Bowling Green University Popular Press, 1997. 159–182.

Smith, Wendy. "An Earlier Start on Romance." *Publishers Weekly* 13 Nov. 1981: 56.

Stern, Lori. "Disavowing the Self in Female Adolescence." *Women, Girls & Psychotherapy.* Eds. Carol Gilligan, Annie G. Rogers, and Deborah Tolman. New York: Hawthorn Press, Inc., 1991. 105–117.

Sunstein, Bonnie S. "'Reading' the Stories of Reading: Nancy Drew Testimonials." *Rediscovering Nancy Drew.* Eds. Carolyn Stewart Dyer, and Nancy Tillman Romalov. Iowa City: University of Iowa Press, 1995. 95–112.

Taylor, Jill McLean, Carol Gilligan, and Amy M. Sullivan. *Between Voice and Silence: Women and Girls, Race and Relationship.* Cambridge, MA: Harvard University Press, 1995.

Teen Romances. "Writing for the Teen Market." *Romantic Times* (Summer 1982): 5.

Wood, Leonard. "How Teenage Book Tastes Change." *Publishers Weekly* 25 July 1986: 39.

———. "Teenage Book Buying Matches Adult Purchasing." *Publishers Weekly* 22 Aug. 1986: 106.

Yost, Edna. "The Fifty Cent Juveniles." *Publishers' Weekly* 18 June 1932: 2405–2408.

Chapter 4

Girlhood Pastimes:
"American Girls" and the Rest of Us

Sarah Eisenstein Stumbar and Zillah Eisenstein

In this essay, my mom and I present a dialogue between ourselves about how it feels to be twelve and a girl, and a feminist author/ professor/mother in a culture dominated by boys and men. We agree about a lot but feel it differently sometimes. My mom (Zillah) says she learns a lot from me, and often I get her to change her mind about things. She sometimes gives the consumerist side of culture too much power. I remind her that I have a mind, and think things through in different ways than what is often expected. So when I wanted a Barbie I convinced her that I made Barbie into what I wanted her to be. She still did not get me a Barbie, but all her friends did.

I look at the American Girls Collection—its books, dolls, games, and clothes, etc.—as a fantastic exception to a boy-dominated world. The American Girls Collection creates a world of girls. Samantha, Molly, Felicity, Kirsten, Addy, and Josephina let me experience different historical periods from the dolls' viewpoint. Through their lives, experiences, dreams, parties, and disappointments I learn about colonial America, slave times, pioneer days, the early twentieth century, World War II and New Mexico's past.

It was great fun to explore these stories. They were a jumping-off point for me to think more about girls who lived in time periods different from mine.

I wondered and was a little bothered that none of these girls was poor, except for Addy when she was a slave, but then even she becomes dazzlingly successful. And none of the girls is Jewish, or Muslim, or Korean, or Puerto Rican, like the girls in my school.

Josephina is the exception to this. She is the newest addition to the collection, a Mexican Catholic girl. But she wasn't added to the collection until 1997. Actually, my mom was always bothered by the fact that the collection was called "American." She says: After all, what about all the girls who live in the United States who would not identify themselves as American? And what about South America? I actually agree with my mom—and yet I love the American Girls Collection.

It is this contradiction—that the collection has its faults and its strengths—that keeps my mom and me talking. The American Girls Collection lets me pretend that the world is made up of strong and interesting girls who are taken seriously. Yet, I still know that this is not usually the case: girls are often ignored and their viewpoint questioned. I also know that girls are really very much more diverse than those in the American Girls series. But, in my mind I make the series be the way I want it to be. When the public library did not have all the American Girls books I convinced my mom and dad to buy them for me. They bought me the more than thirty books at $5.95 each. I know that so many girls can't afford this and I know that this is not fair. But this did not stop me from wanting them. And although my mom and dad refused to get me the doll, Samantha (approximately $85), my mom's sister, Julia, as much a feminist as my mom is, did. My aunt and I choose my holiday additions together, and it is great fun.

I'll share with you the way my mom and I agree and disagree about how I will be a twelve-year-old feminist, my way. I will be writing more of the dialogue than my mom, because as a girl I need more space. Our thoughts are somewhat fragmented because my experiences and my mom's ideas keep shifting and changing as we explore new places and spaces. We will share our thoughts honestly and directly, even though they jump around and do not always fit together neatly. So let me start.

Sarah: I am twelve and have always been a girl. I know what it feels like to have boys everywhere; in movies, in books, and in the classroom, waving their hands high. Don't get me wrong! Being a girl is great. Really, I would not want to be a boy. I just wish we girls could have more room to express OUR ideas. I also think that our culture would be more interesting and fun, especially for girls, if girls could be more of a jumping-off place for films, books, etc.

I think that girls have to create their "own" popular culture and use what exists to do so. The American Girls Collection is a chance to do this and that is why it has grabbed me and pulls me along.

Zillah: It is amazing to me how the American Girls Collection knows how to commercially tap into girls' interests. The magazine tells them how to make birthday parties and do different crafts; tells stories of girls across time and place; and most of all, takes girls seriously. Sarah, for her eight-year-old birthday party, made petits fours like Samantha did in her Victorian times. She *and* her friends loved dressing up old fashioned and pretending to live like girls used to. The whole process amazes me.

Sarah: When I was three it seemed like all the books were about boys. Because I read so much it made me feel like everything was focused on boys: everything. My mom and dad would read me stories with boy characters but would change the names so that there were some girls.

Wherever I turned there were boys. I was drowning in a culture where it was all boys. Names, pictures, stories, all my earliest memories were of boys, and I was a girl.

My mom, dad and I searched and searched for books that put girls in the spotlight without making them always seem boy-crazed and stupid. When we found them I felt triumphant. I loved stories with girls, so we continued to scavenge and search for them.

I have already told you that I think it is great to be a girl and I am glad that I am who I am. I don't want you to think that my search for my own space and mirrors makes me feel inferior, or less than. I am glad that I am a girl even though I know that boys are given more freedom, time, and recognition—almost always.

I am sure that this has much to do with my family life. It probably matters that my name, Sarah Eisenstein Stumbar, is a result of my parents' desire to be fair rather than follow patriarchal boy custom. My parents decided before I was born that if I was a boy, my last name would be my mother's. If I was born a girl, I would have my father's last name.

My dad was the first to hold me when I was born, and he bottle-fed me half the time; my mom breast fed me the other half. In short: I feel like my earliest beginnings challenged the usual boy/girl dividers.

Zillah: It is an amazing process to grow up a second time with an
          adolescent daughter. We have just been through a hard year at
          school where Sarah's classroom was obnoxiously dominated
          by boys who were aggressive and mean spirited about girls
          and sex and sexuality. I remember one day Sarah wore a gay
          rights pin to school and several of the boys in her class went
          wild. They taunted Sarah, demanding that she tell them if she
          were gay. Her answer was fabulous and really got them going:
          she simply said she did not know yet.
               I just finished reading *Reviving Ophelia* by Mary Pipher
          and I've been reading lines from it to Sarah. The book de-
          scribes the enormous insecurities of adolescent girls. Sarah is
          keen to make sure she knows her true self and is amazed when
          she finds parts of herself described in Pipher's book. When
          Sarah starts yelling that she cannot figure out her "advanced
          math class" problem I remind her of *Reviving Ophelia*, then
          she calms down and invariably figures it out.
               Adolescence seems fabulously tricky. For Sarah it mixes
          and marbles several selves: her love of history ("herstory," as
          she says) and her studies of World War II, especially of chil-
          dren in hiding in those years; her love of sports and athletic
          challenges; her devotion to friends and friendship; her politi-
          cal commitments to racial, sexual, and economic equality; and
          her phantasmic imaginings with her dolls, especially Samantha,
          of the American Girls Collection. Let her tell you about this
          particular happiness.
Sarah: The American Girls Collection is really one of the only main-
          stream/popular culture things I do. I do not really watch much
          TV or see most movies made for kids. I hated *Clueless* but
          loved *The Incredibly True Adventure of Two Girls in Love*,
          Antonia's Line, and *Sense and Sensibility*. But I'm still a
          girl who likes to have fun and pretend with my dolls and friends.

The American Girls Collection and Me (by Sarah)

In second grade my teacher, Cindy, read a book, *Kirstin's Surprise*,
to the whole class. **Kirsten** lives in 1854. She is Swedish and lives on
the prairie in Minnesota. When I realized she was part of a "collection," called the American Girls, I could not wait to find out more. I
was really happy to have a whole series of books to read about four

girls' lives (Addy and Josephina hadn't been created yet). There were twenty-four books in all. I liked reading about Kirsten because she was a girl and seemed to be a girl with a dream, and a dream she reached for. Kirsten's stories centered on her feelings, and as a girl I felt at home. She was part of *her*story, and made me feel included. Because Kirsten was the first girl in the series that I read about, she holds a magic that none of the other American Girls hold. What I love about Kirsten is that her story feels true: language doesn't come easy to her, and she isn't overjoyed about her mom's new baby, but life still goes on. She can't always go to school because of housework, but she makes do.

Addy is an exslave who is growing up in Philadelphia in the 1860s. I was really happy when American Girl added Addy, the only African-American girl in the series. I had never thought that the American Girls books really represented the variety of girls that exist, but they are closer now that there is Addy. What I like about Addy is she has the seriousness of someone who has known much pain, but still she celebrates her happiness and laughs a lot. She knows that she is lucky to be in Philadelphia, where she is free, and reminds me to appreciate freedom. Addy's stories taught me a lot about the people who helped newly freed slaves and what their lives were like. What I don't like about the Addy books is she learns to read and write very quickly. Everything works out perfectly. In the last book the whole family is together, except for her aunt and uncle. This didn't happen much in real life for exslaves. Even though I find some parts of Addy's books unrealistic given the reading I have done about slavery, I still love them.

Samantha is a young girl growing up in the Victorian era. Until the Addy books were written, Samantha was my favorite girl. Samantha was my favorite girl/doll because she does not let herself be held captive to the beliefs of her time. She climbs trees and says what she thinks. I love the way she makes friends with a poor servant named Nelly, who lives next door. In Samantha's lifestory there are many varied views about women of her time. Samantha's grandmother is stuck in the old-fashioned ways, but her aunt is a suffragette. Samantha isn't quite sure what her beliefs are. What I don't like about Samantha is she doesn't know how privileged her life is. She doesn't know about people that aren't as wealthy as she is. I also think that she is sometimes selfish and unthinking. In *Meet Samantha* she runs out in the middle of the night, without telling anybody, because she wants to know why the family's seamstress left without telling her goodbye.

This shows that Samantha is very self-centered and cares much more about herself than anybody else.

Felicity is growing up during the American Revolution in Williamsburg, Virginia, in 1774. I have never really liked Felicity. Whenever I go to the shelf to choose a book from the American Girls Collection, her books are never my first choice. I do not like Felicity because I think she is a rich snob. In *Happy Birthday Felicity*, Felicity gets her grandmother's old guitar as a birthday present, and she takes it to her lessons, disobeying her parents. Then she loses the guitar by leaving it on a bench. She does not care, thinking that everything and anything can be replaced. True, she is not all bad and she does help people. In *Felicity Saves the Day* she helps Ben, her father's apprentice who ran away, but she would not have done so if that fall Ben hadn't kept her secret about a horse named Penny. Because she loves horses, Felicity had helped Penny run away from Nye, her evil master. I think that if someone asked Felicity to help them, but they could give nothing back to her, that Felicity would not help. She is selfish and self-centered.

Molly is growing up on the homefront in the United States in 1944, during World War II. I like the setting and time in which the Molly books take place, but I think that they do not represent enough about what was going on in the war. The books only discuss what was happening in the United States and how Americans were fighting against the Germans. Nothing is said about the Japanese in the United States or abroad, or the horrors in Europe and Africa. I also do not like the plots of the books. *Changes for Molly* is all about tap dancing and her dad coming home. There is little said about her feelings about war, or about Hitler, or about the devastation of Europe. I like Molly as a person but I think that she could help us know more about the sadness of war.

In Sum

Sarah: Even though I do not think that all of the American Girls books are great, I love the American Girls series because it lets me read about girls and imagine them and myself in different times in *her*story.

　　　　The American Girls Collection lets the part of me— and it keeps getting smaller—that wants to be a part of the popular culture belong. That is both good—a space for girls— and bad—it's still exclusionary of many.

Zillah: The American Girls series clearly introduced Sarah to pieces of *herstory* that she then explored further on her own. At the same time it also directs girls toward "shopping" as a way of experiencing their culture and history. This is tough. Sarah knew some of the stuff was silly and unnecessary, and yet she also wanted to take part.

Sarah: I do not like it when the Pleasant Company—the makers of the American Girls Collection[1]—tries to sell you stuff that you do not need for tons of money. Girls who are not wealthy cannot buy from the catalogue. And even middle-class girls cannot buy lots of the things advertised.

Recently the Pleasant Company marketed a new series called The American Girl of Today. This consists of items that Kirsten, Felicity, Samantha, Addy, Molly, and Josephina would wear if they lived in the 1990s. Supposedly these items are what the "average" girl would use and wear today. When I say average, I mean girls who wear jeans, shorts, baseball caps, and rollerblades. In all of the "new stuff" to buy for one's dolls, there is not a book or a multicultural item. Yes, I do have the jeans for Samantha and a pair of shorts for myself. But I wish that there were different choices of how one can look, and be, today.

I think the Pleasant Company is best at marketing historical items, not the things of today. I think that the only reason the Pleasant Company developed this line is that they are running out of ideas to make money on. And then I get annoyed.

Zillah: As Sarah enters middle school I wonder what her outlets for celebrating her girlhood will be. Samantha still sits on her bed, but I wonder for how long.

Afterthoughts

Zillah: It is important to recognize that alternative media—like *New Moon*, a magazine for girls and their dreams, *Stone Soup*, a journal of young people's writing, and *Skipping Stones*, a multicultural children's magazine—exist to help young girls find their voice. Given popular culture's representation of phallocratic privilege in particular "adolescent" form, girls must reinvent spaces for themselves. And many of them are doing so.

These girls—and consumer culture—are a complicated product of the partial successes of feminism and feminism's commercialization. My daughter and many of her friends are thriving, even though phallocratic culture uses feminism for its own market purposes, which are hardly in girls' interests.

Clearly the American Girls Collection was important to Sarah between the ages of eight and eleven. This year, at twelve, and in middle school, she no longer seems interested in American Girl in the same way. She is engaged elsewhere. Nevertheless, Samantha still sits on her bed, and she'll get the newest Josephina books from the library.

Sarah is annoyed that only the Josephina books are translated into Spanish. She says if The American Girls Collection was serious about multilingual access all the books would be available in Spanish. Sarah clearly feels free to both embrace and criticize the American Girls empire. Maybe this is all we can ask for given the constraints and pressures of a consumer culture that markets male violence right alongside girl's empowerment.

Note

1. Mattel Inc., the maker of Barbie, bought Pleasant Co. for $700 million in June 1998. ("Mattel Agrees to Buy Maker of American Girl Dolls." *New York Times* 16 June 1998: D4.)

Chapter 5

The "Superbowl of All Dates": Teenage Girl Magazines and the Commodification of the Perfect Prom

Sharon R. Mazzarella

Led by Angela McRobbie's groundbreaking semiotic analysis of the British teen girl magazine *Jackie*, recent years have yielded a multitude of quantitative and qualitative analyses of teenage girls' magazines both in the United States and Great Britain. The majority of these analyses have focused on the discourses of beauty and romance prevalent in these magazines. In her study of *Seventeen* magazine, for example, Kate Peirce found that the major focus of the magazine was beauty and fashion. Looking specifically at messages (including both advertising and editorial content) about nutrition and fitness, Eileen Guillen and Susan Barr found that such messages typically focus on weight loss and physical attractiveness. Similarly, Ellis Evans, Judith Rutberg, Carmela Sather and Charli Turner found that, taken together, the predominant message of *Seventeen*, *Young Miss*, and *Sassy* is on self-improvement as defined by "fashion dressing and physical beautification" (110). According to Margaret Duffy and J. Micheal Gotcher (32), the teen magazine *YM* presents "a social reality in which the only power available to young women is achieved through seduction, beauty, and fashion." Yet, as Meenakshi Durham found, *Seventeen* and *YM* often give girls conflicting messages. These magazines inform girls of the need to be beautiful and therefore sexually attractive to males, but at the same time warn them to be sexually responsible. In addition, recent studies have documented the often negative effects of such magazines on adolescent girls (Levine, Smolak, and Hayden; Martin and Gentry; Martin and Kennedy).

In this essay I narrow the analysis of teenage girl magazines in the United States by focusing on the way in which these magazines market and sell one particular component of female teen culture—the high school prom. Specifically, the purposes of this essay then are to (1) articulate how the "perfect" prom is defined by the articles and advertisements in these magazines, (2) identify the ingredients (i.e., commodities) presented as necessary to the creation of such perfection, and (3) analyze the underlying discourses about gender roles, dating, leisure, and consumption presented to young women via these magazines.

To conduct this study, I analyzed the editorial content and advertising of two issues each of four magazines targeted to adolescent girls. These include the March 1994 and March 1995 issues of *Seventeen* and *'Teen*, both of which feature lengthy prom sections in addition to their regular content. Also analyzed were two magazines devoted exclusively to proms—*YM*'s special prom issue (1994 and 1995), and the 1994 and 1995 issues of *Your Prom* (a once-a-year spring publication by the publishers of *Modern Bride*).

"The Night of Your Life"

The rhetorical strategy of these magazines is to build the prom up to be "the most wonderful night of your life" (*Seventeen* 1995, 22). In fact, the articles and fashion layouts within these magazines are replete with hyped-up labels for prom night, including: "the big night" (*Seventeen* 1995 34; *YM* 1994, 10), "one amazing evening" (*Your Prom* 1995, 119), "the night of your life" (*YM* 1994, 50), "a night to remember" (*YM* 1995, 13), "the best night ever" (*Your Prom* 1994, 15), and "the Superbowl of all dates" (*YM* 1994, 57).

Even advertisements get in on the "big night" act. For example, a multipage ad for Finesse hair care products exclaims:

> Your evening is here and your time has come . . . turn the page and get ready with FINESSE. You've got the ultimate dress, and the date of your dreams, now prepare your hair for the best night of your life. Grab a friend, and get ready to FINESSE your prom way in advance! . . . Your prom night can be nothing short of perfect. . . . Let the prom begin! . . . set yourself up for a magical night! . . . Your dream night is underway, so make sure your hair makes the same statement it did when you made your big entrance!

All of this, of course, can be accomplished by using the "right" hair care products.

Similarly, an ad for Cathy's Concepts costume jewelry declares its products to be "For Memories that Last a Lifetime." "Prom night is one of the most exciting nights of your life," the copy tells us. "Let Cathy's Concepts help you make a statement they will never forget!" Even an ad for personalized prom garters beckons the reader with the promise of "Once-In-A-Lifetime Memories."

While the overwhelming message of these magazines is that prom is the ultimate evening and that everything should be perfect, there are a few isolated instances of dissent. In giving advice on how to help one's date get over his "fear of formals," the 1994 issue of *YM* (10) advises: "De-emphasize the 'big deal' aspect of the date. Don't feed the hype machine. Saying anything that reinforces the idea that the prom is the date of all dates will only convince him he'd have more fun bowling with Grandma."

Similarly, the 1995 issue of *YM* offers yet another dissenting message in an article titled "The 10 Biggest Prom Pressures (and How to Deal)." The article acknowledges that the reader's prom expectations may be too high. "You're so obsessed with making your prom perfect that you've been in a total planning frenzy" (54), the reader is told. She is then advised to "remember the prom doesn't have to be perfect to be fun. Besides, no matter how much you plan, something's bound to go wrong" (54). This is an interesting tactic, since on the next page is a sidebar titled "Prom-Trauma Survival Guide" which begins: "It's supposed to be perfect . . ." (55).

Despite these rare anti-hype messages, the overwhelming theme is that prom is a rite of passage of such immense importance to young women that everything must be perfect. To ensure such perfection, the reader is told, she must do everything in her power to create the perfect prom, whether it be by purchasing and using the right products or by avoiding one or another "prom disaster." Part of the strategy of building the prom up to be the ultimate night is the threat that things can, and often do, go wrong, resulting in some sort of "prom horror story."

In fact, these magazines prominently feature articles detailing assorted prom horror stories from prom "veterans," or "survivors" (as they are sometimes called). For example, both the 1994 (6) and 1995 (6) issues of *YM* include articles on readers' most "mortifying" or "humiliating" prom experiences. In both, readers' prom horror stories are rated on a four-star scale with four stars describing the "ultimate supremo humiliation."

Similarly, readers of YM's 1995 "Prom-Trauma Survival Guide" (55) are warned: "It's supposed to be perfect, but the prom can turn out to be one major mortifying moment just waiting to happen." An example of one of these "major mortifying" moments is arriving at the prom only to find that someone else is wearing the same dress.

Words like "panic," "trauma," "nightmare," and "horror" are used quite liberally in these magazines to refer to everything from the inability to find the "perfect" dress, to drunken dates, to the pressure to have sex. In fact, deciding on the "perfect" prom dress is presented as being just as stressful (and potentially life-altering) as deciding whether to have sex on prom night. Coordinating one's dress with the right accessories is presented as being as important as deciding whether to get drunk at the prom.

Nowhere is this phenomenon more evident than in YM's "The 10 Biggest Prom Pressures (and How to Deal)" (52–55). According to the article: "The prom is about as stress-free as a pop quiz. . . . Here, the biggest prom nightmares, plus advice from survivors on how to keep your cool" (53). The number one "prom nightmare," as identified by this article, is when "you and your mom have a major dress disagreement" (53). Interestingly, pressures to have sex and drink are only numbers three and four, respectively.

Just about anything, however, is a potential prom disaster waiting to happen. 'Teen informs the reader of "5 ways to avoid a prom makeup disaster," complete with prominent references to Bonne Bell cosmetics (1995, 67). Even eating can have disastrous consequences. While several prom horror stories involve people eating tainted food and getting sick at prom, YM (1995, 94) offers a listing of foods (including spaghetti and lobster) to avoid on prom night, in an article inviting the reader to "read on to avoid a prom dining disaster." By building the prom up to be the ultimate date/evening, and by warning of the potential for disaster, these magazines set themselves up to function simultaneously as sage advisors and fairy godmothers, providing the reader with helpful hints, step-by-step guides, and all the commodities she needs to "make it a night to remember, not a nightmare [she'd] love to forget" (YM, 1994, 56).

This tactic is certainly not unique to articles and magazines devoted to the prom. According to Robert Goldman (132), women's magazines in general "proclaim themselves as the voice of 'expertise'—addressing readers in an imperative voice as well as that of an intimate friend engaging us in personal dialogue." A quick glimpse at the opening statements by the editors reveals this strategy. For example, Bonnie Fuller, editor-in-chief of *YM* (1994, 4) informs the reader: "If you think you're the only girl who's ever suffered from pre-prom jitters, think again. . . . we want to make your prom as horror-free as possible. So, to get you completely prom prepped, here's an entire issue packed with 100 prom-perfect dresses, tons of accessories, great new hair and makeup looks, tips on how to be the ultimate date and how to help your guy overcome his prime prom problem. Dig in and get psyched for your big night out!" Similarly, Cele Lalli, editor of the 1995 issue of *Your Prom*, (8) acknowledges: "We know what an exciting time this is for you, and *Your Prom* magazine is here to help you successfully plan and enjoy this big event."

Prom-oriented magazines offer guidance by tailoring the standard content of women's/teen girl's magazines to prom. Like most magazines for women and teenage girls, these magazines include advice columns (for instance, *YM*'s 1995 (10) sidebar "7 Prom Pitfalls (and How to Avoid Them)"); horoscopes (so that you know which guy will be the perfect date); and quizzes (including ones on how well you know your prom date, how well you can handle a "prom crisis," and how well you know your "prom style").

Angela McRobbie and Naomi Wolf have observed that magazines for females (teens and women) typically include step-by-step guides to a variety of things, especially physical beautification. Similarly, in their analysis of *YM*, Duffy and Gotcher (1996) argue that teen magazines purposely employ expert, "credible sources" to advise teenage readers, thereby creating "the illusion that the information provided is for the good of the reader without exposing the true objective, which is to sell a product or service" (37). Prom-oriented magazines are no different, except that the guides are on how to do one's hair and makeup especially for the prom. Whether these articles are makeovers of "typical" promgoers or simply instructions, they make conspicuous references to product brand names so that the reader doesn't inadvertently purchase the wrong brand of hair spray, for example. One can't use just any brand of hairspray to get that "prom-perfect hair."

Further, it is assumed that the reader needs advice on how to do just about anything and everything. The 1994 issue of *Your Prom* includes a special segment on "tips and ideas for the best night ever," and gives the reader advice on how to "make the most of [her] glamorous gams," (15), on "purse packing" (18), and on taking photos (22). There is even a section titled "Undercover Blues," a "primer" designed to help the reader "make the right undergarment choices before the big night arrives" (22).

The need to plan everything down to the smallest detail is the key to having the perfect prom. From shopping for the "perfect" dress well in advance to making sure she has enough film in her camera, from "practicing" her makeup techniques prior to prom night to coordinating hose, shoes, and dress, the reader is told she has power and is in control. Yet these magazines coopt the true meaning of power and control. What they present is a form of power and control that comes from commodities.

"All Dolled Up"

Not only do these magazines equate power and control with consumerism, but the power and control they offer are mainly limited to physical beautification. Nowhere is this more evident than in a layout titled "All Dolled Up" in the 1995 issue of *Seventeen* (192–199). The premise of the layout is that the reader can become like that icon of femininity, the Barbie doll. According to the layout, "Barbie's not just a doll—she's a plastic powerhouse. She can be anything she wants." While the rhetoric is that of power, it is obvious that the only thing Barbie (and presumably the reader) has control over is her physical appearance. One page of the layout features the copy: "She may be the boss, but Barbie still does her own filing (you've got to hand it to her—she's always picture perfect)." The accompanying photograph presents a young model in a short pink dress filing her nails. On another page, the reader is told "Barbie's got a gift for putting on the glitz—and for wielding a mean curling iron." This is a blatant cooptation of power, control, and even talent, as they all come from products and exist solely in the realm of physical beautification. The final page of the layout shows a model holding a large, pink suitcase, while the copy reads: "You won't catch Barbie toting a tiny backpack to the postprom party—she's got way too much stuff." And, of course, these magazines tell the reader that she, too, must have lots of "stuff."

The 1995 *Your Prom* offers the reader a checklist to make sure she is organized in her planning for prom (54). According to the checklist, the planning should begin two or three months before the prom, at which time the reader is advised she should: (1) start clipping pictures of dresses from the magazine and browsing in stores, (2) begin a diet, (3) start taking care of her hair and nails, and (4) work on her tan. As prom night approaches, the young woman is advised to purchase her dress, shop for accessories, make an appointment for her prom hairstyle, practice applying her makeup, and wear her prom shoes for a few minutes here and there to break them in. Almost every item in the checklist involves the physical beautification of the reader, culminating in the final checklist item: "Congratulate yourself on how great you look!"

Everything about the reader's appearance can and should be planned and "perfect." This is not, however, an easy task. *Seventeen* (1995, 30), for example, warns: "Wayward bra straps, problem panty lines—and you thought finding a dress was the hard part." In a similar tone, *YM* (1994, 78) tells the reader, "If you think tracking down the perfect dress was tough, try dealing with the details" (that is, accessories).

A major component of this planning and perfection is buying and using the right commodities so that the reader has perfect makeup, perfect hair, perfect skin, and perfect accessories (jewelry, shoes, etc.). The need to look "perfect" (as defined by the editors, writers, and advertisers) permeates the discourse of teenage girl prom magazines, as both articles and advertisements present to young women the commodities necessary for having the perfect prom.

When it comes to commodities, however, nothing is more important to achieving "perfection" than the prom dress. A question asked by the editor of the March 1994 issue of *Seventeen* exemplifies the pervading rhetoric of these magazines. "When it comes to the prom, what's more important—who you're going with or what you're going to wear? We vote for the dress" (10).

As can be seen in Table 1, three of these four magazines (*Seventeen*, *'Teen*, and *Your Prom*) allot a significant number of pages to advertising.[1] Depending on the magazine and year, between 45.3 percent and 66.9 percent of pages in these three magazines are advertisements. This is not atypical for women's and teen girls' magazines. For example, Evans et al. found that nearly 57 percent of *Seventeen* magazine is allotted to advertising. Although Evans et al. calculated "space" and this study calculates "pages," the results are remarkably similar. While the amount of advertising is comparable to that in other magazines for adolescent girls, these prom issues do feature advertisements specially targeted to female promgoers.

While the purpose of this study is not to compare differences across magazines, as would be expected, the two magazines devoted solely to proms (*YM* and *Your Prom*) allot between 63.6 percent to 100

Table 1
Breakdown of Advertising Pages
Devoted to the Prom in Percent

Magazine	Total Pages Devoted to Advertising[1,2]	Ad pages Devoted to Prom Ads[3]	Prom Ad Pages Devoted to Prom Dresses
Seventeen			
3/94 (n=229)	57.6% (n=132)	35.6% (n= 47)	85.1% (n= 40)
3/95 (n=243)	56.8% (n=138)	41.3% (n= 57)	86.0% (n= 49)
'Teen			
3/94 (n=151)	49.7% (n= 75)	40.0% (n= 30)	70.0% (n= 21)
3/95 (n=137)	45.3% (n= 62)	38.7% (n= 24)	79.2% (n= 19)
YM (Special Issue)[4]			
1994 (n=137)	26.3% (n= 36)	75.0% (n= 27)	70.4% (n= 19)
1995 (n=103)	10.7% (n= 11)	63.6% (n= 7)	100.0% (n= 7)
Your Prom			
Sp. 94 (n=155)	65.8% (n=102)	97.1% (n= 99)	85.9% (n= 85)
Sp. 95 (n=151)	66.9% (n=101)	100.0% (n=101)	92.1% (n= 93)
TOTAL 1,306	50.3% (n=657)	59.7% (n=392)	84.9% (n=333)

1. The total number of pages includes inside front, inside back, and back cover pages.
2. The total amount of advertising was calculated by counting every page devoted solely to advertisements (including both individual full-page ads and pages full of multiple ads but no editorial copy). Clearly these numbers yield a slight under-representation of the total amount of advertisements in these magazines as there are many half-page, quarter-page, or even smaller advertisements that were not counted.
3. Prom ads include ads for prom-related products (dresses, dyeable shoes, garters, limos, etc.) as well as ads for more generic products (hair care, jewelry, makeup, etc.) which make specific reference to proms.
4. See endnote 1 at the end of this essay for the total amount of advertising in YM, which does not include advertising-type layouts of prom dresses bearing designer names and prices.

percent of their advertising pages to prom-related advertising, while the more general interest magazines devote just over one-third of their advertising pages to prom ads. In terms of what types of prom-related products these magazines are advertising, Table 1 clearly shows that the dress is the most frequently advertised product. Depending on the specific magazine and issue analyzed, 70–100 percent of prom-related ads are for prom dresses—the single most important commodity for the perfect prom (or so these magazines tell us.)

The emphasis on finding the "perfect" prom dress is evidenced by more than the sheer number of pages allotted to advertising and dress layouts. The copy of these magazines trumpets the need to find the perfect dress, the search for which could lead to panic. As *YM* (1994, 28) announced in the opening of a fashion layout: "Here's the ultimate cure for the what-am-I-going-to-wear-to-the-prom panic." The cure? A black dress.

Another tactic of prom dress layouts is to link the dress (and prom) to romance, fantasy, and fairy tales. Often themes like "One Enchanted Evening," and "Fairy Tale Prom" (both in the 1995 *Seventeen*) are employed. While the 1994 issue of *'Teen* invites the reader to "find the dress of your dreams" (112), the 1995 issue of the same magazine asks, "Got a date with a prince? Slip into a dress reminiscent of Cinderella" (92). The "Fairy Tale Prom" layout in the issue of *Seventeen* mentioned above is a multipage layout retelling the tale of Cinderella from her ragged beginnings to her triumphant enchantment of a handsome prince—a transformation accomplished with the aid of a fairy godmother and a multitude of commodities.

The Cinderella theme is repeated in advertising, too. Payless shoes offer two variations on the Cinderella theme. One reads: "Let's not forget, Cinderella snagged a prince with the perfect shoe." The other reads: "Here's your glass slipper. Have a ball!" Similarly, one ad for Loralie dresses includes the copy, "Enchanted evening awaiting you may all your prom dreams come true."

While many of the ads for prom dresses feature no text other than the name of the designer and the location(s) where one can buy the dress, they tend to be multiple-page spreads, often printed on thicker paper than the rest of the magazine. By offering no text, these ads allow the reader to devote her full attention to the dresses, which speak for themselves. There are, however, some dress labels that do include text in their ads, foremost among them Loralie and Flirtations. Loralie exemplifies the notion that the dress is the single most important element of the perfect prom: "Over the years, you may forget the flowers. Or the band. Or even the boy. But you'll never forget the dress. Or the way it made you feel!"

Some articles and ads stress the idea of using the prom as an opportunity to express individuality. For example, Phyllis Ehrlich's "editor's message" in *Your Prom* (1994, 3) informs the reader: "Whatever your personality and style, we have pages and pages of fashion and beauty to help you create the look that's uniquely yours." Yet this is a form of individuality and uniqueness created by consuming the right mass-produced commodities.

For example, a nine page advertising layout for Flirtations dresses contains the following copy written one line per page: "(Don't tell me it's what all the girls are wearing—that's the last thing I want to hear—I'm not 'all the girls'—I don't want to be part of the crowd—never have—I want something that's unique—like me—it's time to make some waves—as always—maybe red will get their attention—or black—very sexy—a real knockout,—that's what I'd like them to remember about me—now that's not something everyone can say.)" Yet another multi-page Flirtations ad contains the following copy: "(Special—I want to look special—not like the other girls—maybe something fun and short—something Mary, my older sister, could never wear—I want something unique, something that no one else will be wearing.)"

In these advertisements, individuality is reduced to wearing a dress that no one else at the prom will be wearing. (Or so the reader hopes.) While the reader is told that such consumption will allow her to express her individuality, Robert Goldman contends that this results in nothing more than pseudo-individuality—in which our personal histories are erased by the commodity, which becomes the source of our individuality. According to Judith Williamson (70), advertisers offer us an "identikit" comprised of the appropriate commodities that will enable us to create the identity we desire. Through purchase and consumption, "we create ourselves, our personality, our qualities, even our past and future" (Williamson 70).

Further, advertisers dissect us into a myriad of disparate parts, each of which needs to be fixed, altered, and/or improved by consuming a particular commodity (Williamson). While Goldman and Williamson refer specifically to advertising, I would argue that their observations and theories are just as relevant to the "editorial" content of these magazines. Whether it be a fashion layout, a makeover, or a "how-to" feature, this editorial content makes abundant references to specific product brand names. Most of these magazines even contain a page or two in the back informing the reader of exact locations where she can purchase the clothing, accessories, etc. featured in the "editorial" content. It is not atypical for magazines like Seventeen (1995, 34, 37) to feature an article detailing something like a "pre-prom spa-athon," including advice on aromatherapy, how to give yourself a facial and a manicure, as well as how to exfoliate your skin and keep your hair from frizzing on prom night. Each section is replete with specific product and brand name identifications.

Such features as the "pre-prom spa-athon" also exemplify another theme of these magazines: physical beautification is fun! It is presented as a form of leisure and recreation that the reader and her friends can engage in together. The photos accompanying the features, showing groups of ecstatic teenage girls with curlers in their hair and cream on their faces, send a clear message. The process of physical beautification is both fun and something the reader can share with her friends.

"Prince Charming"

I have mentioned that these magazines stress the need to plan for prom carefully. While much of this planning involves purchasing the right products, there are other, less commercial elements of prom that need to be carefully planned and controlled—including sex and drinking. Like most of these magazines, *Your Prom*, 1994 (85) includes an article asking "How Far is Too Far on Prom Night?" Even more, the young reader is told that she needs to have control over her date. Whether she accomplishes it by being so alluring and sexy that "he's under [her] spell" (*YM* 1995, 51) or by making sure he looks good and has a good time, the success of the evening rests squarely and solely on her shoulders.

The young reader of *Seventeen* (1995, 182) is warned about potential "prom-date fashion blunders" in an article advising her on how to get her date to dress appropriately for the prom. When the article offers the reader "a few cautionary tales about getting him dressed right" (182), it is telling her that it is *her* responsibility to make sure *he* dresses right.

But it is not just a potential fashion *faux pas* the reader needs to worry about. She also must allay his "Fear of Formals," or so she is told in an article detailing teenage guys' biggest prom fears. The article includes "expert" advice on "how to get them over it" (*YM* 1994, 10–13). Once again, the problem rests with him, but the young woman reader is told it is *her* job to help *him* get over it.

While she needs to control her date, she also needs to make sure he has a good time. As such, the reader is offered a list of "the 12 worst things you can do on prom night," all of which involve things which would make her date feel uncomfortable (flirting with other guys, complaining, clinging, vanishing, etc.) (*YM* 1994, 12–13). Similarly, the same issue warns the reader not to "go down in high school history as the prom date from hell," and advises her on "how to be a great prom date" (56–58).

A related tactic is to have teen males tell what they like/don't like about prom. For example, an article in *YM* (1995, 80–82) titled "What Guys Really Want On Prom Night" is designed to dispel myths about sex, romance, drinking, etc., and includes a sidebar titled "What Guys Really Hate" about prom.

Of course, while she is busy making sure he is dressed right, over his fear of proms, and is having a good time, she also must look perfect, not to mention sexy. After all, this is the real source of her power, or so these magazines tell her.

Over and over again, these magazines tell the reader that she must look good for her date. Nowhere is this message clearer than in the prom dress layouts of these magazines. Whether she is being told she can "take his breath away in a pastel ballgown" (*'Teen* 1995, 92), "charm and bewitch him" in a little black dress (*YM* 1995, 44), or "melt his heart in this hot little number" (*YM* 1994, 96), the reader is made aware both of the need to impress her date, and the fact that her physical beauty affords her some measure of power over him.

But it's not just the dress which will impress him and empower her. While an article titled "Prom Date Perfect" (*'Teen* 1994, 94) reports on what teenage guys say are their favorite dress colors and styles, it also identifies how they like girls to wear their hair, nails, and makeup. The subhead of the article is: "Want to dazzle your prom date?" If you do, then simply follow the guidelines.

In an intriguing merger of advertising and editorial content, this same issue of *'Teen* includes several one-page ads for various dress companies. Each ad includes a box containing assorted editorial content, such as shopping tips for dresses. In addition, each ad also features a quote from a different teenage boy about the dress. For example, an ad for a Mike Benet dress includes a quote from a sixteen-year-old named Michael. "Keep it short, and I won't be able to keep my eyes off her."

In many respects, these prom magazines are reminiscent of another staple of teenage girl popular culture, the romance novel, which also perpetuates a "code of beautification" (Christian-Smith 43). Like romance novels, these prom-oriented magazines emphasize how important it is for girls to be attractive to boys, a feature that raises Linda Christian-Smith's concern. "In becoming the girl of a boy's dreams" she "accepts another's version of reality as her own: how she should behave, think, and look. The ability to define reality for another is certainly one of the more important forms of social power" (54).

Of course, the fact that she's being manipulated is not obvious to the reader, since the language of these fashion layouts and ads implies that *she* is the one with the control. Of course, she can have power only if she makes the right consumer choice—that is, purchases the "perfect" prom dress. Further, this power is, again, directly attributable to her physical appearance.

Conclusion

The excessive emphasis magazines for adolescent females place on physical appearance has been well-documented (Duffy and Gotcher, Evans et al., Guillen and Barr, Peirce). Naomi Wolf labels this emphasis on women's physical appearance, "The Beauty Myth"—a phenomenon directly related to advertisers' need to sell products to women.

Clearly, these special prom issues of teenage magazines are no different. A main component in the planning and control of a prom is planning and controlling one's physical appearance, a control that is directly linked to commodities. As Wolf has observed:

> This obligatory beauty myth dosage the magazines provide elicits in their readers a raving, itching, parching product lust, and an abiding fantasy: the longing for some fairy godmother who will arrive at the reader's door and put her to sleep. When she awakens, her bathroom will be full of exactly the right skin-care products, with step-by-step instructions, and palettes of exactly the required makeup. The kindly phantom will have colored and cut the sleeper's hair to perfection, made over her face, and painlessly nipped and tucked it. In her closet she will discover a complete wardrobe arranged by season and occasion, color-coordinated and accessorized on shoe trees and in hatboxes. . . . She will deliver herself into a world of female consumer apotheosis, beyond appetite. (70)

In addition, much of the consumer rhetoric of these magazines is similar to Goldman's concept of "commodity feminism," in which "the commercial marriage of feminism and femininity plays off a conception of personal freedom located in the visual construction of self-appearance" (133). Feminist goals of individuality, independence, and control over one's life are commodified and translated as the freedom to choose commodities to define one's independence. "Meanings of choice and individual freedom become wed to images of sexuality in which women apparently choose to be seen as sexual objects because it suits their 'liberated' interests" (Goldman 133).

Both Goldman and Wolf stress that the goal of advertising is to create insecurity and anxiety in the reader, both of which can be alleviated by a "commodity solution" (Goldman 145). The four magazines discussed here are no different. Through both advertising and editorial copy, they tell the reader that the prom is the "ultimate" date and that everything about it should be perfect. The road to prom perfection, however, is fraught with assorted "horrors." These magazines present the reader with the threat that any number of horrors could befall her on this night of all nights. As a result, the reader is made painfully aware that she is treading in dangerous waters, and she is kept in a perpetual state of "prom panic," the solution to which is to be found in commodities.

In her analysis of *Jackie*, McRobbie observes that through these magazines, "teenage girls are subjected to an explicit attempt to win consent to the dominant order—in terms of femininity, leisure and consumption" (87). The prom-oriented magazines discussed in this essay do this by promising the reader control, power, and individuality through the consumption of mass-produced commodities. Further, the reader is told that her power, control, and individuality rests with her physical appearance—her femininity. Through the process of commodified self-beautification, the reader is told she can wield this power, control, and individuality to achieve her ultimate goal—the perfect prom.

Note

1. There is one anomaly about the *YM* special prom issues that should be addressed. While Table 1 shows that these issues allot only a quarter (or less) of their pages to traditionally defined advertising, they do not fill the remaining three-quarters of their pages with articles. Instead, 58 pages (42.3 percent) of the 1994 issue and 51 pages (49.5 percent) of the 1995 issue contain prom dress layouts complete with designer names and prices. While all of the magazines make use of such layouts (which in effect function as advertising), none do so to the extent of *YM*. If we add these prom dress layouts to the number of full-page ads allotted to prom dresses, the 1994 issue of *YM* includes 77 (out of 137) pages of prom dresses, while the 1995 issue includes 58 (out of 103) pages. In fact, the cover of each of these issues heralds the emphasis on prom dresses. The 1994 cover announces "100 Dresses! Find Your Dream Dress," while the 1995 cover declares "80 Great Dresses," "Find the Perfect One for You."

Works Cited

Christian-Smith, Linda K. *Becoming a Woman through Romance*. New York: Routledge, 1990.

Duffy, Margaret, and J. Micheal Gotcher. "Crucial Advice on How to Get the Guy: The Rhetorical Vision of Power and Seduction in the Teen Magazine *YM*." *Journal of Communication Inquiry* 20 (1996): 32–48.

Durham, Meenakshi G. "Dilemmas of Desire: Representation of Adolescent Sexuality in Two Teen Magazines." *Youth and Society* 29 (1998): 369–389.

Evans, Ellis D., Judith Rutberg, Carmela Sather, and Charli Turner. "Content Analysis of Contemporary Teen Magazines for Adolescent Females." *Youth and Society* 23 (1991): 99–120.

Goldman, Robert. *Reading Ads Socially*. London: Routledge, 1992.

Guillen, Eileen O., and Susan I. Barr. "Nutrition, Dieting, and Fitness Messages in a Magazine for Adolescent Women, 1970–1990." *Journal of Adolescent Health* 15 (1994): 464–472.

Levine, Michael P., Linda Smolak, and Helen Hayden. "The Relation of Sociocultural Factors to Eating Attitudes and Behaviors Among Middle School Girls." *Journal of Early Adolescence* 14 (1994): 471–490.

Martin, Mary C., and James W. Gentry. "Stuck in the Model Trap: The Effects of Beautiful Models in Ads on Female Pre-Adolescents and Adolescents." *Journal of Advertising* 26 (1997): 19–33.

Martin, Mary C., and Patricia F. Kennedy. "Advertising and Social Comparison: Consequences for Female Preadolescents and Adolescents." *Psychology and Marketing* 10 (1993): 513–530.

McRobbie, Angela. *Feminism and Youth Culture: From Jackie to Just Seventeen*. Boston: Unwin Hyman, 1991.

Peirce, Kate. "A Feminist Theoretical Perspective on the Socialization of Teenage Girls through *Seventeen* Magazine." *Sex Roles* 23 (1990): 491–500.

Williamson, Judith. *Decoding Advertisements: Ideology and Meaning in Advertising*. New York: Marion Boyars Publishers, 1978.

Wolf, Naomi. *The Beauty Myth: How Images of Beauty Are Used against Women*. New York: Anchor Books, 1991.

Chapter 6

What Every Girl Should Know: An Analysis of Feminine Hygiene Advertising

Debra L. Merskin

I was about thirteen when I first noticed that long awaited spot on my underpants. Joy, fear, shame, uncertainty, and, ultimately, relief followed. My first period came and went and I waited. It would be another year before it would happen again. In the interim I was sure there was something wrong with me, that my body had betrayed me, that I was somehow less a girl than my already menstruating peers. I just knew everyone was having "their's" but me.

Not only did the coming of my period suggest that I was growing up but that I was growing vulnerable to the things that affect women. The mystique surrounding "the club" evaporated as quickly as that first drop of blood—what had been promised as a time of fulfillment, of bridging the gap between childhood and Barbies to adolescence and earrings, instead became a time of silence. No longer spoken of with anticipation, my period became "that time of the month," being "on the rag," and "the curse"—ultimately a terrible secret to be kept—especially from boys.

Burdened with practical worries unique to their situations, such as gathering sufficient supplies to keep this function hidden with secretive buying and finding places to change, a girl's body poses special challenges. How we, as a culture, have come to think of menstruation is important as well as how this information influences the way adolescent girls think about their bodies.

Centuries of myth and taboo have created a view of the female body that continues to be communicated in modern society. As part of their socialization, adolescent girls receive the same information that first encourages them to be excited about approaching woman-hood, yet when menstruation occurs, they are told to cover up and hope no signs of femaleness seep through their clothing.

The central argument of this paper is that modern advertisements for feminine hygiene products are compilations of centuries-old myths and taboos associated with controlling women's bodies. Employing the concepts of ideology (Hall, "Encoding"; Hall, "The Rediscovery"; Hall, "The Problem"; Hall, "Ideology") and structural analysis (Williamson), this study presents the findings of a content analysis of advertisements over a ten-year period for feminine hygiene products and medicines in *Seventeen* magazine. Beverly Havens and Ingrid Swenson's ("Imagery") framework for analyzing these ads is used. The findings suggest that today's advertisements perpetuate menstrual myths and dictate appropriate behavior around tales from the past.

The Myths and Taboos

Known by a variety of names (the monthlies, the curse, a red aunt, Going to See Sophie), menses is thought of in hopes of womanhood and feared in anticipation of ostracism. Important to understanding adolescent girls, these beliefs contribute to the construction of body image and self-esteem (Ernster 5–7). Symbolically marked in some cultures while hidden in others, a common theme of menses is the transition to adulthood—the girl becomes a woman (and can become a mother) (Thuren 217). In Anglo and European history, taboos were based on beliefs that menstruating women "caused meat to go bad, wine to turn, and bread dough to fall" (Thuren 217–228). Well into this century in rural England, "menstruating women could not touch milk, fresh meat, or pork being salted, lest it go bad" (de Beauvoir 148). Elsewhere in Europe, women were not to touch wine or any-thing else on the table such as salted pork, preserves, pickles, sauerkraut, or bread. During this time, menstruation and the world outside were made incompatible, hence regulating women's spheres of movement to private (as opposed to public) space. This is reflected in an ancient English poem: "Oh! Menstruating woman, thou'st a fiend from whom all nature should be screened!" (de Beauvoir 149).

According to Patricia Allen and Denise Fortino, "many ancient ta-boos and tales—born of the awe or fear with which men often regard menstruating women (how could they bleed so profusely and still survive?)—are at the heart of many myths and prejudices still with us today" (18). One of the reasons taboos die so hard is that they are "rigorously taught to youngsters, who dare not question them" (Delaney, Lupton, and Toth 22). In dated parlance, these beliefs or myths have been called old wives' tales. Those associated with menstruation are among the most prevalent and persistent:

- Because menstruation is seen as a sign of uncleanliness, a woman's touch during this time is undesirable and should be avoided.
- A woman is not to swim and is to avoid exercising during her period.
- Having intercourse during menstruation is dangerous to her health.
- A woman isn't interested in sex or is easily aroused before or during her period.
- A woman shouldn't eat cold foods while menstruating.
- Regular activities should be curbed because a woman is physically vulnerable during her period.
- Permanent waves in her hair won't take—and neither will dental fillings—when a woman is menstruating.
- A woman should not water plants while she's having her period. (Allen and Fortino 18–20)

Menstruation and Social Taboos

Inspired by fear and often confused with defilement and hygiene, taboos help order a society. A taboo "expresses itself essentially in prohibitions and restrictions" and can be defined as: "forbidden and excluded persons, acts, words, thoughts, and things that supposedly threaten a group's welfare and survival and are, therefore, used to that group's advantage" (Voigt 97). To remain stable, a society needs order and, according to Mary Douglas (92), "dirt offends against order." "The curse" is a taboo that states menstruating women and girls are considered "filthy, sick, unbalanced, and ritually impure" (Daly 248). As a society we have beliefs about separating, classifying, and organizing to create social structures designed to withstand natural disasters, punish transgressions, and demarcate. In many cases it is necessary to exaggerate differences to create a semblance of order. For example, distinctions between men and women are made visible and exaggerated through differences. Given that only women menstruate, the biological fact of blood is used to define cultural and social distinctions. According to Allen Lien, women are subjected to "menstrual discrimination," a kind of contempt and isolation (120).

The periodicity of menstruation fascinated earlier civilizations that had yet to make the associative leap between menstruation and pregnancy (Ellis). Because of frequent pregnancies, continuous nursing, poor nutrition, and daily battles to stay alive, women's periods were probably fairly irregular. Therefore, when menstruation did happen, it was a rather dramatic event (Brownmiller).

Menstruation and the Private Body

Central to understanding why women consider themselves to be cursed are early rituals associated with fertility and confinement of women to private space. Menstruation has historically been, and currently is, used as justification for preventing women from fully participating in society. The view that a woman's monthly bleeding is a biological defect is appropriate to a social system in which women's behavior is controlled by men. Bureaucratic regimes often "subject women's bodies to more control than men's bodies" (Shilling 38). Emily Martin suggests that this is because women are expected to manage and conceal menstruation, pregnancy, and menopause in "institutions whose organization of time and space takes little cognizance of them" (94).

Nearly every religious and cultural tradition stigmatizes menstruating women. For Western societies, the popular reference to menstruation as "the curse" began with the biblical telling of how it was inflicted upon Eve because of her sin (Hoffman). The biblical words of Leviticus [15:19–33] speak directly to fear of women's blood as being at the root of evils: "And if a woman have an issue, and her issue in her flesh be blood, she shall be put apart seven days; and whosoever toucheth her shall be unclean until the even. And every thing that she lieth upon in her separation shall be unclean; every thing also that she sitteth upon shall be unclean" (quoted in Agonito 21–22). The idea that menstrual blood is excess blood that is dirty and toxic can also be traced to the writings of the early Greeks and Romans (Allen and Fortino; Delaney, Lupton, and Toth; Knight). According to Ellen Mahoney, taboos that concerned a young woman having her period were widespread:

- In Persia, a menstruating woman was thought to be possessed by an evil demon. In order to cleanse herself after giving birth to a female child, she had to lie in front of a hot fire for fourteen days.

- In Egypt, a woman was slapped if she complained of cramps.
- In Rome, a menstruating woman was believed to destroy entire crops, wilting plants if she even walked by them.
- In East Africa anything touched by a menstruating woman was considered poisoned. To eat meals she had to crouch in a dark corner, eat, and then throw away or burn her dishes.
- In South Australia, a man who walked by a menstruating woman was considered to be contaminated. The woman had to warn passersby that she was menstruating. If a man was not so warned, the belief was he would weaken and suddenly grow old.
- In Alaska, women of the Dene tribe had to wear a hat called a "menstrual bonnet" and a thick veil to cover their faces during their periods.

Yet these myths aren't necessarily cast entirely in past ideas of behavior. In 1923, a British school board published a report that identified the "strains" schooling imposed on growing girls (Dyhouse). It suggested that girls have less energy than boys as menstruation posed periodic disturbances that condemned many of them to recurring, if temporary, diminution of general mental efficiency (133).

In modern times many have heard the argument that it is not possible to have a woman president as she could not be trusted to handle the stress of office if it were "that time of the month." In 1982, during a United Nations debate on the Falkland Islands, a diplomat stated that "Prime Minister Margaret Thatcher's actions had to be understood in the context of the glandular system of women" (Hoffman 201). A 1996 story reported that United Airlines was sending its flight attendants through "cultural diversity training to make them more sensitive to other cultures" (Gingold and Rogan 172). This means taking into consideration some cultures' religious taboos around menstruating women. If a man who is being served food or beverages by a female flight attendant asks her, "are you clean?" and she is menstruating, she must get a male attendant or nonmenstruating female to serve him.

Menstruation and the Public Body

Puberty—the biological process—is an ambivalent time when coupled with adolescence—the social and personal process. There is embarrassment and excitement. It is nasty and yet remains a "sweet secret," signifying the transition from girlhood to womanhood. Either way, it is affirmation of femaleness, as Anne Frank noted in her diary: "I get the feeling lately of being embarrassed. . . . I never discuss myself or any of these things with anybody; that is why I have to talk to myself about them. Each time I have a period—and that has only been three times—I have the feeling that in spite of all the pain, unpleasantness, and nastiness, I have a sweet secret" (Frank 30).

Girls now begin menstruating earlier than ever before, even earlier than they did in the 1950s (Pipher 53). Changes in nutrition and diet, growth hormones added to food, and the influence of light exposure are all thought to contribute (Pipher 53). Although the average age of menses for American girls is twelve and a half years, some begin menstruating as early as age nine. An already anxious time, many American girls are dealing with their first period at the same time they're trying to adjust to junior high school (Mann 173).

Coupled with messages that reinforce the beauty ideal of thinness, the physiological changes associated with menstruation also influence a girl's developing body image: "Sometimes my body looks so bloated, I don't want to get dressed. I like the way it looks for exactly two days each month: usually, the eighth and ninth days after my period. Every other day, my breasts, my stomach—they're just awful lumps, bumps, bulges. My body can turn on me at any moment; it is an out-of-control mass of flesh" (Hayne 213).

Confusion about bodily changes is typical for the adolescent girl. Early socialization includes direction on appropriate behavior during a girl's period. Control of activities is central to that process, particularly during menstruation.

Important to understanding how girls comprehend their bodies through menstrual myths is the fact that, in modern life, popular culture and the media provide a great deal of information once obtained through interpersonal sources. Advertising serves as a kind of social glue, binding together parts of society and communicating critical information and taboos about participating in it. The following section provides a theoretical framework that describes how and why dominant beliefs are incorporated into advertising.

Theoretical Foundations

According to Kate Kane, advertisements for feminine hygiene products are "powerful weapons in an ideological battle for control of women's sexuality" (82). The information advertisers use to construct their messages carries the weight of the dominant culture—the ideology—which incorporates taboos. Stuart Hall ("The Problem" 28–44) defines ideology as, "the mental frameworks—the languages, the concepts, categories, imagery of thought, and the systems of representation—which different classes and social groups deploy in order to make sense of, define, figure out, and render intelligible the way society works." By using the structuralist approach exemplified by the work of Hall and Williamson, it is possible to understand how meanings are constructed through advertising.

Life's events do not inherently have meaning. Rather, through social agreement, meaning is created. In modern society, through language, social practices are organized into symbolic products and meaning is made. According to Hall, by using ideology as the theoretical foundation, we can focus on the symbolic influence of media on audiences and explore the ways this activity "exercises symbolic power" ("Ideology" 309).

Anxiety is a state of mind associated with a girl's period and is reflected in advertisements, as well as the themes of cramps, bloating, peace of mind, trust, security (Delaney, Lupton, and Toth). The dominant view that menstruation can be equated with sickness is communicated through ads for "women's medications" and "feminine products." Preparation for a woman's period involves "assembling a suitable array of products, which are conveniently packaged and available by mail order. Menarche is then portrayed as a hygienic rather than a maturational crisis" (Whisnant and Zegans 809). Robert Goldman suggests that femininity is a commodity, made possible through purchase. In this way of thinking, it is also possible to conceal femininity through purchase.

Williamson suggests that modern advertising thus teaches us "to consume not the product, but its sign" (43). Therefore, what the product stands for is more important than what it is. An example of this is the marketing of diamonds. When likened to eternal love, diamonds are marketed to create a symbolism in which "the mineral means something not in its own terms as a rock, but in human terms, as a sign" (12). The diamond is no longer the means of securing eternal love but rather is eternal love. The image-making process and its symbols can also reinforce less positive beliefs.

Samuel Becker suggests that ideology "governs the way we perceive our world and ourselves; it controls what we see as 'natural' or 'obvious'" (69). Owing to the physical constraints of the media they appear in, advertisements are capable of defining a situation quickly. In fact, it is critical to the success of an advertisement that it makes an immediate connection to the target audience by drawing on shared understandings. By doing so, ads confer status, reinforce dominant belief systems, and, through signification, communicate fundamental information to the audience. The tools we use to make these connections are referred to as referent systems (Williamson 17–19). This is "the social knowledge of the audience" from which advertisers and audiences draw their materials and turn them into messages that reflect the views of the dominant society (Jhally 132).

As a conduit for personal information, advertising represents a version of reality, one that is vitally connected to the dominant ideology. According to Katherine Toland Frith, an advertisement "is both a marketing tool and a cultural artifact" (185). If we accept the idea that advertisements reflect the dominant ideologies of the society that produces them, it becomes important to look at the entire advertisement in terms of text, visuals, and context. Vickie Rutledge Shields suggests that "the production of visual texts takes place within dominant ideological structures" (25). According to Kane, hygiene advertisements "situate the body in a complex of pollution beliefs that reconcile the individual body to society" (83). Although the advertisements might not speak directly to the curse of Eve, they do mention secrecy—"no one knows but you"—which is consistent with our collective understanding of menstruation.

Advertising as Myth Maker

The first Kotex ad appeared in 1921 in *Good Housekeeping* magazine. In the ad, a young woman was pictured skating, and the headline read: "Meets the most Exacting Needs" (Marchand 21–22). The copy shyly mentioned that Kotex "completes toilet essentials" for active school girls, "guards against emergencies," and has "been accepted as the most satisfactory article of its kind" (21–22). The ads of this time featured, in a scientific way, the value and convenience of the product. Facts were presented as inoffensively as possible, leaving the reader to come to her own conclusions, assuming an innate and intimate understanding of the subject.

In the 1930s, the sanitary protection industry reminded women that "menstruation was naughty; as irrepressible evidence of sexuality, news of its arrival, departure, and duration had to be kept under wraps" (Houppert 31). Shame and secrecy were key words used in advertisements. For example, a Kotex tampon was called Fibs. The

ads reminded women that the "ultimate humiliation would be any indication that they're menstruating" (Houppert 32). A 1934 booklet offered the "Voice of Experience" about menstruation and discouraged
cold or hot baths, swimming, horseback riding, lifting heavy weights,
"athletic dancing," or arduous household duties during a girl's period
(Delaney, Lupton, and Toth 94). If one defied these guidelines, irregular menstruation and fallen organs would be the punishment: "Girls
should not exercise, play tennis, or wear high-heeled shoes during
their periods; such activity can cause a prolapsed uterus. Girls should
wear tight-fitting bloomers during the winter menstrual cycles; otherwise, they are likely to develop a 'catarrhal condition' in the delicate
vaginal tissues" (Delaney, Lupton, and Toth 94).

For those of us who grew up in the 1950s, booklets from school
nurses and counselors, films produced by Kotex and Modess, and
"training kits" from manufacturers provided information on becoming
a woman. Of course, the message behind all this material was to buy
and be loyal to **a** brand. The point was to use "our" product because
"nothing will show"; "no one will know"; "your secret will be safe"
(Delaney, Lupton, and Toth 94). We were meant to deodorize, sani-
tize, remove any evidence, and hide all shame. Above all cover it up!
Hide yourself! In the 1996 guide, *The Period Book: Everything You
Don't Want to Ask—But Need to Know*, adolescent girls were given
advice on the major "what ifs" of menstruation that are commonly
seen in advertisements:

- What if I get my period at school?
- What if I bleed through to the back of my skirt or pants and
  people can see it?
- What if I get my period unexpectedly and there isn't any way to
  buy a pad or tampon?
- My parents are divorced. What if I get my first period when I'm
  at my Dad's house?
- What if I can't get a tampon out?
- What if I go to buy pads or tampons and the check-out clerk is a
  guy in my class?
- What if my mother hasn't said anything to me yet about getting
  my period? How do I get her to talk to me? (Gravelle 83–95)

Since early times, advertisers have given hygiene products a social
persona with euphemistic names that are seemingly more sensitive to
consumers. Even today, when advertising is considerably more direct,

constipation is referred to as "not being regular." Advertisers have
created some of the most brilliant affectations for feminine hygiene
problems. For example, women are addressed with talk about "that
time of the month" and "not feeling fresh." Ann Treneman notes that
"the language of the ads is often coy and euphemistic to the point of
being adolescent" (160–61).

The accompanying images are just as allegorical—heart and flowers—
suggesting the delicacy of femininity. Even the names of the products
reflect an attempt to reassure women, even liberate them, from the
burdens of menstruation—New Freedom, Always, Rely, and Stayfree.
The underlying message has been fairly consistent, however, playing
on both hopes and fears—"hopes that the woman will not have to
change her ordinary life too much during 'that time of the month';
fears of betrayal by dripping blood, revealing outlines, or odors"
(Treneman 160–61).

Many advertisements attempt to recapture the interpersonal aspect
that many feel has been lost in modern life. At times, the adolescent
advertising reader finds herself eavesdropping on a private conversation between a mother and daughter. At other times she encounters
the product in another girl's bathroom or on the dressing table in a
bedroom. The text often presents a "knowledgeable version of our
mothers" (Treneman 159–60). Letter/response formats are also used
for this purpose in ads. For example:

> Reader: I've never used tampons before, but I think I'd like to try them now.
> The only thing stopping me now is that I don't really know how to use them.
> I got my first quite early, so none of my friends know any more than I do. And
> before you tell me to discuss this with my mother, you should know I'd rather
> die than talk to mum about that sort of stuff.
> Dear Early-Bird: The first thing you should do is get to know your body a little
> better. There's a very useful little pamphlet inside every pack of Libra Fleur.
> This will help you get to know where and how to insert the tampon . . . For
> more information and a free sample, send your name and address to "Libra
> Personal Product Adviser." (Treneman, 159–60)

The Previous Research

Very little research has been done in the past on advertising for feminine hygiene products. In 1988, Havens and Swenson found that these
advertisements depicted menstruation as a "hygienic crisis" best managed by an effective "security system" that would afford a girl "peace
of mind" ("Imagery" 95). The ads suggested that women were always

"running the risk of failing, evidenced by soiling, staining, embarrassment and odors" (89). Further, the authors suggested that such imagery and information in ads may "encourage guilt and diminished self-esteem in the adolescent who does experience discomfort" (96). A lack of maternal teachers and of male figures in the ads is evident; the importance of peer support is reinforced. Kane studied the ideology of freshness in television commercials and argued that feminine hygiene commercials are "powerful weapons in an ideological battle for control of women's sexuality" and that the "ideology of freshness" is central to that battle (83).

Several scholars have investigated messages concerning menstruation in commercial educational materials. In 1989, Havens and Swenson reviewed educational, audiovisual media that depict aspects of menstruation. They found that the majority presented anatomical information, acknowledged fear and embarrassment, and encouraged discussion with female adults and peers. Lynn Whisnant, Elizabeth Brett, and Leonard Zegans interviewed girls nine to eighteen and found that commercial educational materials are an important source of information about menstruation. The researchers also found, however, that the information may not be complete, accurate, or realistic.

Through personal interviews, other researchers have investigated American adolescent girls' experiences. Whisnant and Zegans interviewed pre- and postmenarcheal girls and found that the experience is highly emotional and influences a girl's emerging identity as a woman. The researchers suggest that American culture, however, tends to ignore the importance of this experience and in fact conveys the view that it is a hygienic crisis. Elissa Koff and Jill Rierdan interviewed sixth-grade girls about their coming periods, their understanding of menstruation, and their views of themselves. The researchers found that the girls claimed they were prepared for menarche, but their information was in fact incomplete at best and, more typically, filled with misconceptions. The major findings revealed a lack of information about how often menstruation occurs and how long it lasts, lack of clarity about physiology, and negative attitudes about menstrual related changes in the body.

Others have conducted interviews in an international setting. Muhammad Nazmul Haq, for example, found that urban schoolgirls in Bangladesh began menstruating earlier than rural girls, and found a positive correlation between age at the onset of menarche and body weight. Britt-Marie Thuren interviewed girls and women in Spain about how menstruation influences beliefs about the female body and sexuality. She concluded that beliefs are culturally relevant and that change comes slowly in traditional cultures. Merete Gainotti interviewed adolescent boys and girls in southern Italy. She found a consistent lack of accurate information about menstruation in general and that girls expressed a negative evaluation while boys tended to ignore the information about menstruation.

In addition, essays have come from the cultural studies tradition. For example, Berkeley Kaite provides an historical analysis of the growth of the feminine hygiene market and women's participation in the labor force. Treneman describes the irony of images associated with flowers and freshness and menstrual myths.

The Current Study

To determine whether dominant myths associated with menstruation and adolescence persist, a content analysis was conducted replicating an earlier study (Havens and Swenson, "Imagery") that analyzed ads in *Seventeen* magazine over a ten-year period (1976–86). In the current study, advertisements for sanitary products were analyzed for the ten-year period, 1986–96. The ads were selected from the same publication as the Havens and Swenson study—*Seventeen* magazine. *Seventeen* was originally selected for its wide circulation: 1.5 million in 1985; 2.3 million in 1996 (Havens and Swenson, "Imagery"; *Advertising Age*). A random sample of available issues from 1986 to 1996 was selected. Of the 126 issues published between 1986 and 1996, all were available for this study. A 25 percent sample was selected for each year, yielding three issues per year.

All advertisements in the thirty issues were examined for products associated with menstruation. Among the 102 ads for feminine hygiene products, 47 were duplicates and 55 were distinct. Given that a goal of advertising placement is repetition, it is important to account for duplicate ads when considering the impact of repetition for building brand awareness. As the focus of this study was content, however, duplicates were removed. After removal of duplicates, 55 advertisements were analyzed. The findings are presented below. Consistent with the original study, nearly all the ads were full-page (87 percent). In some cases there were combinations of quarter- or third-page ads (9 percent), followed by two full pages or one-half page ads (2 percent each).

Each ad was evaluated for recurrent themes (text, context, and tone) as in the original study. Two central themes guided the coding for both studies: scientific and athletic approaches. Scientific themes included the depictions of special designs (wings), schematics of the pad's or tampon's construction, special coverings (shields), or sizes (slim). Athletic ads showed young women engaged in a variety of activities—ballet class, swimming, bicycling, and gymnastics. Often, these women were wearing, if not white then at least tight clothing such as leotards and leggings. In some cases the photographs focused on the buttocks and/or perineal area. One example is an Always Ultraplus ad with the headline "Introducing the No-Worry No-Show Maxi." In the ads, the women appear happy, confident, and in control — even if pondering their menstrual dilemmas.

In the original study the findings were limited to a narrative analysis, whereas in this analysis the findings are quantified. In addition, this study examines the context, themes, and tones of the ads more deeply.

Table 1 compares the overall product advertising in the two studies. As the statistics reported in the original study were limited to products advertised, only Table 1 makes available comparative data. The table shows that in 1976–86 pads were advertised most, whereas in 1986–96 tampons appeared most often. There has also been a decline in advertising for pantiliners. In terms of the brands advertised, Tampax is dominant (31 percent), followed by Always (22 percent) and Playtex (14 percent).

Table 2 describes the context of the ads—that is, the story or circumstances each advertisement is constructing. The context of these ads were categorized as either the worries of physical embarrassment; the practical concerns of finding supplies; becoming ill with her period; or having to leave class and miss lessons. Primarily the ads focused on worries about staining, odor, and the resultant embarrassment (73 percent). This was followed by a concern with the practicalities of finding the necessary tampons and pads quickly should a girl's period come unexpectedly (18 percent), while feeling ill (5 percent) or having to leave during class lessons (4 percent) followed.

Table 1
Products Advertised

	Havens & Swenson		Present Study	
Product	Frequency	Percent	Frequency	Percent
Pads	NA	44	22	40
Tampons	NA	43	30	55
Pantiliners	NA	13	3	5
Total		100	55	100

Table 2
Context of Ad

Context	Frequency	Percent
Worries	40	73
Practical Concerns	10	18
Illness	3	5
Lessons	2	4
Total	55	100

The tone of the ads—how the audience was addressed and by whom—was examined. Role models were used most frequently (56 percent). These were often girls who addressed the reader as a peer or friend. Sometimes the girl's name and age were provided or a sports or fashion figure was used. For example, in one ad, college freshman Eileen Travell gives advice on pantiliners, accompanied by the headline "Why Does a Busy Student Like Eileen Travell Use Lightdays Pantiliners?" A matter-of-fact, conversational tone was taken in approximately 30 percent of the ads, humor in 11 percent, and self-confidence in 4 percent.

Attributes of the product were often presented in the ads including the comfort of the product (53 percent), ease of use (56 percent), lack of bulk (20 percent), and its biodegradability (4 percent). (Note: multiple features were often listed.) An example of comfort includes an ad for Tampax that compares its cardboard applicator with the Playtex plastic applicator under the headline "Hardware. Software." Ease of use was played on in a Playtex ad that read: "I thought tampons would be hard to use." And lack of bulk was emphasized in another ad for Playtex that read: "I hate pads—they're like wearing diapers."

Table 3 describes the overall theme of the ads. The theme is the dominant voice, what the headline or key topic of the advertisement emphasizes. "Trust" was the dominant theme (64 percent). This was the headline used by the major advertiser, Tampax, whose ads claim: "Trust is Tampax." An example of the freedom theme is shown in the advertisement, "No one ever has to know you have your period," and an ad depicting a ballet class. Both are examples of the secrecy theme and were used respectively by Stayfree Ultra Thin and Tampax. The theme of fear was most often associated with the use of tampons, such as: "I felt funny about using a tampon" (Playtex), and "Are you sure I'll still be a virgin?" (Tampax).

Table 3
Theme

Theme	Frequency	Percent*
Trust	35	64
Freedom	16	29
Secrecy	15	27
Fear	8	15
Other	1	2

* In some cases more than one theme was present, therefore column does not total 100%.

The number of models in the ad was not included in the Havens and Swenson study, but is reported here. Typically, one model appeared in the ad (46 percent), followed by none (illustrations or schematics were used) in 25 percent. Sixteen percent of the ads featured two models, and a group of individuals were shown in 13 percent of the ads. These group photos often featured both men and women.

Conclusion

The focus of this essay has been an exploration of the dominant myths surrounding menstruation and the ways they are articulated in advertising. An analysis of advertisements for feminine products provides evidence of a dominant ideology, one that reinforces taboos through the shaping of advertising messages. Despite increased knowledge of women's physiology, feminine hygiene advertising continues to present a situation much akin to that in the past. Women are warned of the social humiliations possible if they purchase a product likely to fail them. Themes of impending discovery, and hence failure, are still very basic concepts in advertising. Although ads in general rely more and more on visual—versus copy—intensive treatments, the messages remain the same. Consistent with other behaviors (dieting, using drugs), having one's period is another activity to be kept secret. The women typically wear revealing white clothing that dares their bodies to betray them, thus reinforcing taboos about pollution and discomfort.

The findings of this study, in terms of tone, context, and theme are similar to the original Havens and Swenson study that argued that the ads in question depict a "hygienic crisis best managed by an effective security system affording protection and peace of mind" (95). By rep-

licating the earlier study, it is possible to assess whether copy plat-
forms have changed in the last twenty years. By extending the analysis
to include a more in-depth look at the copy techniques the ideology of
the ads becomes clearer.

According to Hoffman, in male-dominated cultures, the most successful women are those who best "sublimate their femaleness, they
minimize monthly discomforts, fluctuations, flashes, and cramps" (201).
This suppression of signs and symptoms is evident in modern advertisements for hygiene products. Critical researchers have suggested
that advertisements reflect the dominant ideologies of the society that
produces them. Consistent with Williams' analysis of signification, the
present study illustrates the use of carefully selected images and head-
lines by which the ads deliver information laden with age-old myths
signifying shame, physical discomfort, and secrecy.

Although few of us like to admit it, as consumers we have become
increasingly dependent on advertising for information. Adolescents,
in particular, may have fewer personal sources for private information
or may prefer not to confide in them. In this way, advertising becomes
a forum for discussing personal matters, a kind of social guide on how
to remedy problems. Through the process of socialization, girls learn
what society expects of them, how as women they are to look, feel,
behave, and how they can expect to be treated by others—particularly
by men. Perhaps owing to the availability of birth control, the significance of a girl's period has changed, but the weight of the culture still
determines how this event is perceived and how a girl's sense of self
develops. Self-esteem becomes intimately connected with body image, an image increasingly prescribed by media images.

Despite the liberalization of body-related thinking and the increased
presence of women's issues in advertising, particularly since the 1970s,
menstruation has not been redefined as something positive. The dominant ideology of American culture suggests that evidence of femininity, the fact that women bleed, is best kept hidden. Women are responsible for hiding this shame as well as the accouterments of this
activity.

Kerry Carrington and Anna Bennett, on the other hand, suggest
that advertising for feminine hygiene products is not an example of
media manipulation, given that girls routinely need these products,
they say the advertising is not creating artificial desires. These authors approach the advertising question of "Will I be a virgin after I
use tampons?" not as a perpetuation of myths but rather as a debunk-

ing of them. However, given the current research and the international preponderance of these myths, it is doubtful that a few years of advertising could dislodge thousands of years of stigma. It is more likely that: "By circulating and recirculating negative images and myths about women and nature, advertising supports the dominant ideological themes that undermine environmental consciousness and that allow not just gender—but a global region and a particular vision of life—to remain dominant" (Frith 195).

In American life, Puritanical notions of impurity, shame, and fear have been used to physiologically control women, with fear of incurring the wrath of a "Puritan ancestor, stiff-necked, dress in black" (Vonnegut 75). Menstruation has been socially constructed as a problem—something shameful and dirty. However, by exploring the myths and working to explode them, women and girls can come to see that their social and private space has been regulated by their bodily functions, that this regulation is as much a social construction as are other myths surrounding ability, intellect, and physicality. If young girls are given positive information about their bodies, and put this knowledge into perspective, they can be proud and vocal about their experiences of growing up.

Works Cited

Advertising Age Sept. 1996. (*passim*)

Agonito, Rosemary. *History of Ideas on Woman.* New York: G.P. Putnam's Sons, 1977.

Allen, Patricia, and Denise Fortino. *Cycles: Every Woman's Guide to Menstruation.* New York: Pinnacle, 1983.

de Beauvoir, Simone. *The Second Sex.* New York: Vintage Books, 1952/1989.

Becker, Samuel. "Marxist Approaches to Media Studies: The British Experience." *Critical Studies in Mass Communication* 1 (1977): 66–80.

Brownmiller, Susan. *Femininity.* New York: Fawcett Columbine, 1984.

Carrington, Kerry, and Anna Bennett. "'Girls' Mags' and the Pedagogical Formation of the Girl. *Feminisms and Pedagogies of Everyday Life.* Ed. Carmen Luke. Albany, NY: State University of New York Press, 1996.

Daly, Mary. *Gyn Ecology: The Metaethics of Radical Feminism.* Boston: Beacon Press, 1978/1990.

Delaney, Janice, Mary Jane Lupton, and Emily Toth. *The Curse: A Cultural History of Menstruation.* Rev. ed. Urbana: University of Illinois Press, 1988.

Douglas, Mary. *Purity and Danger.* New York: Praeger, 1966.

Dyhouse, Carol. *Girls Growing Up in Late Victorian Edwardian England.* London: Routledge & Kegan Paul, 1981.

Ellis, Havelock. *The Psychology of Sex.* Vol. 1. New York: Random House, 1936.

Ernster, Virginia L. "American Menstrual Expressions." *Sex Roles* 1 (1975): 3–13.

Frank, Anne. *The Diary of a Young Girl.* Geneva: Bantam Books, 1952.

Frith, Katherine Toland. "Advertising and Mother Nature." *Feminism, Multiculturalism, and the Media: Global Diversities.* Ed. Angharad N. Valdivia. Thousand Oaks, CA: Sage, 1995. 185–196.

Gainotti, Merete Amann. "Sexual Socialization During Early Adolescence: The Menarche." *Adolescence* 11 (1986): 703–710.

Gingold, Alfred, and Helen Rogan. "If You're 'Unclean,' Do You Still Get Pinched on the Bottom?" *New Woman* Sept. 1996: 172.

Goldman, Robert. *Reading Ads Socially.* New York: Routledge, 1992.

Gravelle, Karen. *The Period Book: Everything You Don't Want to Ask—But Need to Know.* New York: Walker and Company, 1996.

Hall, Stuart. "Encoding and Decoding in the Television Discourse." Occasional paper. Birmingham England: University of Birmingham, 1973.

———. "Ideology." *International Encyclopedia of Communication Vol. 2.* Ed. Eric Barnouw. New York: Oxford University Press, 1989. 307–311.

———. "The Problem of Ideology: Marxism Without Guarantees." *Journal of Communication Inquiry* 10.2 (1986): 28–44.

———. "The Rediscovery of 'Ideology': Return of the Repressed in Media Studies. *Culture, Society and the Media.* Eds. Michael Gurevitch, Tony Bennett, James Curran, & Janet Woollacott. New York: Routledge, 1982. 56–90.

Haq, Muhammad Nazmul. "Age at Menarche and the Related Issue: A Pilot Study on Urban School Girls." *Journal of Youth and Adolescence* 13.6 (1984): 559–567.

Havens, Beverly, and Ingrid Swenson. "A Content Analysis of Educational Media about Menstruation." *Adolescence* 24 (1989): 901–907.

———. "Imagery Associated with Menstruation Advertising Targeted to Adolescent Women." *Adolescence* 23 (1988): 89–97.

Hayne, D. "Body Vision?" *Mademoiselle* April 1987: 213.

Hoffman, Eileen. *Our Health, Our Lives.* New York: Pocket Books, 1995.

Houppert, Karen. "Pulling the Plug on the Sanitary Protection Industry." *Village Voice* 7 Feb. 1995.

Jhally, Sut. *The Codes of Advertising.* London: Routledge, 1990.

Kaite, Berkeley. "The Body and Femininity in Feminine Hygiene Advertising." M.A. Thesis, Carelton University. Ottawa, Canada, 1984.

Kane, Kate. "The Ideology of Freshness in Feminine Hygiene Commercials." *Journal of Communication Inquiry.* Winter (1990): 83–92.

Knight, Christopher. *Blood Relations: Menstruation and the Origins of Culture.* New Haven CT: Yale University Press, 1991.

Koff, Elissa, and Jill Rierdan. "Early Adolescent Girls' Understanding of Menstruation." *Women & Health* 22.4 (1995): 1–18.

Lien, Allen. *The Cycling Female: Her Menstrual Rhythm.* San Francisco: W. H. Freeman and Company, 1979.

Mahoney, Ellen V. *Now You've Got Your Period.* New York: Rosen Publishing Group, 1988.

Mann, Judith. *The Difference: Growing Up Female in America.* New York: Warner Books, 1994.

Marchand, Roland. *Advertising and the American Dream: Making Way for Modernity, 1920–1940.* Berkeley: University of California Press, 1985.

Martin, Emily. *The Woman in the Body*. Boston: Beacon Press 1987.

Pipher, Mary. *Reviving Ophelia: Saving the Selves of Adolescent Girls*. New York: Ballantine Books, 1994.

Shields, Vickie Rutledge. "Advertising and Visual Images." *Journal of Communication Inquiry*, 14 (1990): 25–39.

Shilling, Chris. *The Body and Social Theory*. London: Sage, 1993.

Thuren, Britt-Marie. "Opening Doors and Getting Rid of Shame: Experiences of First Menstruation in Valencia, Spain." *Women's Studies International* 17 (1994): 217–228.

Treneman, Ann. "Cashing In on the Curse: Advertising and the Menstrual Taboo. *The Female Gaze*. Eds. Lorraine Gamman and Margaret Marshment. London: The Real Comet Press, 1989. 153–165.

Voigt, David Quentin. "A Tankard of Sporting Taboos." *Forbidden Fruits: Taboos and Tabooismin Culture*. Ed. Ray B. Browne. Bowling Green, OH: Bowling Green University Popular Press, 1984.

Vonnegut, Kurt. "Miss Temptation." *Welcome to the Monkey House*. New York: Bantam Doubleday, 1956.

Whisnant, Lynn, Elizabeth Brett, and Leonard Zegans. "Implicit Messages Concerning Menstruation in Commercial Educational Materials Prepared for Adolescent Girls. *American Journal of Psychiatry* 132 (1975): 815–820.

Whisnant, Lynn, and Leonard Zegans. "A Study of Attitudes toward Menarche in White Middle-Class Adolescent Girls." *American Journal of Psychiatry* 132 (1975): 809–814.

Williamson, Judith. *Decoding Advertisements: Ideology and Meaning in Advertising*. London: Marion Boyars, 1978.

Chapter 7

Disney's *Pocahontas*: Conversations with Native American and Euro-American Girls

Amy Aidman

Acknowledgments: The reception research for this essay grew out of earlier research with Debbie Reese. I gratefully acknowledge her work and her insights, as well as her help in making contacts with Native American[1] girls for this study. I would also like to thank Renee de la Cruz of the Audubon School Native American Elementary Program of Chicago. Many thanks to the girls who participated in the study.

The purpose of this essay is to analyze preadolescent girls' comments about Disney's animated feature film *Pocahontas* in light of conclusions drawn from a critical textual analysis of the movie (Aidman and Reese). Background information is presented concerning the story of the historical figure Pocahontas and the Disney movie based on her, followed by a textual analysis of the movie. Comments from three focus groups of girls ranging in age from nine to thirteen are included in this essay. The final section presents conclusions drawn from the interviews and the textual analysis. The ethnic and socioeconomic background of the young people in this analysis include: a group of middle-class Euro-American girls from a midwestern university town, urban working-class Native American girls from a large midwestern city, and girls of working-class families from a rural reservation in the Southwest with one Native American parent and one Euro-American parent.

While the research on minority children and media has increased over the decades, there is scant literature when the focus turns specifically to American Indian and Alaska Native children (Geiogamah and Pavel 196). Because of the lack of studies on media and American Indian children (Morris; Geiogamah and Pavel), it is difficult to generalize about American Indian children's interactions with media. The studies that have been done point to a need for reform in representations of Native Americans in television and film to overcome the lack of nonstereotypical, positive representations. "Overall, the media's track record for socializing American Indian and Alaska Natives is lamentable" (Geiogamah and Pavel 198). Joann Sebastian Morris expresses concern that no matter how diligent American Indian parents may be in socializing their children to be proud of their culture and heritage, their children's healthy psychological development can be undermined by mass media's general lack of positive representations of Native Americans. Mistaken, inappropriate images of Native Americans in film and television have not only a direct negative impact on the young but also an indirect impact, created by the negative impressions the images make on the majority population, which can include peers and teachers.

The study discussed in this essay begins to fill a gap in research on Native American children's understanding of mass media texts. The study addresses three questions: (1) How do Disney's claims to creation of positive prosocial representations of women and Native Americans in the movie *Pocahontas* hold up or collapse when viewed from a critical perspective which takes gender and class into account? (2) How do girls of different ethnic, socioeconomic, and geographic backgrounds relate to the romanticized story Disney has chosen to tell? And (3) how do the girls' responses to the movie compare between groups and with those of the researcher?

The Legend of Pocahontas

Disney's *Pocahontas* is a full-length animated feature film that can be classified as historical fiction. Released in the summer of 1995, the movie builds on the story of Pocahontas, reputedly the first Native American woman to marry an Englishman and to visit England. Pocahontas has been credited for a peaceful period between the Indians and the English during the early 1600s. While the historical details are difficult to document, the legend of Pocahontas is that as a young girl she saved the life of the English explorer John Smith by throwing herself between him and the executioner's weapon. Later, she married another Englishman, John Rolfe, and went to England with him. She was the first Native American to accept Christianity and English ways. She died at the age of twenty-one on a ship heading from England back to North America (Barbour; Lemay; Mossiker).

Disney's version of the Pocahontas story is a romantic fantasy in which Pocahontas and John Smith meet and fall in love in spite of the enmity between their peoples. The English, led by the greedy Governor Ratcliffe, reach the shores of North America, claiming the land as their own, determined to find gold and to fight off the Indians, whom they call "savages." The Indians watch the movements of the invaders and prepare to defend their land. While the high-spirited Pocahontas dreams of future adventures along an uncharted path, her father, the chief, Powhatan, tells her that Kokoum, a young heroic warrior, wants to marry her. Pocahontas privately rejects the idea of marrying Kokoum because he is too serious, and she consults Grandmother Willow (a 400-year-old tree spirit) about the future and the meaning of her dreams.

After her talk with Grandmother Willow, Pocahontas spots the English ship and begins to secretly trail John Smith as he explores the area. When she and John Smith meet, they are instantly romantically attracted to each other. Pocahontas is quick to understand John Smith's exploitive approach to the land and is upset by his characterization of her people as uncivilized. She educates him in a philosophy of life that is anathema to the profiteering motive Smith employs. Respect for the land, plants, and animals as living spirits is at the core of the life view Pocahontas imparts to John Smith. While Pocahontas and Smith spend more time together, falling in love, the English are establishing a settlement and searching for gold, and tensions are rising between the English and the Indians. Both sides prepare for battle.

Caught in a bind between their illicit love for each other and their loyalty to their own peoples, Pocahontas and Smith meet to form a plan to talk with their respective leaders to head off the battle. Kokoum, worried about Pocahontas, who keeps running off from the village, goes out to look for her on a tip from her friend Nakoma. When Kokoum finds Pocahontas with the white man, Kokoum attacks Smith. Meanwhile, one of the Englishmen, Thomas, has been sent to look for Smith. When Thomas sees Kokoum go after John Smith, he shoots and kills Kokoum. Smith quickly sends Thomas away and takes the blame for killing Kokoum. Smith is captured and his execution is ordered. The following morning, with both sides up in arms, the execution is about to take place. Powhatan stands poised over Smith to kill him, but at the last possible moment, Pocahontas throws herself over Smith's body, proclaims her love for him, and makes an effective call for an end to the fighting. Hearing the wisdom in her words, Powhatan declares that he will not start the battle. At that moment, the greedy English governor, Ratcliffe, aims his gun and fires at Powhatan. Smith leaps before Powhatan, taking the bullet himself. The wound is serious and it is decided that the only hope for Smith's recovery requires him to return to England for treatment. Pocahontas decides that she has to stay with her people rather than go with John Smith to England. She feels a sense of duty at home. The story ends with the romantic, bittersweet parting of Pocahontas and John Smith.

A Textual Analysis of Disney's *Pocahontas*

The intertwining of race and gender is central to this critical textual analysis of the movie *Pocahontas*. The later Disney movies, and in particular *Pocahontas,* appear to be attempts to respond to growing cultural diversity, as well as to calls for multiculturalism and strong female role models in the United States. The character Pocahontas has been called a "Disney girl for the nineties" by her creator, Glen Keane. She was intended to be more muscular and beautiful than any of the Disney heroines ("Disney Discovers the Super Model" 40). The Native Americans in *Pocahontas* have "come out from behind the rocks" (Appleford 98) and are not merely the stereotypical stealthy enemy typical of Hollywood westerns (Stedman). Predictably, new issues of representation have arisen. Disney's *Pocahontas* may be prosocial, but it is far from unproblematic.

Disney's Pocahontas is a character who brings mixed messages to young viewers. The focus in this section will be on the construction of Pocahontas and her relationships, as well as her legend. How does Pocahontas compare with other Disney heroines, and how may we interpret her story in relation to that of Disney's other animated female stars? How does the "imperial imaginary" (Shohat 69) figure in the construction of the Native American Pocahontas and her romantic involvement with the Anglo explorer John Smith? It is important to note that *Pocahontas* is the only animated Disney movie based on a real person. Unfortunately, it is also the only Disney movie of its genre whose protagonist is Native American. A common stereotype of Native Americans is that of a people who *once* lived on this continent. The movie reinforces this common misconception (especially among young white children) of Native Americans in North America as extinct or even mythical peoples (Shaffer 202). Disney is riding the wave of recent North American films that "reflect a pronounced interest in Indians not as faceless savages who fire arrows at the good guys from unseen hiding places but as members of dynamic cultures" (Appleford 98). In addition, the movie reinforces the stereotype of Native American as noble savage, which springs from the ideological notion of "primitivism." Stuart Hall refers to this as the good side of the "native," "portrayed in a certain primitive nobility and simple dignity" (21) and points out that this is an image produced out of white ambivalence.

The first scene of the film in which Pocahontas appears establishes her as a young woman who possesses great beauty and grace. She has a Barbie doll body—tall, with long, muscular legs and arms, huge breasts, a tiny waist, a long neck. Feminist arguments point out that holding up these unrealistic body images to young audiences is unhealthy. Not only can girls' self-esteem be endangered when they compare their own bodies to Hollywood's representations of the ultimate desirable woman, but judging from the epidemic of eating disorders in this country, it is clear that aspiring to unrealistic body shape and weight can cause serious illness, both psychological and physical (Gonzalez-Lavin and Smolak).

Reports indicate that Disney's Pocahontas was drawn from blended images of top fashion models, Iman and Kate Moss, and Princess Tigerlily from Disney's *Peter Pan* (Muldoon 21). She has long, flowing black hair, dark skin, high cheek bones, big black eyes, a full mouth, and an ethnic nose—not the button nose of Snow White or Cinderella. She has more in common with Disney's other ethnic heroine—Princess Jasmine of Aladdin. She has been called a character that just about any (heterosexual) male, animated or otherwise, would love. Compared with other Disney heroines, such as Snow White, Cinderella, or Belle (from *Beauty and the Beast*), she is just as beautiful, only sexier, more sensual, and exotic.

Early in the movie the character and personality traits of Pocahontas are made clear. First of all, she is off by herself enjoying nature. She is independent, adventurous, courageous, and athletic—no stumbling through the woods as a helpless female when she is pursued by some villain. Her dive off the waterfall is a moment that frames her as a thrill seeker, confident in her physical ability, and sensual in the pleasure she takes in nature. She is spontaneous, mischievous, playful, and defiant. In comparison with her more sedate friend and foil, Nakoma, she is clearly a high-energy, dominant female figure.

With respect to strong female role models, it is gratifying to see Disney departing from the female leads who are forever in need of rescue by the hero. Cinderella would have continued as a servant without her fairy godmother and her prince. Snow White would have been killed if not for the kindness of the woodsman, or forever banished without the dwarfs, and her prince. Sleeping Beauty would have slept forever without her prince. Even Jasmine, who shows some intelligence and independence, ultimately has to be rescued by Aladdin in order to have some choice as to her future mate.

Unlike other Disney heroines, Pocahontas does not live happily ever after with her Prince Charming. She pays dearly for all of those strong character traits. At the end of the movie John Smith is wounded and has to be taken back to England for medical treatment. Pocahontas decides that she is needed by her people and cannot go with him. The resolution of the relationship between the two is to always be together in spirit. This ending to the movie is not necessary for dramatic purposes. Since the real Pocahontas ended up marrying a white man and traveling to England, it is not necessary for historic accuracy. It can be viewed on the one hand as a subtext that a strong woman cannot have it all, and on the other hand as Disney's inability to imagine sanctioning an interracial relationship in one of its animated films.

This is particularly intriguing when considering the barriers other animated characters have had to overcome on the way to romantic fulfillment. Snow White and Cinderella had help in battling the evil intentions of wicked and powerful stepmothers. Their beauty and goodness entitled them to supernatural assistance and to an enchanting future.

The issue of class has to be overcome in a number of the movies. Only magic is able to conquer the class barrier. Cinderella is a servant and has to be transformed by her fairy godmother's magic before she can win her prince. Princess Jasmine is under a decree to marry only royalty, and it is the genie's power that helps Aladdin, the "diamond in the rough," to reveal his inner prince to become an acceptable match for her. Ariel in *The Little Mermaid* and Belle from *Beauty and the Beast* both have unproblematic liaisons with animal-like characters. Disney sanctions cross-species romantic involvements in these two films yet cannot entertain the possibility of the consummation of an interracial romance.

Like the other Disney heroines, Pocahontas has the animals and birds on her side. This is a feature that is part of virtually every animated Disney movie but the relationship of the barefoot and scantily-clad Pocahontas with animal and plant life goes beyond the others. She has a mystical, spiritual relationship with nature. The spirits of the earth, water, and sky are actively instructing her, helping her to see her future and to make important decisions. The scenes in which she consults Grandmother Willow (an anthropomorphised tree) exemplify her mystical relationship with nature. While it makes for enchanting visuals, this heightened spirituality also represents a stereotypical image of the Native American "in the person of the peaceful, mystical, spiritual guardian of the land who is in vogue in the 1990s" (Bird 2).

Most, if not all, of the Disney heroines are motherless. If there is a living mother, she is an evil stepmother. Pocahontas' grandmother is a tree spirit and her dead mother is immortalized and personified in the wind. Her father tells her that the people look to her mother (the wind) for leadership and that one day they will look to her. One reading of this is that Pocahontas, too, can hope to be as ephemeral as the wind.

Another way in which the postcolonial imaginary of Hollywood's movie makers comes into play is through Pocahontas' choice of love interests. Her rejection of the notion of marrying Kokoum, a heroic man among his people, is quite shallow. "He's so serious," she says. She figures that marrying him would be the end of her life. With that rejection of the familiar, she embraces a Western perspective on individual destiny. The notions of tradition and the common good are sacrificed for a sense of fulfillment through involvement with the unknown. It also conveys to young girls that a dangerous man is preferable to a solid, serious man for a mate. Pocahontas' immediate attraction to John Smith is really a bit questionable. Her friend Nakoma's reaction on first sight of him is more natural. She is shocked by such an unusual looking human. The movie does not provide a reasonable explanation for Pocahontas' attraction to this Nordic-looking character. He is constructed to fit Hollywood notions of the white male hunk and that should be good enough to make him "universally" attractive.

On several levels, Pocahontas, "as a metaphor for her land, becomes available for Western penetration and knowledge" (Shohat 57). To the character John Smith, Pocahontas is clearly one more conquest. She has to disobey her father and betray her people to be with him. Her desire to be with him is responsible for Kokoum's death. To the producers of the film, the metaphor is taken one step further. The character is the product of the colonial gaze, not only in her physical features and attitudes but in the way she is rescued from a life of serious pursuit of the common good by an adventure with the irresistible John Smith. By the movie's end, Pocahontas realizes the importance of her people's need for her as a leader. This seems almost an afterthought for the movie makers, an excuse to keep her from the romantic fulfillment that has traditionally been the reward of the animated Disney sisterhood. So, as she must be satisfied with a tree for a grandmother and the wind for a mother, she has to learn to live with the ghost of a romance sacrificed for the future of her people.

Although the filmmakers ridicule the greed of the English explorers, depicting them as destroyers of the land, disrespectful of nature, crude and barbaric invaders with no regard for the native inhabitants of their new world, the conflicts are diffused by the end of the film. John Smith and Governor Ratcliffe return to England. Pocahontas has a broken heart but will rise to lead her people. John Smith is physically wounded but will heal. Kokoum, whose only fault was his seriousness, is dead. As a man of color in competition for the white man's female object of desire, he had to die. This ending neatly eliminates the need for the filmmakers to deal with the suffering of Native American people throughout history at the hands of the European settlers and their descendants.

It is important to emphasize the complexity of the subtexts in Disney's *Pocahontas*. The messages about strong women and Native Americans are mixed. While perpetuating some stereotypes, others are diffused. In *Pocahontas* we have moved beyond earlier depictions of women as wilting heroines and Native Americans as the bad guys, but it should be remembered that the characterizations in the movie are part of an ongoing process of change, and as such still have their problematic elements with which we must grapple.

On the plus side, the movie *Pocahontas* begins to fill a void in film offerings for children with strong female, ethnic role models. The portrayal of indigenous people is more well-rounded than earlier representations in Hollywood children's films. Native people are shown within their communities and families rather than as the isolated enemy. For parents and teachers, the movie can be used as a springboard for discussion with children of issues related to native peoples. It can also provide a starting point to delve into the history of this period. Finally, the underlying theme of respect for nature, or eco-consciousness, is important and timely.

While noting Disney's socially conscious intentions, they cannot be considered out of context. Obviously, the driving force behind the movie is economic. For example, the Pocahontas costume was the best-selling Halloween costume at Toys R Us in 1995 ("Ten Most Popular Halloween Costumes Sold"). Pauline Turner Strong (1995) articulates the inherent contradictions well:

> Pocahontas raises a number of difficult and timely issues . . . a tribute to its seriousness and ambition. Indeed, the film begs to be read as a plea for tolerant, respectful, and harmonious living in a world torn by ethnic strife and environmental degradation. That Pocahontas is rife with tensions and ironies is also a testimony to the limitations of serious cultural critique in an artistic environment devoted to the marketing of dreams. That our children are surrounded with Pocahontas-hype while being called to treat other cultures and the land with respect requires us to clarify for them the difference between consuming objectified difference and achieving respectful relationships across difference.

Another troubling aspect of the movie is its glorification of Native American religious beliefs. Today, that spirituality is increasingly exploited for commercial purposes. Laurie Anne Whitt (1995) makes the point that, intentional or not, this kind of cultural imperialism serves to "extend the political power, secure the social control, and further the economic profit of the dominant culture. The commodification of indigenous spirituality is a paradigmatic instance of cultural imperialism" (2).

In concluding the textual analysis of Disney's version of the Pocahontas legend, I want to draw attention to other possible interpretations of the Pocahontas story (beyond the Euro-American myth). While the Pocahontas story is viewed by Euro-Americans as a tale of cross-cultural understanding and tolerance (and the movie reinforces that view), it can also be seen as a tragedy for the woman Pocahontas, not to mention a turning point in the conquest of native peoples and their land. Pocahontas, as the first indigenous person to convert to Christianity, is a symbol of the acceptance of European cultural domination. She went from being an adventurous, free, high-spirited child to a tightly bound proper Christian woman, married to a man for whom she reportedly felt no great passion, far from her home in a foreign land. Ultimately, she died of disease contracted in England. According to reports, grave robbers attempted unsuccessfully to sell her remains. In spite of attempts to locate them, Pocahontas' remains have never been found (Mossiker). The historical record says that after being kidnapped by the English, Pocahontas willingly and quickly accepted Christianity and English customs. Perhaps her willingness was really resignation. Her father wasn't coming up with the ransom—what could she do? Although she was a favorite at court, it is possible that she was primarily a curiosity. There is no indication in the written history that her English hosts changed their ways or ideas because of their interactions with her. What is traditionally celebrated about Pocahontas are the ways in which she was expedient to European imperialism. While the Disney movie version of the Pocahontas story does not end in the usual romantic fulfillment viewers expect, it leaves the impression of a far gentler fate than the real-life Pocahontas and the descendants of her people suffered.

The Girls' Responses to *Pocahontas*

Three focus groups, with three to five participants in each, were conducted with girls ranging in age from nine to thirteen. In Group 1 there were five girls, from nine to thirteen years old. These girls can best be described as middle-class, Euro-American from a midsized midwestern university town. Group 2 included four girls, from ten to twelve years old. These were Native American girls of working class families from a large midwestern city. In Group 3 there were three girls, ages nine to eleven years old, from a rural reservation in the southwestern United States. Their families are working class and they are of mixed Native American and Euro-American descent but identify themselves as Native Americans. Differences in ages between the groups was not significant.

The girls were asked to recall how many times they had seen the movie *Pocahontas*. The urban Native American girls claimed to have seen the movie an average of eight times (Group 2), whereas the average number of times the others saw it was 2.3 for the girls from the rural reservation (Group 3) and 1.4 for the Euro-American girls (Group 1). Significant differences were found between the urban Native American girls and the Euro-American girls (t=3.00; p<0.05). Aimee Dorr (1982) points out that research provides evidence that children prefer programs and characters that are ethnically similar to them. Table 1 below supports that idea and provides detailed information about the groups.

The girls and the researcher screened the movie together immediately preceding the interviews. After viewing the movie the girls were asked to rate it on two scales. The first measure asked how much they

Table 1
Demographics

	Group 1 n=5	Group 2 n=4	Group 3 n=3
Mean Age	11.4	10.8	10
	[9,11,12,12,13]	[10,10,11,12]	[9,10,11]
Ethnicity	Euro-American	Native American	Mixed EA/NA
SES	Middle class	Working class	Working class
Regionality	Suburban Midwest	Urban Midwest	Rural west
Average Number of Times Viewed Movie	1.4	8	2.3
	[0,1,3,3,0]	[5,12,3,12]	[3,3,1]

liked the movie on a 1 to 5 scale (1="hated it"; 5="loved it"). The second measure asked them to rate the movie's quality on a 1 to 5 scale (1="thought it was a terrible movie"; 5= "thought it was a great movie"). Table 2 illustrates their responses.

While the numbers in Table 2 are too small to talk about statistically significant differences, the urban Native American girls (Group 2) liked the movie the most, followed by the Native American/Euro-American girls (Group 3). The Euro-American girls in Group 1 liked the movie the least, giving it an overall neutral rating. Since the two groups of girls with Native American backgrounds (Group 2 and 3) scored similarly, their scores were combined and compared with the Euro-American girls (Group 1). Girls of Native American background liked the movie significantly more than Euro-American girls (t=2.80; p.<.05). As to the movie quality, the girls in Group 3 gave it the highest rating. The Euro-American girls in Group 1 rated the movie lower than the other groups on quality. When quality ratings of both groups of girls with Native American backgrounds were combined, they were significantly higher than those of the Euro-American girls (t=2; p<0.05).

Table 2
Mean Ratings of Movie

	Group 1	Group 2	Group 3
Like Movie	3.0	4.25	4.0
Quality of Movie	3.2	4.25	4.3

The Interviews

This section summarizes each group's comments about the movie. Although the interviewer proceeded from a predetermined interview schedule, the format was open-ended to allow the researcher to probe certain issues or to give the participants the opportunity to expand on their ideas. The girls were asked to speak one at a time, but were told that it was okay for them to enter the conversation if something another girl said made them think of a point they wanted to make.

Questions about the movie focused initially on the girls' descriptions of the character Pocahontas with regard to her physical and personality traits. The issue of identification with the character was raised by asking the girls if they thought they were like the character in any way, would like to be like the character, and in what ways they might be different from her. The girls were asked to think about Pocahontas' judgements and choices, especially with regard to rejecting Kokoum and falling in love with John Smith. Finally, the girls were asked what they thought of the movie's representation of Native Americans and Englishmen. Results of the interviews with each group are summarized below.

Group 1—Euro-American Suburban Girls: Pocahontas' hair was immediately mentioned as a salient characteristic: "Her hair always gets in the way." Another girl commented, somewhat cynically, "She speaks with wisdom beyond her years." In addition, the girls labeled her as "kind of preppy," "silly," and not as pretty as all the other "Disney girls" and too heroic in comparison with the other Disney heroines. Referring to Pocahontas' jump off a cliff above a waterfall, one of the girls called her a "suicidal maniac." When asked what younger female viewers might think of Pocahontas, the girls in this group thought younger girls would think she's pretty and would want to copy her and be like her when they grow up. They explained that younger girls would want to buy the product spin-offs from the movie in order to be like Pocahontas. When asked why the younger girls would want to be like her, one girl jokingly said, "because she can jump off cliffs," while another submitted that it was because she was pretty, tall, has a boyfriend, and her father is a chief—in other words, she is the ideal of what every young girl aspires to be. There were also comments about her body being out of proportion. They mocked the way she spoke as being like a phonetics lesson.

John Smith, according to one of the girls, was not masculine. He had a "wussy attitude" that did not match up with the way the animators drew him. "He's too understanding for a guy." To this comment another girl replied that he was just trying to be nice to Pocahontas so she would like him. One girl commented that she had not wanted to see *Pocahontas* because the character seemed "too lighthearted" for an Indian. Her idea was that Indians are serious and that Pocahontas was not an authentic Indian because she was not serious enough. Another girl said she had not wanted to see the movie because Pocahontas "goes around doing good deeds," and that all the current popular movies and books for youth are about characters who are trying to do good. The theme is always the same and it makes for boring stories. She said, however, that it was okay to make these kinds of movies for smaller children. Yet another argued that Disney twisted the facts of the historical Pocahontas and that it is wrong for Disney to create a happy ending just for the sake of the movie. She was concerned that younger children would believe that the version offered in the Disney movie is the truth and that they would have misconceptions about history because of that, while another said that Disney created a happy ending so that the children watching it wouldn't be sad. Concerning the movie's ending, the girls agreed that it was mixed, both happy and sad. One noted that Pocahontas' father would be happy his daughter came back instead of going "off with some guy."

When asked if there were any ways they would like to be like Pocahontas, one of the girls said she liked where Pocahontas lived, while some others replied that it is no longer like that. Another envied Pocahontas' freedom to be off by herself, while another remarked that Pocahontas did not have to go to school. They also liked her friend, Nakoma. One of the girls said that while it would be nice to be one of those kinds of people who everyone likes, a heroine and popular, on the down side it would be too glamorous and in that way not appealing. Another expanded on that thought, saying, "It's too fake. It's like being the decorative frosting on a cake. It looks pretty . . . but, it's not real." While they admired her bravery and even admitted to aspiring to being a little more brave, they concurred that Pocahontas was too brave for her own good.

The girls in this group, while overall very cynical in their response to the movie, said that they had favorite Disney movies when they were younger and that they had acquired some of the spin-off products. One said she especially liked the music to the movies. Several remembered having had the Disney paper dolls, and another remembered pretending to be Beauty from *Beauty and the Beast.*

One said that Disney is trying to become more "ethnic" in its movies, while another said they are trying to become more geographically diverse and modern.

The girls were asked how they were different from Pocahontas. One girl said that she is "civilized," and would not consider throwing herself between a raised club and someone else in order to save them. Another girl referred to the mystical side of Pocahontas, noting that Pocahontas' dream had a meaning but that as far as she could tell her own dreams have no meaning. Another girl said she didn't have the bravery of Pocahontas, while another girl said it was stupidity rather than bravery.

When the girls were asked what they thought about Pocahontas' deciding not to marry Kokoum and then falling in love with John Smith, one response was that she was the type of character who wouldn't have wanted anyone who was "thrown at her." Another expanded on this by saying that Pocahontas did not want what anyone else wanted her to have, she just wanted to be different. Yet another added that Pocahontas was a typical teenage girl in that she did not want what her father wanted for her. One girl called Pocahontas' rejection of Kokoum "hypocritical," since both he and John Smith were the "hero type," but others argued that Kokoum would have tried to tell her what to do and squelch her free-spirited nature and rule over her and hold her back. On top of that, while Pocahontas was for peace, Kokoum was a warrior, and that would have created problems between them. One of the girls said she didn't understand why Pocahontas was upset that Kokoum had been shot, since she had rejected him. She interpreted Pocahontas' shock at seeing Kokoum killed as a sudden love for an unattainable person. "She wants what she can't have."

The girls were asked to comment on the movie's representations of Native Americans and the English. Concerning its depiction of Native Americans, one girl called it stereotypical, referring to the chanting of the medicine man. She said today they have houses and water and that they don't live like that any more. In general, the girls rejected Disney's representation of Native Americans as stereotypical. One girl pointed out that there were similarities in the way the two groups were portrayed. Both the Indians and the English were obsessed by the same kind of worries. Yet she said that in a way Disney had turned the stereotypes around, making the English out to be savages, while the Indians were the wise ones. Another girl pointed out that the English were portrayed as very greedy.

The tone of this group's comments was often cynical, and eventually the girls began to talk about how at their age they enjoy making fun of movies for younger children. They talked about the fun of watching these movies with others their own age and laughing about certain parts. One girl said she thought the filmmakers intentionally add parts for teenagers to joke about in order to widen the audience. These girls seemed to enjoy second-guessing the filmmakers as well as critiquing and lampooning the movie.

Group 2—Native American Urban Girls: The initial response to the character Pocahontas from this group was one of liking and approval. "She's pretty." "She's nice." In contrast with the comments of the girls in the first group, which began in a cynical tone, these girls took the character more seriously. "She's pretty smart . . . she knows which path to take." There was an appreciation of her efforts to stop the fighting and curb the "path of hatred." There was also approval of the playful, adventurous, childlike aspects of her personality, as well as her freedom, her risk-taking behavior, and her desire to dream.

The question of identification with the character produced mixed responses. While two of the girls did not think that they had anything in common with the character, another identified with the childlike nature of Pocahontas, saying "people say that I act like a little kid . . . I want to keep having fun." However, this girl labeled herself as shy, saying she would not speak out the way Pocahontas did, and later said she admired that in the character. She also mentioned a similarity between herself and Pocahontas in that both of them seem to have contact with protective spirits that help out when there is trouble. She said she would like to be around animals the way Pocahontas was. Another girl also identified with the desire to have fun and have exciting things happen. The same girl said that she, herself, stands up for her own and other people's rights. In that respect, she identified with Pocahontas when Pocahontas stood up for John Smith.

When asked in what ways they might want to be like Pocahontas, in addition to wanting to have adventures, one of the girls remarked that Pocahontas lived in a beautiful place. She also admired Pocahontas' decision to stay with her father at the end of the movie rather than going off to England with John Smith. The girls raised the issue of Pocahontas' service to her people as a positive attribute. They also talked about wanting to be like Pocahontas physically. "She's very beautiful. She's sleek," noted one of the girls, while another said, "I would like to be pretty like her, she's very beautiful." The girls liked

Pocahontas' wisdom, heroic nature, and adventurous spirit as well as her strength and power in standing up for herself and her people. "I would like to stand up for myself more than I do," one of the girls said.

When asked how they think they are different from Pocahontas, one of the girls replied, "I don't look like her. I don't live like her. I live in a bad place, where there are gangs." Another girl mentioned that it was not polluted where Pocahontas lived but that she lives on a noisy main street. Still another talked about how in contrast to where she lives, in an apartment in a neighborhood where it is dirty outside and there are gangs, Pocahontas lives in a place free of these problems where the water is clean. She also said, "I am not really wise like her. Sometimes I don't choose the right path. And she's really pretty . . . and I am not that pretty."

Other differences in culture were noted. One of the girls said that she has a big family, but that in contrast with Pocahontas' family, all of whom live in one place, her family members live in different places. She also pointed out that while today young people go to school, Pocahontas did not go to a formal school, and that there are differences in the ways they have celebrations. Another girl mentioned that while Pocahontas was able to harvest her food, her own family goes to the store to get food.

On the topic of Pocahontas' decision to reject Kokoum, the girls agreed that it was a good decision. They agreed that Kokoum's seriousness was a problem. If she married him, it would prevent her from doing all the things she had dreamed of doing. They thought he would be an authoritarian and jealous husband. "He would boss her around." "She wouldn't be able to jump off waterfalls." "She would have to stay home." "She would be stuck cooking for him . . . he wouldn't go out to have some fun with her . . . If she had married Kokoum the fighting wouldn't have stopped. He would have convinced Powhatan to keep fighting." One girl said that if two people of different backgrounds, like Pocahontas and John Smith, love each other, their love might contribute to an improvement in the relationship between their people. In addition, Pocahontas was old enough to decide for herself rather than her father telling her what to do. They agreed that it is right to marry the person you love rather than to end up in an arranged marriage. They thought John Smith would allow Pocahontas to continue to have fun and exciting adventures. One said that, as Grandmother Willow concluded, John Smith had a good soul.

When asked how the movie represents Native Americans, the girls' comments were generally very positive. According to them the film shows that "we're not savages. We're the same as anybody else. We have feelings, and blood, and everything that other people have. We don't like to start wars. We stop wars." "They want to be peaceful, to live and have fun." "Even though the culture's different, it doesn't make them savages." "They're powerful. Everybody's the same. The skin color doesn't matter." "Indians aren't really savages. They can take care of themselves." One girl expressed the feeling that if they had been left alone, the Indians could have continued living the way they were and it would have been better. On the negative side, one girl said the movie shows that Native Americans like to start to fights, since Kokoum started the fight with John Smith.

Responses concerning the movie's representations of the Englishmen were generally negative. According to one girl, the English had to learn that the Indians, in spite of their outward differences, are not savages. Another comment was that the English were blind to any way of valuing nature other than their own. The English were convinced that they were the greatest and the smartest people. The girls agreed that the movie showed the English to be greedy and prejudiced against the Indians. It showed them as wanting to kill the Indians. One girl pointed out that the English called the Indians "Injuns" and said that the Englishmen seemed like savages themselves. However, they said that the representation was not totally negative, since by the end of the movie the Englishmen understood the Indians better, realizing that the Indians did not want to fight.

Group 3—Mixed Native American, Euro-American Rural Girls: The first thing the girls in this group had to say about Pocahontas was that she's an Indian. In addition, they said she is different from other people. Her skin is different. Her behavior is different from that of other people in that she doesn't follow the rules. They said it is clear that she cares about people. She stopped the fighting, and that shows that she cares about people. It was also mentioned that she is pretty.

When asked about how they might identify with Pocahontas, they all said just that she's an Indian and so are they. They admired the fact that she is pretty and likes to be different. "She's really pretty and nice and she cares about other people." They would like to be different the way she is and to be helpful to other people. They all admired her independence, and they felt that they, too, were independent.

When asked how they are different from Pocahontas, they mentioned that they wear different kinds of clothes and that their tribal ways are different, in particular their language. They talked about differences in appearance, saying that Pocahontas has darker skin and longer hair. With regard to the character's personality, one girl said Pocahontas is probably kinder than she is, and another said she did not help others as much. When asked about her physical bravery, the girls said that although they had recently jumped off waterfalls they did not think they were always as brave as Pocahontas. The girls in this group were unsure about the correctness of Pocahontas' decision not to marry Kokoum and did not offer any thoughts or comments on that situation.

When asked about how the movie represented the Native Americans, one of the girls said it was good because it showed how they really lived, while another said it was a mixed portrayal. According to one, the fact that the Indians in the movie did not start the fight contributes to a positive representation, but the fact that they wanted to kill John Smith shows them in a negative light. One of the girls commented that the song "Savages" (in which the two groups dehumanize each other with this label), especially bothered her.

They thought that the English people were represented in a general, but not totally, negative light. The way they wanted to fight and to keep John Smith from being with Pocahontas were the negative aspects of the portrayal, along with how they talked about killing and called the Indians savages. Also, the Englishmen killed two Indians in the movie, they wanted to build houses without asking permission, and they claimed the land as soon as they reached the shores. The only good thing the English did was to stop fighting. According to these girls, John Smith was nice because he liked Pocahontas.

When asked about the movie's end, they said they thought it was good that Pocahontas stayed home rather than leave for England with John Smith, because if she had gone it would have been a betrayal of her people.

The tone of this session was low key. The girls seemed a bit shy and reticent about engaging in the interview process. Interestingly, after the tape recorder was turned off and the interview officially ended, the girls warmed up, became more animated, and asked me to ask them more questions about movies, while they waited to be picked up. They considered *Pocahontas* too juvenile for them, a movie that is more interesting for their younger siblings and cousins.

Analysis of the Interviews

Any analysis of the girls' responses to the movie should make it clear that what they said tells as much about them and their life situations as about the movie. While there were a number of common issues raised by the groups, each had its own particular ambience. The Euro-American girls were somewhat cynical and sarcastic. It seemed at times as if they were engaged in gossip about a girl whom they all knew. Their reading of the film contained some elements of an oppositional reading, in which they criticized Disney for its version of the Pocahontas story, and enjoyed making jokes about various aspects of the movie and its characters.

Group 2, the urban Native American girls, had a very different tone. A much more serious consideration was given to the movie. The girls seemed to take the character and her story to heart. There was a feeling of authentic connectedness to the movie. Judging from the number of times these girls had previously seen the movie, it can be assumed that it had significance for them. Their talk about the movie could be characterized as in line with a dominant reading. Not having many positive media images of Native Americans with whom they want to identify might lead them to embrace the movie and the character wholeheartedly and uncritically.

The girls in Group 3, of mixed background from a rural reservation, responded seriously to the movie, but they gave the distinct impression that the movie was not very important to them nor did it have any meaning for them beyond that of any other Disney movie. Perhaps the reality of their lives on the reservation, in which their own tribal identity and culture is strong, limits the significance of mediated representations of Native Americans for them.

All three groups mentioned Pocahontas' physical beauty, but only the girls in the urban Native American group talked about wanting to be pretty like her. The girls in the other groups did not in any way indicate dissatisfaction with their own physical appearances in comparison with Pocahontas. In fact, the comment was made by one of the Euro-American girls that Pocahontas was not as pretty as the other Disney heroines. In considering why it might be that only one of the groups of girls expressed the desire to be pretty like Pocahontas, one has to wonder about these girls' notions of what constitutes beauty in society. Clearly, for them Pocahontas represents an ideal of Native American beauty against which they measure themselves as inadequate.

This supports the notion raised earlier in this essay that representations of women with unrealistic body images can be unhealthy for the self-esteem of girls and young women.

Each of the groups addressed Pocahontas' inner qualities—her adventurous nature, courage, caring for others, and wisdom—but to varying extent and with different conclusions. The Euro-American girls related to Pocahontas as an exaggerated figure, a caricature. They questioned Disney's motives and made judgments about the filmmakers' intentions, interrogating not just the characterizations but the fictionalized version of the Pocahontas story.

The urban Native American group gave wholesale approval to the character Pocahontas, her personality, her choices, her judgements. The girls in this group seemed to desire to be more like Pocahontas. The girls from the reservation also approved of Pocahontas and her ways, but the desire to be like her was not an issue. These girls admired her independence, but they thought they were independent themselves. The Euro-American girls thought Pocahontas' dives off of waterfalls indicated that she was a "suicidal maniac" and the urban Native American girls approved of her risk-taking behavior, while the rural girls from the reservation related to it as something they had also done. Perhaps because of their experience of daily living on the reservation, the rural Native American girls were not engaged in the fantasy of *Pocahontas*, either as a Native American ideal or as a representation of a lost past.

All of the groups related to the natural environmental setting of the movie. One of the Euro-American girls expressed a kind of longing to live in such a beautiful place, while another added that it does not look like that anymore. However, it was in the group of urban Native American girls that a kind of nostalgia for a perfect past was inspired by the movie. Not only did some of the girls say they would like to live in the place Pocahontas lived, one of the girls wondered aloud if she might not be living like that now if the Europeans had not come and conquered and changed the ways of life and the land. The girls from the rural reservation thought the movie represented well the way Indians really live and that this was a positive aspect of the movie, even though their own clothes and customs are different.

In contrast with the textual analysis that critiques the movie for presenting Native Americans as peoples of the past, the girls of Native American descent did not appear to be concerned with that aspect of the film. In fact, stereotypes were mentioned specifically only by the Euro-American group. It may have been uncomfortable for the girls of Native American background to address the issue of stereotypes in the presence of a non-Native American researcher. On the other hand, both groups with Native American backgrounds showed a concern for the use of the word "savages." (The word "savage" falls under the definition of an ethnic slur and is therefore a taboo term.) Girls in both groups pointed out that the movie showed that Indians want peace, not war, and that they are like other people—the color of the skin does not matter. They thought that in general the Indians were represented positively and were not troubled by the ending of the movie, in which Pocahontas and John Smith are separated, even though they approved of the relationship. None of them mentioned the fact that only Pocahontas, among all the Disney heroines, did not live happily ever after with the hero. This was an issue that was salient for the researcher.

Interestingly, the Euro-American girls thought that Kokoum would have made as good a mate for Pocahontas as John Smith, but the urban Native American girls foresaw problems if Kokoum and Pocahontas would have married. They agreed with the idea presented in the movie that Kokoum was too serious and that Pocahontas' fun would have ended if she were to marry him. They extrapolated from the movie that Kokoum would have been an authoritarian husband. They also thought it was important to marry for love and that ethnic background should not be a roadblock to a relationship. The girls from the rural reservation had no comment on Pocahontas' decision to reject Kokoum. It might be a non-issue for them, being of mixed Euro-American and Native American background themselves. None of the girls mentioned any hesitation concerning Pocahontas' readiness to go with a strange and unknown man.

One of the urban Native American girls said that she related to Pocahontas' spirituality because she also felt that she had helping spirits. While this issue was not specifically raised by any of the other girls, one of the Euro-American girls was a bit wistful about the fact that Pocahontas' dream had a meaning, in contrast to her experiences of her own dreams. The only other mention of spirituality was that one of the Euro-American girls found the depiction of the medicine man to be stereotypical.

One final methodological note should be made in concluding this analysis. The interviewer's identity as a middle-class, Euro-American may have influenced the moods of the interview sessions. For the

Euro-American girls, the similarity between the interviewer and themselves may have led them to "cut loose," whereas the girls of Native American background were seeing a person dissimilar to them ethnically, coming from a very different social background, and it may have contributed to a feeling of shyness or hesitation. Beyond this, there may simply be different cultural values placed on verbosity that could account for the loquacious, interactive nature of the session with the Euro-American girls, and to the quieter sessions with the Native American girls. Whatever the explanation, it would be desirable to have interviewers who are ethnically similar to the interviewees in future research.

Conclusion

This essay set out to critically analyze the animated Disney movie *Pocahontas* with respect to gender and race and to examine interviews with preadolescent girls of different ethnic, socioeconomic, and geographical backgrounds in light of that analysis. It is evident from the interviews that although there were points of agreement, in general, the girls' responses and attitudes toward the movie varied widely both between the groups and with respect to the researcher's conclusions about the movie.

In some respects, the Euro-American girls produced a reading that could be labeled as "negotiated." However, on a certain level, they considered the movie in terms of the traditional interpretation of the history of that period which is taught in U.S. schools—that is that the good guys were the Europeans, and the fact that they won was a positive outcome. Their ability to joke about the movie may be related to the fact that *Pocahontas* is just one more animated Disney movie for them, a genre that was important to them as little girls but is now considered a vehicle for budding adolescent sarcasm and cynicism.

For the urban Native American girls, *Pocahontas* is clearly an important movie. This can be concluded judging alone by the number of times they saw the movie. Given the lack of positive media representations of Native Americans, it is not difficult to understand why they would relate so strongly to the movie and the character Pocahontas. Some of the movie's themes, such as respect for nature and the value of family and community, are themes that are in line with their traditional cultural values. While their reactions to the movie were far afield from those of the researcher, their reactions support the need for and importance of positive, nonstereotypical representations of Native Americans in contemporary popular culture.

While the Native American girls from the rural reservation were not as enthusiastic about *Pocahontas* or as engaged in the discussion, as the girls in the urban group, they also produced a dominant reading of the movie. As pointed out earlier, the movie did not seem to be of great importance to them. This might be the result of the culture of their daily lives strengthening their personal and cultural identities in such a way as to make media representations of Native Americans less significant for them.

None of the girls questioned the lack of a romantic ending or Disney's choice not to let the characters live happily ever after in an interracial romance. None of the girls questioned Disney's Eurocentric view of the Pocahontas story or of the history of the period, although among the Euro-American girls there was dissatisfaction concerning Disney's misrepresentation of historical "truth," with regard to Pocahontas' age and her relationship with John Smith.

The girls' readings of the film produced three very different conversations that can be related in part to their ethnic, class, and geographical backgrounds. To the researcher's initial claim that *Pocahontas* is a mixed bag, "prosocial yet problematic," the girls' conversations add a number of interesting insights. Taken as a whole their responses attest to the complexity of the representational issues in the movie; reaffirm the importance of continuing to deconstruct the texts and subtexts of children's popular culture particularly as they relate to gender and race; and emphasize the necessity of talking with girls about their understanding of popular culture.

Note

1. The use of the terms "Native American" and "American Indian" is contested. After seeking advice about this, the author has decided to use the terms interchangeably in this essay. When quoting or referring to another's writing, the term used by the source is used in this essay.

Works Cited

Aidman, Amy, and Debbie Reese. "*Pocahontas*: Problemitizing the Pro-Social." Paper presented to the International Communication Association. Chicago, Illinois. May 1996.

Appleford, Robert. "Coming Out from Behind the Rocks: Constructs of the Indian in Recent US and Canadian Cinema." *American Indian Culture and Research Journal* 19.1 (1995): 97–118.

Barbour, Philip L. *Pocahontas and Her World: A Chronicle of America's First Settlement in Which is Related the Story of the Indians and the Englishmen. Particularly Captain John Smith, Captain Samuel Argall, and Master John Rolfe*. Boston: Houghton Mifflin Company, 1970.

Bird, S. Elizabeth. "Tales of Difference: Representations of American Indian Women in Popular Film and Television." *Mediated Women: Representations in Popular Culture*. Ed. Marian Meyers. Cresskill NJ: Hampton Press, 1998. 91–109.

"Disney Discovers the Supermodel." *Good Housekeeping* June 1992: 40.

Dorr, Aimee. "Television and the Socialization of the Minority Child." *Television and the Socialization of the Minority Child*. Eds. Gordon L. Berry, and Claudia Mitchell-Kernan. New York: Academic Press, 1982. 15–31.

Geiogamah, Haney, and Michael D. Pavel. "Developing Television for American Indian and Alaska Native Children in the Late 20th Century." *Children and Television: Images in a Changing Sociocultural World*. Eds. Gordon L. Berry, and Joy Keiko Asamen. Newbury Park: Sage Publications, 1993. 191–204.

Gonzalez-Lavin, Andrea, and Linda Smolak. "Relationships Between Television and Eating Problems in Middle School Girls." Poster paper presented at the Society for Research in Child Development; Indianapolis, Indiana, 1995.

Hall, Stuart. "The Whites of Their Eyes: Racist Ideologies and the Media." *Gender, Race, and Class in Media*. Eds. Gail Dines, and Jean M. Humez. Thousand Oaks: Sage Publications, 1995. 18–27.

Lemay, Joseph A. *Did Pocahontas Save Captain John Smith?* Athens: University of Georgia Press, 1992.

Morris, Joann Sebastian. "The Socialization of the American Indian Child." *Television and the Socialization of the Minority Child*. Eds. Gordon L. Berry, and Claudia Mitchell-Kernan. New York: Academic Press, 1982. 187–201.

Mossiker, Frances. *Pocahontas: The Life and the Legend*. New York: Alfred A. Knopf, 1976.

Muldoon, Paul. "Barbie, But No Bimbo." *Times Literary Supplement*. 13 Oct. 1995: 20–21.

Shaffer, Denise D. "Making Native American Lessons Meaningful." *Childhood Education* 69.4 (1993): 201–203.

Shohat, Ella. "Gender and Culture of Empire: Toward a Feminist Ethnography of the Cinema." *Quarterly Review of Film & Video* 13 (1991): 45–84.

Stedman, Raymond W. *Shadows of the Indian: Stereotypes in American Culture.* Norman: University of Oklahoma Press, 1982.

Strong, Pauline Turner. "H-Net Movie Review: '*Pocahontas*'" *http://www.cris.com/ ~nlthomas/articles/pokyrevw* htm, 30 June 1995.

"Ten Most Popular Halloween Costumes Sold Nationwide Last Week at Toys R Us." *Time* 6 Nov. 1995: 22.

Whitt, Laurie Ann. "Cultural Imperialism and the Marketing of Native America." *American Indian Culture and Research Journal* 19.3 (1995): 1–31.

Chapter 8

A Guided Tour through One Adolescent Girl's Culture

Angharad N. Valdivia with Rhiannon S. Bettivia

RHIANNON: Mom, do you have anything to read?
ANGHARAD: Well, all I have is this book called *Foucault for Beginners*.
RHIANNON: What's that about?
ANGHARAD: It's about this French thinker who influences a lot of theories about popular culture and some about gender.
RHIANNON: Cool! (Later on she asks) Do you have *Simone de Beauvoir for Beginners*? She sounded so cool in that Foucault book! And could you order me a virgin Piña Colada?

We are on vacation, lounging around the pool of a Howard Johnson's, resting after playing in the water. Rhiannon is getting a tan. Everything about this moment underscores the connections between popular culture, critical theory, feminism, adolescence, parenting, and femininity. I, of course, am having a real piña colada in the shade and reading the entertainment section of a local newspaper, hoping they have a horoscope. I probably should be reading Foucault or something serious like that, but it's too sunny for high theory. As well, I hope that Rhiannon won't become a Foucaultian theorist and abandon her tendency for trenchant materialist critique.

As a parent, a scholar, and a feminist, the whole notion of "the personal is the political" goes without saying. In fact, I must amend this old U.S. feminist slogan to "the intellectual is the personal is the political." Furthermore, there are no special moments when these three areas merge; rather, they are inextricably entwined every second of the day. I am always a mother, and also a professor, and also a feminist scholar. I have to think about gender in a theoretically grounded manner as I attempt to raise my children in a culture that remains largely sexist, racist, and classist. I have to do this knowing that we occupy pockets of privilege while simultaneously intersecting with vectors of oppression. I believe that the knowledge and experiences derived from feminism and from the study of popular culture will help us in this process.

This essay explores the tensions and pleasures in trying to navigate this terrain as my daughter Rhiannon, currently thirteen, grows up. Before continuing, we must both admit two things. First, the dominant voice will be mine, the mother.[1] Second, the bumps are there for both of us. For just as it is difficult to mother in this culture, it is no easier growing up with a feminist mother. Many times after a movie or show Rhiannon will comment, "I know you did not like that for some feminist reason!" Likewise, it was difficult to see Rhiannon go through her Barbie stage until it became obvious that Ken was cleaning up the house so Barbie could finish her dissertation! The same pressures that cause a feminist mom to cringe at much of popular culture cause a daughter to cringe at how this response will set her apart from most other girls and their mothers. As much work as feminists have put into changing our culture, there remains a lot of work to be done so that taking a progressive stand does not automatically generate feelings of otherness.

Based on an admittedly small sample of two, this will be a theoretically grounded conversation between a feminist mother and an adolescent daughter about the place and role of popular culture in our everyday lived experience. Among the popular culture texts to be discussed will be the more traditional mainstream ones of television and Hollywood film as well as the more girl-targeted ones of the American Girls book series, dolls, and other related catalog items (Brady, "Reading"), Barbies, and Playmobile dollhouse sets. Alternative production of poems, books, and newspapers will round out the discussion.

Theoretical Musings

Until quite recently, we paid very little attention to girls' consumption and production of popular culture. Indeed we paid very little attention to girls in general! While within feminist studies there is an increased interest in understanding the role of popular culture in women's lives in a holistic sense, we have a small but growing amount of research on girls aged nine to fifteen. Feminist research on popular culture reveals both that most mainstream texts are highly gendered and that there are possibilities and spaces for oppositional and negotiated readings of these texts—that is, girls can interpret against the grain altogether or finds parts within the text that they will rework to validate their experiences. In addition, the utopian potential of new communications technologies is being borne out by some segments of the female adolescent population—for example, Riot Grrrls and producers of zines.[2] Thus, we can surmise that at least some adolescent girls receive mainstream cultural texts and produce alternative forms of popular culture.

That girls are exposed to a huge amount of popular culture is undeniable. Much of this exposure occurs during "leisure" hours, and the literature on this age group (see Hendry et al., for example) suggests that this is the one luxury "bestowed on adolescents" (2). It is estimated that adolescents spend about eight hours per day with some sort of popular culture as a primary behavior, often as a secondary or tertiary activity (Fine, Mortimer and Roberts, as cited in Williams and Frith). In sum, at this age media and peers replace family and parents as a source of influence and a form of time expenditure.

That leisure-time media, whether it be mainstream or subcultural, underrepresents or stereotypes adolescent girls is now an understood fact (McRobbie, *Feminism and Youth*). However, as Angela McRobbie (*Postmodernism*) notes, we must acknowledge that there have been some representational changes in particular texts, such as *Sassy* magazine, that are partly a result of the participation of women who grew up influenced by the women's movement. Consequently, girls gravitate toward these texts over the more traditional "romance" magazines.

Though girls spend considerable amounts of time with popular culture, we ought not forget that their school time is laced, if not soaked, with interactions and representations that are gendered masculine. Research shows that girls are nearly erased as subjects within the schooling experience, whether it be in terms of how teachers and administrators pay attention to them or in terms of their representation in instructional materials such as textbooks and other classroom aides (Gilbert and Taylor; Mann; Pipher; Roman, Christian-Smith and Ellsworth). Additionally, McRobbie (*Feminism and Youth*) suggests that precisely because girls have less access to freedom than their brothers, their cultural activities are incorporated into the "safe" spaces of the home and school. Considering that nearly all adolescent girls attend school for about seven hours a day, excluding extracurricular activities, this is an area of study that we must not forget. Indeed Jeanne Brady (*Schooling*) provides us with some very useful guidelines to carry out what she calls "a feminist pedagogy for liberatory learning."

Context is all important to understanding the interaction between adolescence, gender, and popular culture (see Nava). To begin with, the research is still rather new. There are all sorts of topics that are just beginning to be studied, and we have similar phenomena occurring in related and intersecting areas of study. Within adolescent studies (see Danesi) we are just beginning to pay attention to girls and to question the nearly biological understanding of this age group—that is, rather than considering social or cultural aspects, to assume that hormones and other physiological factors guide the behavior of adolescents. Within feminist scholarship we are beginning to focus on adolescence, though pioneering scholars such as Carol Gilligan have been urging us to follow this path for quite a while. Finally, within popular culture studies, feminist scholars such as Angela McRobbie and Lana Rakow have made a loud call for the inclusion of women and gender. Within this body of work we have a multiplicity of approaches ranging from the study of content to production and reception of popular culture. If we replace women with adolescent girls in this suggested path of scholarship, we can see that we have huge areas to begin studying. Thus we have the beginning of what promise to become fruitful topics, such as girls and subcultures, schooling and popular culture, production of alternative media, etc.

This flurry of new research is partly influenced by the presence of a generation of feminist scholars schooled in a theoretically expansive body of work. But the influences are not merely academic. Relevant to this particular essay, we have many members of this generation of feminist scholars whose daughters are nearing or passing through adolescence. Remember: The intellectual is the personal is the political. Increasingly, theories of adolescence take on a very personal meaning. Most frightening, these theories seem to predicate an inescapably divisive period between mothers and their adolescent daughters and a dip in self-esteem for the girls during this same period (see Pipher).[3]

In a way this essay represents an effort to work through the battleground that adolescence seems to pose for mothers and their daughters. Drawing on and being inspired by a body of literature that includes coauthored conversations between mothers and daughters (Koffinke and Jordan) and guidelines for alternatives (Brady *School-*

ing), this is an attempt to build a prophylactic bridge for the upcoming divide. In other words, if, as recent feminist scholarship on adolescent girls suggests (for example, Finders), adolescence is an essentializing category that effectively glosses over sociopolitical issues of race, class, and gender, then would not a theoretically grounded approach based on precisely a problematization of these issues lead to a practice that by taking these issues into account, removes some, most, or all of the potential for that inescapable divide and dip?

Much of the support for such a utopian vision comes from the seemingly contradictory findings in the study of girls and popular culture. For example, while much of the research suggests that adolescents generally reduce family interaction in favor of media and peer-group involvement, recent feminist scholarship cautions us to consider the class biases of that finding (Finders). In an ethnographic study of middle- and working-class girls as they crossed the passage from upper elementary to junior high school, Margaret Finders challenges us to revisit our notions of adolescence and the popular media's role in it. In an impassioned plea for an awareness of the heterogeneity of the essentialist category of "adolescence," Finders argues that neither peer and media involvement nor resistance and rebellion are necessarily predominant components of adolescence. Additionally, her work suggests that the inevitable split between mothers and daughters in the adolescent period is not universal. The working-class girls in her study, in fact, remained close to their mothers or got even closer as a result of their entrance into the increasingly alienating experience of junior high school. This finding is supported by a 1995 study (Taylor, Gilligan, and Sullivan) that finds this to be true of working class and African-American girls and their mothers. Finally, Finders erases the divide between school hours and leisure hours, for she demonstrates that they are inextricably entwined. Girls read magazines during English classes and classic books after they go to bed. Any study needs to at least acknowledge both the heterogeneity of the adolescent girl population and the ubiquity of popular culture in their lives.

Topics of Conversation

Admittedly, the area of popular culture is a huge one. Therefore, we had to come up with some limits to our conversation.[4] First, we'll discuss the site of schooling. Second, we will discuss what's available to adolescent girls in their leisure time. Third, we will discuss what appeals to girls. Fourth, we will discuss sites of intervention or areas of production.

Schooling as a Site of Gender and Popular Culture

The first category of conversation involves the daily attendance of school. Though Rhiannon attends her last year of middle school—that is, eighth grade—looming ominously over us is the specter of high school. Thanks largely in part to the review of the literature for this particular article, I face this transition from middle school to high school with great trepidation. This is not assuaged when school personnel confirm my worst fears. Thus the following exchange took place just last night (February 4, 1997) when I had the opportunity to attend the open house at Rhiannon's prospective high school.

I went over to the counselor to find out what the counseling staff's approach was to adolescent girls' issues. The conversation went as follows:

> ME: Hi, I came over to talk to you because I am a little concerned about all of the literature that suggests that because of the classroom and hallway climate (books, teachers, classmates, etc.) girls kind of go underground and underachieve at this age. I was wondering if the counseling staff has materials about this for the girls or if there is some sort of effort to deal with these issues.
>
> SHE: Oh, I've never heard about that research, but I do know the facts.
>
> ME: What are those?
>
> SHE: Well, that in high school girls slow down intellectually and boys excel more at academics . . . of course, girls still do well in English and Social Studies. (I must have looked aghast for she continued) Why don't you talk to the Dean?
>
> ME: Oh, really? What is she in charge of?
>
> SHE: Oh, you know, discipline issues, so she can address your "climate" questions. (she calls the dean over)
>
> ME: I am concerned by some research I've been reading about issues of low-level hallway harassment toward girls which affects their self-esteem and such . . .
>
> DEAN: I am not aware of any such thing here at Central. . . . But of course teenagers will be teenagers!

Double yikes!!! Not only is the first counselor spouting the worst of sexist assumptions regarding girls and education, but the Dean herself is reifying "teenagehood" as a category that serves to accomplish an erasure of the consideration of issues of gender, class, race, and ethnicity that go to the core of understanding the adolescent experience! I am dumbfounded. I want to find an all-girl school run by feminist teachers. I want Jeanne Brady to quit her job, move to Champaign, and open an all-girl school run on the principles she outlines in her book, *Schooling Young Children*. The only saving grace of the entire depressing night was the math teacher's comment, after checking out Rhiannon's feminist T-shirt ("10 years of feminism in ICA") that "four of five of the math teachers are women!" She smiles at Rhiannon.

Meanwhile Rhiannon comments:

I don't know why they keep doing research on girls in schools. (She is reading the Finders book and finds it too simple. Plus girls do not use those labels anymore.) Obviously, girls in school aren't going to tell people everything that goes on in their daily lives, and you can't find out by just observing. Even if you observe and talk to them long enough, you are not going to know more than teachers, and they don't know what it's like to be an adolescent girl. Only the girls would know because most of the girls' lives are secrets. A lot of the things that happen, that you don't want to talk about, that you are thinking, a lot of things are secret. Stuff like being mad at your friends or having crushes, you have to keep it a secret. Because everything is so tightly knitted together and intertwined so that if one person finds out they can tell the entire student body and everyone will find out right away.

When I am absent from school, I don't worry about missing math because it's easy. It's like $y = mx + b$. I worry about missing gossip because it's much more complicated, and you don't get a formula for that!

I don't notice the teachers treating the girls any differently than the boys, although they do separate us by gender at lunch and stuff. It's easier to control the different groups of people that way.

Some people tell a couple of the teachers about their lives. Ms. Trumbull is really involved with the "g-funks,"[5] we call them the "g's." She really is a "g-funk." The "grungies"[6] are entirely separate and don't really talk to the teachers. I guess there is no "grungie" teacher. Grungies are more into computers: they know everything about computers. But they don't like Macs, they like IBMs. They listen to Nine Inch Nails, and the girl grungies listen to No Doubt. Everybody listens to Smashing Pumpkins. What's even more popular now is Ozzy Osborne.

Clearly my concerns differ wildly from Rhiannon's. Miraculously, she doesn't seem to have noticed the gendered aspects of her education yet. Maybe she is outspoken enough that she gets equal time.

Maybe she's bored enough that she checks out. I'll have to go observe her classroom, though that makes her uneasy. She tells me all of her teachers are scared of me! I still remember Mr. Rogers in fourth grade. He'd sweat so profusely when I talked to him that he'd literally soak his shirt by the time I left. My concerns then centered on inclusion of multicultural aspects into U.S. history. He answered my questions with, "I really don't touch on that but Rhiannon always brings it up."

She also prioritizes the social. She is keenly aware of subcultures within the school setting, being very careful not to be considered a member of any one group. She doesn't articulate the racialized character of the subgroups she mentions. G-funks are mostly African-American. Consequently, she has a tendency to hang out with the mostly white "grungies," even though she lives in a Mac house. I noticed we end up listening to Alanis Morrisette, No Doubt, and Sheryl Crow a lot lately—that is, when she is not on the phone catching up on all the gossip. Schoolwork takes but a minimal amount of time; gossip goes on forever.

What's Available to Adolescent Girls

From the perspective of a feminist mother, both too much and too little is available for adolescent girls. There are so many magazines, books, TV shows, movies, and CDs targeted at this age group—*Teen*, *Sassy*, *Romeo and Juliet* (the movie), *My So-Called Life*, etc. Some of the stuff looks promising, but much more of it looks very traditional in terms of gender roles, the ideal of beauty, consumerism, and all that. Besides, it seems like the really good stuff doesn't last long, as in the case with *My So-Called Life*.

Critics didn't like that. All the girls liked it. They would have watched it. Everyone likes Claire Danes.

It also appears that a considerable portion of popular culture consumption is coincidental: It's just there so why not pay attention to it? Though the viewing or reading of certain texts is usually done in an openly ironic way (*I don't know why I am watching this but it's on TV*, or *I don't like teen magazines, they're just kind of funny*), they still form part of the daily diet. These texts are so ubiquitous that they cannot be avoided. This includes random TV watching of shows on the Cartoon Network.

Hardly! Adolescent people don't watch the Cartoon Network.

How about *Scooby Doo*? You watch that all the time!

Well, I am a rare child! I really don't like to watch TV all the time. Singled Out *and* Saturday Night Live *are pretty funny. Some-*

times there are some nifty guests on David Letterman. *Some of the really, really preppy people are dedicated to* Friends. *They wear the* Friends *sweatshirts; they watch the show; they buy the* Friends *notebooks. Some of my "grungie" friends watch* The Simpsons.

Likewise, attempting restriction of certain forms usually serves to increase their allure. I still remember that whenever Aunica, a friend of Rhiannon's, came over she'd head straight to Rhiannon's Barbie collection since her parents forbid her to have one. That was seven years ago. I feel similarly about the overabundance of advertising images, for I know that I am affected by them despite my best efforts, yet I can do little to curtail Rhiannon's exposure.

I think they over advertise Barbies. I hope they get at least some of their money back. I think too much money is spent on advertising. They should spend it on other things. I think when they try to target people my age, they don't know how to do it so we end up thinking the commercials are stale.

Girls' magazines appear to have a mixture of very traditional content as well as articles that would have not appeared when I was growing up: about sex, pregnancy, AIDS . . .

Just write STDs (sexually transmitted diseases). They never write about AIDS in those magazines. Sometimes HIV but most of the time STDs. Because there are so many STDs they talk a lot about them generally but not about any of them specifically. Can I go take that nap now?

Movies are still quite popular. Except they need help getting there. Romance movies such as *Romeo and Juliet* and *In Love and War* as well as comedies such as *Beavis and Butthead* appeal. What about other stuff like books, video games, etc.?

"Grungies" are really computer freaks, so I guess they play computer games. I know some of the preppy people play Sony Playstation and stuff. John likes to read Steven King books, and Elaine is a witch so she reads Anne McCaffrey books about dragons and others about magic spells. My girlfriends and I like to read really old books like Gone with the Wind *and* Pride and Prejudice. *The girl "g's" like to read romance novels.*

There is so much available to this age group and these girls. They take the abundance for granted. (*Absolutely everybody but me has a stereo and TV system in their bedroom!*) Yet they are sometimes very astute and cynical consumers of popular culture, something which has been documented by scholars of adolescent girls (Nava and Nava). Yet they find the allure of the available too powerful to resist. It's there so they watch it or read it, but they don't like it, or may not even want to be associated with it. Additionally, at least in their little group, there is a wide variety of interests despite their outwardly homogenous appearances, sartorial and otherwise. They are all aware of each other's predilections and respect them at face value. Elaine the witch is not made fun of for being a witch. She just is.

What Appeals to Girls

There is a difference between what's available and what appeals to girls. Admittedly, here is where this conversation gets very particular, for we cannot generalize from a sample of one even if it includes comments about a more extended social setting. However, this section should provide some ideas as to why certain popular culture forms will succeed where others fail.

I liked reading the Foucault book and Uncle Tom's Cabin, *Jane Austen and the Bronte sisters. The critical theory stuff is really interesting, but I like the beginner's books because the other stuff is too hard to read. I like to listen to Alanis Morrisette, No Doubt, Sheryl Crow, and some of Jewel's stuff is pretty cool, but not all of it. I guess the* Seventeen *magazine is pretty funny. Also,* People *magazine is pretty funny: I love that! I love the witchcraft stuff.* Romeo and Juliet *was pretty cool.* Clueless *was kind of dumb. I think it was a money maker—whoever made it was pretty smart.*

In terms of what I like to do, I like to talk with my friends on the phone. I like to do things with my friends like go to the mall. Otherwise, I think the mall is stupid. I am not a shop-aholic or anything. I am a choc-aholic though.

Sometimes I like to sit alone in my room where it's very quite so I can sort out my thoughts. That, of course, has nothing to do with popular culture.

I like to make things, and model them, and make them look pretty. I wanted a dollhouse and the porcelain dolls not so I could play with them like most girls do. I like to make those picturesque Better Homes and Gardens *scenes. You know, like the ones with the girls' bedrooms where they have the canopy and the pink light— where the girl's room is set in perfect fashion like nobody's room would ever be. I like to make my room to look like that but it's so hard not to mess it up then.*

Rhiannon's interests are all over the spectrum. The CD collection spans from Gloria Estefan through George Winston and Boyz II Men, from Elton John to Sheryl Crow. Books are everywhere! In the bathroom, my room, the living room, the kitchen: tons of them at different stages of being read. American Girl catalogs crowd every magazine rack. An American Girl doll is prominently displayed, as are some of her pricey accessories. The doll collection has grown larger with each trip and special occasion. What becomes patently clear is that everybody loves to buy a little girl a doll. Even people who would not spend $50 on a CD-ROM of the Louvre (one recent request), spend $75 on a bride porcelain doll. So the doll collection grows inexorably, demanding more space and attention. The one common theme here is growth and spread, as all of these items take over the entire household and envelop all of us in an aura of female adolescent culture that we cannot escape. Now we all walk around singing "Jagged Little Pill!" wondering when we will get to use the phone next and hoping Rhiannon is answering the call-waiting beeps.

Sites of Intervention

In the above three sections, most of the focus was on preproduced forms of popular culture, although with a bit of rearrangement. This section involves the creations of girls this age, the spaces for intervention and circulation of popular culture. The resources available to many of the girls in Rhiannon's peer group far exceed those of many others, especially in terms of access to potential media production centers. For example, many of them have computers in their homes. (Rhiannon repeats: *Actually, most of my friends have computers, and TVs, and CD players in their rooms.*) Some have access to computer and media expertise to enhance their creative possibilities. At age nine Rhiannon and her friend Aunica produced and distributed a community newspaper from a desktop computer. Though the veracity of some of the stories was questionable (*Half a million people die daily in car accidents in State College, PA*), the effort was nonetheless admirable. They had produced and distributed a newspaper on their own.

I always encourage students in my classes to create, for few have had access to such resources as they do. In fact, I bought the home computer, with tons of software, in hopes that the children would create stories, books, whatever. More often than not the computer is used either as a word processor, to turn in polished reports, or as a video game site, to play games such as *War Craft II: Tides of Darkness*.

That's not true. You've never looked inside my folder. I have a whole folder full of just story documents that I just did one day.

And instead of playing games, most of the time before I play them, I create my own level. And a lot of the time I just dig around on the hard drive. We have a neat Blockbuster thing where you can find out about thousands of movies. It has like a trivia game about old movies. It asks you stuff like "What was the name of the fourth Rocky movie?" or something like that.

I wrote a bunch of poems but Tobin [her brother] said the memory was getting used up so he made me delete a bunch of them. I am also writing a book about Vietnam with Aunica. I invited her for three weeks in the summer. We plan to spend like two weeks doing research at your [university] library. Then we'll write for two weeks, too. So hopefully we'll get a good start because we've been having problems coordinating long distance. Coordination has been a big problem. We've been writing things, but there's always things we need to cover.

Music is very important to me. I play the clarinet. I would like to play the guitar, the flute and piccolo, the saxophone (baritone, tenor, and soprano) and the piano. But I really won't go into that, because it will just make me upset, and depression really isn't good for my figure. GO FIGURE! A WAIST IS A TERRIBLE THING TO MIND—but I have been hooked by my peers.

There is a ton of creative stuff going on with these girls: They draw, sing, play instruments, write books, create and end major social crises. They are active and self-confident. They are about to enter high school, and we'll see what they are like next year. However, as of today they don't flinch at the prospect of creating their own popular culture and circulating it among peers or keeping it to themselves, for their own pleasure.

Conclusion

To recap the beginning, this essay is a tour of one teenager's life. It is partial, in that life is richer than can be conveyed in one essay, yet representative of this particular adolescent's activities. Since growing up with feminist mothers must be a new and growing area of research, we propose this as one possible intervention in the study of adolescents, popular culture, and feminism. To be sure, growing up surrounded by progressive feminists must have had some impact on the type of activities, reactive and productive, with which Rhiannon is involved. Up to this point the pleasures have far outweighed the tensions of living together. I realize this is partly due to my ability to allow Rhiannon her space and activities, an ability based on knowledge but very much also on material resources, resources that Rhiannon and her friends quite often take for granted. As with my students, I quite often feel like the one who is benefitting from the experience—I learn and this informs my scholarship as well as any future action.

However, we are also at the cusp of a process that has been harrowingly well documented. We are about to enter that dreaded space and time of co-ed high school. If the literature is at all correct, I can expect Rhiannon to recede in her self-assertiveness and self-confidence, and possibly begin getting lower grades. I am much more preoccupied with these findings than Rhiannon is. Nevertheless, I hang onto that utopian component of feminism—the part that reminds me that I am in it to make life better for the next generation. Maybe Rhiannon will navigate the passage more or less calmly. If not, maybe she will emerge strong and ready to continue. Still, as I talked about these issues with a colleague the other day, she wondered what we and the next generation of girls would be like, if we/they didn't have to face a schooling experience that, supported and abetted by much of the available popular culture, silenced, ignored, or muffled our/their experiences, insights, and input. Thus part of our focus as feminist scholars and parents should be at least to facilitate our daughters' passage into young adulthood.

Notes

1. This is a decision made for strategic rather than for egalitarian reasons. Namely, I want to, and have to, get this done, whereas for Rhiannon, this is yet one more demand on her busy after-school schedule.

2. I use the term zine to refer to the homemade and girl-circulated material. Margaret Finders uses this term to refer to magazines.

3. We must also mention that feminist scholars raising sons also grapple with the nearly inevitable masculinization of their offspring (Brady, *Schooling*; Mann).

4. These are semirandom in that after taping conversations, we drew out these four categories as the most salient.

5. A "g-funk" is like a rapper. Basically, it's the black kids who listen to stuff like R&B and rap and dress in jerseys, big jeans, and sport shoes.

6. "Grungies" dress in torn jeans, band shirts, flannels, and torn-up, mismatching shoes.

Works Cited

Brady, Jeanne. "Reading the American Dream: The History of the American Girl Collection." *Teaching and Learning Literature* 4 (1994): 2–6.

———. *Schooling Young Children: A Feminist Pedagogy for Liberatory Learning*. Albany: State University of New York Press, 1995.

Danesi, Marcel. *Cool: The Signs and Meanings of Adolescence*. Toronto: University of Toronto Press, 1994.

Finders, Margaret J. *Just Girls: Hidden Literacies and Life in Junior High*. New York: Teacher's College Press, 1997.

Gilbert, Pam, and Sandra Taylor. *Fashioning the Feminine*. Sydney, Australia: Allen and Unwin, 1991.

Hendry, Leo B., Janet Shucksmith, John Scott Love, and Anthony Grlendinning (Eds.). *Young People's Leisure and Lifestyles*. New York: Routledge, 1993.

Koffinke, Carol, and J. Jordan. *"Mom, You Don't Understand!" A Daughter and Mother Share Their Views*. Minneapolis: Deaconess Press, 1993.

Mann, Judy. *The Difference: Growing Up Female in America*. New York: Wagner Books, 1994.

McRobbie, Angela. *Feminism and Youth Culture: From Jackie to Just Seventeen*. Cambridge, MA: Unwin Hyman, 1991.

———. *Postmodernism and Popular Culture*. New York: Routledge, 1994.

Nava, Mica. *Changing Cultures: Feminism, Youth, and Consumerism*. London: Sage Publications, 1992.

———. and Orson Nava. "Discriminating or Duped? Young People as Consumers of Advertising/Art." *Changing Cultures: Feminism, Youth, and Consumerism*. Ed. Mica Nava. Newbury Park, CA: Sage Publications, 1992. 171–182.

Pipher, Mary. *Reviving Ophelia: Saving the Selves of Adolescent Girls*. New York: Ballantine Books, 1994.

Rakow, Lana. *Women Making Meaning: New Feminist Directions in Communication*. New York: Routledge, 1992.

Roman, Leslie G., Linda K. Christian-Smith, and Elizabeth Ellsworth (Eds.). *Becoming Feminine: The Politics of Popular Culture*. New York: Falmer Press, 1988.

Taylor, Jill McLean, Carol Gilligan, and Amy M. Sullivan. *Between Voice and Silence: Women and Girls, Race and Relationship*. Cambridge: Harvard University Press, 1995.

Williams, Jerome, and Katherine T. Frith. "Introduction: Adolescents and the Media." *Early Adolescence: Perspectives on Research, Policy, and Intervention.* Ed. R.M. Lerner. Hillsdale, NJ: Lawrence Erlbaum, 1994, 401–406.

Chapter 9

Girls Make Music: Polyphony and Identity in Teenage Rock Bands

Carol Jennings

> Sometimes when we play, since we're girls, people just notice that and they're like, "Oh, you're good, we didn't expect you to be good because you're girls."
> —Tina, eighteen-year-old bass player for We're No Dentists

Tina's observation echoes the concerns of many girls I've interviewed who consider themselves serious musicians, who play in bands and perform publicly. In the face of a growing body of research that documents the crisis in self-esteem and consequent loss of voice experienced by adolescent girls, the teenage girl who picks up an instrument and "plays loud and fast" is obviously an exception. Musical virtuosity doesn't necessarily immunize a girl from self-doubt and other plagues of adolescent development, but she is demonstrating, in the words of Andrea Juno, that girls can be "bold, brash and loud, all the things they were taught not to be" (4). Meanwhile, in the history of rock production, women's roles have tended to be limited to those of fan, consumer, singer, or songwriter, while female instrumentalists are rare (Gottlieb and Wald 256).

In her essay "Women and the Electric Guitar," Mavis Bayton describes many reasons why girls are discouraged from playing the electric guitar, the quintessential "masculine" instrument of rock. She identifies low expectations as the most pervasive: "The status 'woman' seems to obscure that of 'musician.' Female guitarists are expected to be sexy and incompetent and these expectations form a hurdle which must be coped with or combated in some way" (47). Furthermore, as Joanne Gottlieb and Gayle Wald recognize, "something potentially radical happens when women appropriate this instrument, with all its ingrained connotations" (258). What set of circumstances, internal and external, afford these women the license to defy gender codes?

This question provides a starting point for exploring the experiences of young women who have ventured into risky terrain and found pleasure and self-assurance there. As these young women articulate their struggles, conflicts, and ambitions, they offer strategies for navigating the common obstacles a woman is likely to confront if she aspires to be a rock musician. More generally, their experiences inform our growing understanding of the ways girls (and women) resist social and cultural pressures to be silent. By listening to the girls' music and their words about themselves, we can more accurately discern the problems as well as the solutions they propose.[1]

The girls included in this essay spoke on-camera for a video documentary about young women who play in rock bands, and how music-making influences their social and cultural development.[2] Tina and Nicky (seventeen years old) have been playing for two years in the band We're No Dentists, which they formed with two friends. To videotape the interview, we meet at their father's home in a middle-class neighborhood on the outskirts of Ithaca in upstate New York. We gather in the basement, where the girls rehearse in a space equipped with a drum set, guitar stands, a keyboard, speakers, and amps. The ambient light has been enhanced by the video crew, which consists of a sound recordist, a videographer, and producer/director (all women). Tina has already explained that the two other members of their band, the lead singer and drummer, are away for their first year at college, and aren't available to play with the band until school break. Nonetheless, Nicky and Tina are willing to play simplified versions of their songs for the documentary. Nicky plays lead guitar and sings, Tina plays bass and sings back-up. Both songs they play are about surviving an emotional crisis and feeling good despite one's troubles. The first is a classic rock-and-roll ballad, which describes a disturbing emotional state of haunting dreams, imprisoning thoughts, isolation, and alienation. As with We're No Dentists' other songs, however, a negative and negating state of mind is resisted through the repetition of a reassuring and affirming phrase in the chorus. This strategy of resistance illustrates the renewing and regenerative possibilities of polyphony, in which consciousness escapes closure by continually inviting internally persuasive voices to the fore.

The second song the girls play is a funk tune, difficult to perform without a drummer, and in fact the girls pause midway through the song to explain the problem. Rather than give up, however, they quickly improvise a solution with maracas, which Nicky doesn't know how to handle, much to the amusement of her sister. Tina shows her how to shake the maracas to produce a variety of sounds and rhythms. After a few minutes, Nicky catches on and they start the song over.

> Feel the funk, hear the funk,
> Feel the funk, get the funk.
> Get the funk, hear the funk.
>
> Stop in your tracks and just sit back and feel the funk,
> So close your eyes and be surprised and feel the funk.
>
> We're not going to sit around all night and get the funk,
> No matter what we do is right, so get the funk.
>
> If you want to feel the funk, you better stop acting like a punk,
> If you want to get off that floor, you better get that big butt out the door.
>
> If you want to feel the funk, better stop acting like a chump,
> If you want to get off that floor, you better get that big butt out the door.
>
> Feel the funk, hear the funk,
> Feel the funk, get the funk.

In this song, the girls juxtapose two meanings of "funk": as both a mood that enervates and a groove that inspires (creative) action. The ambiguity echoes the connotations of the blues as a mood, a style, and a way of meeting hardship with grace. The song celebrates the moment of ambivalence, a state of joyful relativity in which one state of mind can cross over into another.

After they've played these two songs a few times through, the girls lead our crew upstairs and outside to the deck in the back of their house. I explain the documentary is about teenage girls who play rock music, and I hope that by sharing their stories Nicky and Tina might inspire other young women to find strategies for managing the difficulties of adolescence in general and creative expression in particular. Tina immediately identifies low expectations and false expectations as her most troubling obstacle. Being a musician is central to her identity as a young woman; she plans to study music in college, and she's proud of her accomplishments as both a classical and rock musician. People who challenge this identity with expectations of incompetence confuse and confound her. Over the course of our interview, she repeats this central concern about being taken seriously a number of times in a variety of voices. Her initial comments are directly addressed to other young women who share her aspirations:

> TINA: When someone says, "You're good for girls," don't be discouraged by that . . . even though you're female and it's mostly a male thing. More and more women musicians are coming out in the music scene.
>
> Now that I'm going [to college] there are no female bands left in the high school. . . . But I know that from us playing, we've encouraged a lot of girls to play. And they've realized, you know, it's not just a guy thing, and that anybody can do it if you work at it. . . . And you can be better than most guys, which we've found out. (*Laughs*)
>
> You know, it's just like anything else. It seems like it's harder to get started. Because I know when I started . . . it was . . . all guys playing all the time and I didn't know if they'd take us seriously. And they, I don't know if they did at first, but definitely by the end, you know, they even felt us as a threat.
>
> At first, we were the chick band. (*Laughs*) But after a while people didn't think of that part anymore, which is nice. It was nice to just be able to play.

Tina's use of first-, second-, and third-person voices that interplay, interrupt, and contradict each other allows for a vital exchange that combats closure and confounds finalization. Of special significance are the moments when Nicky or Tina speaks in the voice of an "other" (Brown and Gilligan 238). For both sisters, Tina especially, this "other" voice pronounces an authoritative, moralistic, and limited viewpoint that contradicts her sense of self: for example, "You're good for girls," and "Oh, well, we'll give them a little more credit, they're girls." Rather than internalizing this "other" voice, or ignoring it completely, however, Tina absorbs it. By perceiving it, she can exceed it; by speaking its mocking comments out loud, she returns it to the context of her own words about herself. Speaking in the "other" voice, Tina appropriates a conflicting point of view and acts out the struggle to keep her own voice.

Having defied expectations of musical incompetence, Tina describes a second and equally disparaging response by many audience members: People who hear the girls play—and play well—but don't really listen:

> TINA: I think as a discouragement for us being girls, like, the only thing that sometimes annoys us is that we'll play, we'd play a show and we'd be

really funky and whatever and people will just compare us to the only
female band they knew.

NICKY: Like the Go-Go's.

TINA: Even if we sounded absolutely nothing like. . . . "Oh, they're the next
        Go-Go's."

NICKY: Luscious Jackson.

TINA: Yeah, we were totally typecast right away, you know. People would
        just see a picture of us, a poster or something and they'd be like,
        "Oh, they're going to be one of those alternative chick bands." That
        never really went away.

Audience members try to categorize the girls' music by comparing it
with "the only female band they knew." (Tina uses the past tense,
suggesting an awareness that the categories themselves are dated.) By
labeling We're No Dentists as "the next Go-Go's," or lumping the
band with musicians as wildly divergent as Luscious Jackson and
Courtney Love, the speaker reveals a point of view that is blind to
obvious differences in style and is instead focusing narrowly on gender—perhaps the only common trait these performers share. Blunt
categorization such as this is a strategy of containment, prevalent in
media discourse about women and rock, intended to neutralize the
threat posed by women who transgress gender boundaries (Coates
53). Identifying We're No Dentists with Courtney Love or Luscious
Jackson, Veruca Salt or the Go-Go's is just as limiting for Tina as the
more generic categories of "alternative band," "riot grrrl," or "girl
group." Her resistance to these labels and comparisons parallels the
reaction of more established punk bands like L-7, in which members
reject such gender-based pigeonholing (Gottlieb and Wald 254).[3]

How do Tina and Nicky describe and oppose this force of containment? According to Tina, on the one hand people will expect from
their band "no talent, don't-know-how-to-play, shrilly-voiced, scream-
ing kind of music" or, on the other hand, women who sing "really
soft" and are "popular." Tina and Nicky show a healthy resistance to
both ends of the spectrum. Nicky insists, "It's hard to even label what
we play." Tina relates, "When I walk downtown with my bass, I don't
want people to be like, 'Oh, there's Riot Grrrl, blah, blah.' Sometimes
that happens. . . . We just want to be thought of, you know, as musicians." They are demanding that the band's music simply be heard.

Probing further to articulate the complexity of their feelings, Tina
and Nicky both acknowledge that their response to expectations is
actually ambivalent. Labels such as "chick band" and the musical styles
they connote are frustrating and confining, the girls admit. But these

same expectations can also be perceived as a challenge, and the act of defying them can be thrilling:

NICKY: At the same time, there are advantages because when we would go up there and people would expect us to be an alternative chick band and we'd play all these funk songs and then we can impress them, so in that sense it was a little more fun.

TINA: Yeah, so in some ways, we took advantage of that. Proved them wrong.

As Nicky says, defiance can be fun. Showing up with talent and determination is a satisfying way to overwhelm and drown out the opposition, the mocking voice of the "other." As two white teenage girls playing funk, they defy racial as well as gender boundaries.

Nicky elaborates on the challenging nature of the mocking voice, the limiting voice, by acting out an exchange. After hearing repeatedly that her band sounds just like the Go-Go's, Nicky says she "started saying, 'I hate the Go-Go's'." Then she clarifies, saying that her rejoinder actually depends on her relationship to the speaker. If the person is someone she knows, she says boldly, "That's stupid." If she doesn't know the person, however, then she is careful not to alienate a potential fan, and instead acts grateful in a "nice-girl" voice. Nicky's rendering of these distinctions is evidence of the ambivalence Carol Gilligan finds in many girls' struggle for true and authentic relationships: "The sounds of one's voice change in resonance depending on the relational acoustics: whether one is heard or not heard, how one is responded to (by oneself and other people)" (Brown and Gilligan 6).

Nicky's performance of the "nice girl" voice, the conciliatory and self-effacing response to false compliments, segues into her account of We're No Dentists' first failed attempt to compete in their high school's annual battle of the bands:

NICKY: The first battle of the bands we tried out [for] the judges were like college students who happened to get along really well with some girl high school students, and the girls just kind of persuaded their decision toward the senior bands. And that was a little discouraging because the guys, the judges, came up to us afterward and were like, "You guys were great, da, da, da." But then it's like, we didn't get in. And we're like, hmm.

Nicky resists the fake flattery of the judge and focuses on her goal: to be accepted. She's disappointed not simply by the rejection but by the idea that they might have been "good enough" had they only been judged on their talent as musicians. Grown women, of course, are all too familiar with this kind of treatment, but a girl's first encounter with the double standard is, as Nicky says, discouraging. When Tina hears her sister tell this story, she immediately interjects a more upbeat comment, "Yeah, but for the most part, as far as like being a female playing, it was mostly encouraged, you know, because people thought it was so cool to see us play." And Nicky admits, "Yeah, a lot of people were like, 'Go girl!'"

The high school battle of the bands is a potent experience for many young women who begin playing in their teenage years. Often it's the first time girls—and boys—have an opportunity to play in public. For the participants, talent is a marginal component in an event that celebrates personal expression. In contrast with a school environment characterized by rigid social, academic, and institutional hierarchies, the battle of the bands permits transgression and invites excess to take center stage.

In some ways, by temporarily suspending the authority of teachers and administrators, as well as the order of various social cliques, the battle of the bands represents a carnivalized atmosphere of license, reversal, and renewal.[4] Other scholars have viewed music events through the lens of carnival and affirmed the potential for social and political enlightenment in the parodic and deviant gestures found there (for example, Nehring 177). In other ways, however, the battle of the bands represents an extension of the prevailing masculinist tendencies in music production and performance. The event is permissive and inclusive, but only to a point, like all of the music industry. Even in this atmosphere of license and permissiveness, girls are prevented, by internal or external obstacles, from taking the stage. As Tina recognizes, by not participating in the game of flattery and flirtation to win acceptance, her band is marginalized.

The following year, perhaps as a consequence of their assertiveness, or simply because the band had "improved," We're No Dentists not only competed but won. They were the first women to be included in the competition. Nicky and Tina attribute their overall success in booking gigs to their perseverance and growing confidence as musicians, as well as to their strategies for overcoming gender-specific hurdles as women.

Other young women musicians identify additional internal and external obstacles, as well as tactics for thwarting them. Carly, twenty-three, started playing guitar when she was sixteen, shortly after her father died. She had yearned to play since junior high school, but felt discouraged by fear of exposure and humiliation in the face of her peers.

CARLY: The battle of the bands is a big high school phenomenon. You go to the battle of the bands, and there would just be a bunch of boys getting up there and making a lot of noise, and it was just great fun, and all their friends would be there, and it would be cool, no matter what, no matter how awful it sounded, it didn't matter.

But if you get a group of girls up there, okay, or even just one girl in one band, it's either, "Oh, gosh, they're awful," or everyone's watching, no one's just hanging out, no one's just enjoying whatever's going on, hanging out with their friends, everyone's just gonna stare directly at them and . . . instant criticism, "Oh, they're awful, I can't believe they're doing this, dah, dah, dah, she should shut up, her voice is terrible."

It's an awful, awful, awful thing. And if you're in the audience, and you hear this happening to other women, there's just, there's no way, there's no way you're gonna get up there, and try and do that. And never go through that pretty important stage, I think, of being in a band, of getting up there when you're awful. Everyone does it. Except you're just not, you're not as willing to do it, because you know exactly what's coming to you the second you get up there. And that's, I mean, for everything. Not just music.

Carly describes an atmosphere that's inclusive, tolerant, even encouraging, until a woman arrives on stage. Then the atmosphere shifts and becomes overtly hostile. She depicts a cycle of self-censorship that she engages in to protect herself from anticipated verbal assaults triggered by the battle of the bands experience and others like it. The hostility she so vividly illustrates in her story extends to the general atmosphere she experiences in high school. She contrasts how she feels and acts at home with her sense of alienation and self-silencing in school:

CARLY: I don't know, I can't speak for everyone, I just know that when I was growing up, my . . . I was, I guess. . . . It probably goes back to when you're very, very little, when you're growing up, and maybe you have brothers, and maybe you don't, but I grew up with very cool parents and a couple sisters and, but I still, um . . .

It's school. No matter how great your family is, you go to school and it's the boys who raise their hands, it's the boys who talk in class,

it's the boys who oggle at you if you're wrong, it's . . . you either
totally go inward, or you just deal, and you don't care. I went completely inward. I couldn't, I wouldn't talk in class. I wouldn't, you
know. I couldn't. I never. . . . I didn't want to be open to that.

I was very quiet, I just didn't . . . I mean, not when I was alone, not
when I was with my sisters, not when I was at home. [At home] I
was just, you know, crazy. But if I got into a situation at school
where I felt like it was going to be too much for me, I would just lie,
not want to deal.

But it's the same thing when you get older. It's so much easier to
stay on the sidelines. It's so much easier to stay in the corner and
clap when your friends are doing their thing, but . . .

Carly's false starts and ellipses represent a struggle to position herself in the story, to find a way to speak about what she knows. Her use
of the second-person, "You either totally go inward, or you just deal,
and you don't care," acknowledges that her view is personal and sub-
jective, not in any sense the final word. She doesn't want to misrepre-
sent the situation, but she knows what she has experienced and searches
for a way to express that. When she says, "I couldn't, I wouldn't talk in
class. I wouldn't . . . I couldn't . . . I never . . ." she's both discussing
and enacting the process of self-censorship. She simultaneously dis-
tances herself from the experience and relives it. Carly's struggle to
explain the disassociation she feels between her identity at home and
her identity in school exemplifies a conflict young girls and women
experience throughout their development: the struggle to stay in connection with oneself and others in a relationship (Brown and Gilligan
4). Carly understands that by "going inward," by neutralizing the external hostility and silencing herself, she is sentencing herself to the
sidelines in both the classroom and the music scene.

Even though "all her [guy] friends" were in bands, and she thought
this was the "coolest thing," and "too much fun," she wouldn't begin
to play an instrument. She didn't know any girls who played in bands,
so "it just wasn't an option." The boys she befriended, however, "would
just all randomly pick up instruments and say, 'let's form this band!'"
She liked the music, she enjoyed the scene, she identified with the
musicians, so Carly became, she says, "their number one fan." "It
didn't occur to me," she says, to play an instrument, "I was always on
the sidelines. I was always involved, I was always putting on the shows,
I was always helping the bands." But not playing. All that changed one
day when she went to New York and saw Kim Gordon in Sonic Youth.

CARLY: When you saw a band full of boys . . . maybe you liked their music
          and you'd have a great time, and you'd be with your friends, but it
          wasn't the same as when you went to the show and there was a
          woman up there. It wasn't the same at all.

          When there was a woman, it was very exciting. . . . You took it
          very personally. . . . When you have so few people in your circle
          doing that and you go to a show and see all these other people
          [boys] doing what you want to be doing, but no one's really giving
          you the personal inspiration to be doing it. . . . Then when you go
          to a show and there's a woman, forget it, you're excited. . . . You
          know deep inside that you can do it. . . . It just kind of drives it
          home when you see other women do it.

Kim Gordon has probably inspired many girls to learn the bass guitar,
and Carly was one. For a girl who aspires to play rock, a female role
model helps silence the critical voices that insist a woman can't or
shouldn't do it. By contradicting a status quo that marginalizes and
excludes women, she opens up a whole realm of possibilities. The
other factor that influenced Carly's choice of the bass guitar was that
"fewer strings [made it] less intimidating." Mavis Bayton describes the
technology of the guitar—the speakers, amps, electronic components—
as deterring to many young women who lack confidence in this "masculine" realm (42). By helping her male friends set up for gigs, Carly
had gained confidence in this area, so when she started playing, she
found the technical demands less disconcerting.

In addition to seeing and identifying with other women musicians,
Carly emphasizes the importance of "zines"[5] for similar reasons:

CARLY: Zines women write are important because then women read, and
          then they do it. It's the same thing as when you see a woman play-
          ing. You know you can do it, so you do it. When you're listening,
          when you're reading articles written by women in either women-
          run zines or any zines, it's so much more inspirational because the
          articles are always personal anecdotes, personal stories about what
          it means to be a woman. Or even if you read an article written by a
          man that's about women, what's going on with women, why we're
          being such jerks, da, da, da.

          It's so important, when you're thirteen years old, and you're a girl
          and you're in high school or junior high . . . you're sitting there not
          necessarily doing anything, everyone's probably doing something
          cool around you, but you feel like, I felt like I wasn't going to do
          anything. Then you start reading these things and it becomes so
          much more important to you.

> When I wanted to play, and I wasn't doing it, and I was reading
> articles written by people who do, or who aspire to, or people who
> support women in music, I felt like I was going to be a traitor if I
> didn't do it. . . . [A traitor] to the other women, to myself, to every
> one. I mean, what am I doing here? I want to do something and I'm
> not. What is that, you know?

Zines in general, and girl zines in particular, offer community and
connectedness, a forum for rehearsing and disseminating oppositions
to the dominant culture. By privileging girls' personal testimony, they
amplify the voices marginalized in a male-oriented society (Duncombe
67–68).

Another setback Carly encountered as a novice bass player in high
school was finding other musicians, male or female, to play with in a
band. Her male friends "all had their bands already from eighth, ninth,
tenth grade. No one needed a bass player." And the other boys she
knew, "They wouldn't play with me. I still wasn't part of that club."
No other girls wanted to play, so it wasn't until college that Carly
"started actual bands and started being comfortable with it." She recognizes her late start is a handicap, because "the only way to get
better is to be in a band. The only way to get better is to play shows.
The only way to get some sort of stage presence is to do it, and you're
just not given the chance." The lack of opportunities, then, extends
well beyond public performance to the sphere of everyday practice.
To develop as a rock musician, it's extremely important to sit in on
informal jam sessions that include demonstrations and discussions about
technique and styles. But women rarely get this opportunity. Bands
consisting of male players often resist the inclusion of women instrumentalists, especially as novices, and even tend to be possessive of
tips, technical information, or other insider knowledge that will speed
a new player's progress (Bayton 40).

For Carly, zines and role models magnified her sense of disassociation from the muted part of her "authentic" self. She felt increasingly
distanced from the "true" part of herself that wanted to be a musician,
and knew this was possible. Fear of not being good enough, and consequent criticism, prevented her from acting on her desire. She describes an internal battle between two halves of a divided self which
had been escalating since she was thirteen, and peaked when her
father died three years later:

> CARLY: I obviously went crazy, and I just didn't know what I was doing or
> what was going on, so when I started playing, I started because I

saw zines, because I saw girls in bands, but also because I needed something to do, I needed to distract myself. I needed to feel like I had a handle on something, I needed to do something that I could control.

There [were] two completely different sides of what was going on with me. I was totally, totally insecure, totally sensitive to everything, to little things, I was basically completely socially inept, you know. I mean maybe not, maybe this is just in retrospect. (*Laughs*) But that's how I felt, that's the way I was. And then my whole world was turned into chaos and I was just like, aughhh, I had to get some of it out. I had to do something, and that's what I did.

The outcome of this battle between her strong desire to play, a voice felt and spoken internally for two years, and the critical "other" voices that kept her silent, was finally resolved by her decision to pick up an instrument and play:

CARLY: At that point I just said, forget it, I'm just going to do this and I don't care and I'm going to do my best, and that's the best I can do, you know. What am I going to do? I have to do something or I'm going to go crazy. So that was my thing that I decided to do. And now, definitely, once you're brave at the first thing it's easier to be brave at the next.

Once I started the cycle of gaining confidence, I just changed my whole life. . . . I'd find myself in little social situations, or in school, when I knew the answer, I'd probably say it, which was definitely a change for me.

Finally, by playing the bass, Carly integrated the warring parts of herself and expressed in public what she felt in her heart. Later, in college, she formed her own bands and continued to evolve as a musician. She also started her own record label to distribute punk and hardcore music. Her teen-age impulse to help other bands evolved into a professional effort to promote bands she likes and to expose audiences to a wider range of underground music.

Recently, while on tour helping market and manage a band called the UK Subs, Carly's career as a bass player took an unexpected turn. When the band's bass player dropped out, Carly realized she was "the last person" they would consider as a substitute, and "they were a fairly big band, playing fairly big shows, bigger than I'd ever played." Nonetheless, after she "yelled and screamed a lot" they finally auditioned her and, to her amazement, invited her to join. She's proud of herself because "that was the bravest thing I've ever done." Moreover, the tour, she says, brought her full circle to where she started, and gave her a chance to give something back:

CARLY: All of a sudden I was in the band and there would be a clump of ten women right in front of me the whole time. And I'd get off stage, and they'd be, "Oh, you were great!" And I knew exactly how they felt. . . . I even talked to a woman a week later about it [who] had seen me in a show, and [she] said, "I saw this great band last week and this woman was on stage, and she—she really rocked, and I'm gonna go get a bass now!" I was like, "That was me!"

When a girl overcomes internal fears and decides to risk exposing herself to false expectations and violent criticism, the first concrete obstacle she's likely to encounter is actually obtaining an instrument. Unless she has a friend who will lend or sell her a guitar, drumset, or bass, she'll need to enter a music shop, which can be a humiliating, and sometimes absurdly humorous experience for a woman.

Portia, Rachel, and Sasha are women in their late twenties who started playing as teenagers and now live in New York City and play in a band called Trixie Belden, with Portia on drums, Rachel on guitar, and Sasha on bass. Their encounters with sales assistants in music shops demonstrate how a woman who wants to buy an instrument, strings, or other equipment is likely to be either harassed or ignored. As Bayton writes, guitar shops are "male terrain" where boys feel welcome and exhibit assertive behavior in trying out instruments and talking shop (41–42). In contrast, women often feel alien, judged, or mocked, which seriously undermines their self-confidence and sense of entitlement.

RACHEL: I hate that feeling, going in and then walking over and looking at the guitars and immediately everyone's going, "You know she doesn't deserve that really nice SG," immediately assuming that I don't. Not that they really think that, but that's always my feeling, that they're like, "What's she doing looking at the nice guitars?" or, "What's she doing in that section, she doesn't know anything. Do you want me to tune that for you?"

It makes me so angry. It's awful.

SASHA: I went into this guitar store once with my friend Morgan, who's a guy, and I've been playing guitar for about a year and half, and he's been playing for like three months. And we went into the acoustic room and I wanted to play this acoustic plug-in, because I wanted to see how loud it could get and what it would sound like. And so this salesman came in, and I would ask him a question about it, and . . . he would look at my friend, who's a guy, who's not holding the instrument, who does not even know anything, and would respond to him. And I was like in this alternative uni verse, I was like . . .

RACHEL: It feels like you're speaking a different language, and you're like, "Can I ask my interpreter? Tell him . . . "

SASHA: Who has a penis.

PORTIA: Who obviously, therefore . . .

RACHEL: Is a member of the country . . .

PORTIA: Who has the translating tool, the little-known translating tool.

SASHA: Of course my friend felt so bad.

RACHEL: When I go to the guitar store with a guy I know who's been playing guitar for a long time, sometimes I realize, like you think they're speaking some special language, and they're like, "Well, what's the pick up like?" And they're saying all these things, and you're like, wait a second, this person doesn't know anymore than I do, it's just they feel more authoritative. And they sound more authoritative when they're talking about it, because the person initially treats them with more respect than they would treat a woman who walked in and asked the same question. It just happens all the time.

SASHA: I buy my strings from a woman.

Portia argues that the salesperson's attitude depends in part on what instrument you have in common. Drummers, she believes, treat you differently from guitarists.

PORTIA: I don't really have that same kind of trouble because drummers are different. Drummers are like the black sheep of the music world, to some extent, because what you do is quite different from what guitarists and bassists do. So everybody is just sort of treated equally, that I've noticed, so far, certainly everybody is friendly.

And you know what it is? Drummers are good in different ways if you know them, but on the surface drummers do the same job. Fundamentally, they do the same job. And so, when you go in, the guys behind the counter are always really eager to me. They're always like, "Oh, you play, oh, how nice, blah, blah, blah. Well, I play, and I do this, and what do you use?"

But I have the same experience when I go into the guitar part to get strings for Rachel. When I used to get strings for her, I mean, it was ridiculous. I would walk in and they would ignore me, and they're over on the other side and they're doing nothing, you know, clearly doing nothing, you know, maybe having a conversation.

> Then they'll be like, "SIGH," walk over. Clearly I don't want any
> thing, because I don't know anything about anything.

This difference in attitude might be attributed to the electric guitar's "masculine" connotations, which for the clerks render suspect any woman's ability to access the instrument or the rigging associated with it. Portia characterizes drummers as less likely to call attention to themselves, less invested in personal recognition, and thus more co-operative.

A girl who's intimidated by condescending behavior might benefit from Portia and Rachel's suggestions.

> RACHEL: You have to figure as long as you get the information it's probably
>   fine.
> PORTIA: True. And the other thing is, you know you can see how it would
>   be intimidating for a young girl to walk into one of those places
>   and have these guys be completely condescending, but on the other
>   hand, what we learn as we go there more and more is that they're
>   always like that. So, it's like you never overcome it, so you just get
>   used to it.
> RACHEL: You just learn to be like, "Hey you loser," or you just learn to joke
>   with them and be extra assertive so you get what you want, and
>   they do respect you. Because if you go in there and you're like
>   (*Baby voice*), "Can I have some strings, I don't know, the purple
>   kind . . ." But if you're like (*Deep voice*), "I know what I want, the
>   Dario Elevens . . ." they see you as more of a serious person, who
>   must know something, and you do develop like a harder exterior,
>   definitely.

Rachel, Sasha, Portia, Carly, Tina, and Nicky all acknowledge the hazards and impediments confronting a young woman who ventures into the masculine world of rock music production. Each emphasizes the tactics for evading, neutralizing, and outwitting internal and external obstacles. The pleasure and self-confidence they derive from their music making reinforce their efforts and suggest a prescription for countering the false expectations that endanger self and voice. Carly offers some closing advice.

> CARLY: It would be very easy for me to say, just play, just get better, do what
>   you want to do, yell and scream and be crazy, but even if someone
>   said that to me, I wouldn't have listened. It's all about what's in your
>   head. I've seen a lot of girls quit if they don't see instant improve-
>   ment, same with boys, but it breaks my heart a million times more
>   when I see girls start and then quit, because they didn't get good

fast enough. It's a lot of work, you know. The best thing is just to persevere, people are gonna tell you you're awful, people are gonna tell you you're good. What people say to women is a lot different than what people say to men.

You're always a woman first before you're a musician, to the audiences, and that's not fair. So when people are reacting to you after a show or whatever, you have to be able to see what they're really saying. If people are like, "Oh yeah, you're so great!" You've got to be like, well, I don't know if it was that great, I'm not doubting myself because of it, but I don't think that's an honest response to what I just did on stage, you know? (*Laughs*)

You have to be able to discern the honest responses from the gender-specific response. You'll get a lot of those, but that's really important to a lot of girls who are thirteen years-old—it's the response.

Notes

1. Brown and Gilligan outline methods for discerning and interpreting the polyphony of voice in *Meeting at the Crossroads*. They also reference Mikhail Bakhtin's *The Dialogic Imagination* (Trans Caryl Emerson and Michael Holquist. Austin: University of Texas Press, 1981).

2. Since the interview reflects a relationship between the girls and video crew, I've described the setting and technical circumstances in this first encounter so that the girls' comments can be interpreted in context. Also, the presence of a camera and microphone always alter in some way the "reality" they are meant to record. All subsequent interviews excerpted in this essay were conducted under similar circumstances.

3. Ironically, while more established bands like L-7 and Hole defy limiting monikers such as "angry-women-in-rock," younger bands, like We're No Dentists, will inevitably be compared with them despite stylistic and often political differences.

4. Describing carnival, Bakhtin (*The Problems* 122–123) writes: "The laws, prohibitions, and restrictions that determine the structure and order of ordinary . . . life are suspended during carnival: what is suspended first of all is hierarchical structure . . . that is, everything resulting from . . . inequality among people."

5. "Zines" are underground publications circulated mostly by mail to readers interested in a particular topic or subject. The zines Carly discusses, which are written and distributed by women, often include letters, artwork, and personal testimonies from readers. See also Stephen Duncombe's *Notes from Underground: Zines and the Politics of Alternative Culture*.

Works Cited

Bakhtin, Mikhail. *The Problems of Dostoevsky's Poetics*. Trans. Caryl Emerson. Minneapolis: University of Minnesota Press, 1984.

Bayton, Mavis. "Women and the Electric Guitar." *Sexing the Groove: Popular Music and Gender*. Ed. Sheila Whiteley. New York: Routledge, 1997. 37–49.

Brown, Lyn Mikel, and Carol Gilligan. *Meeting at the Crossroads: Women's Psychology and Girls' Development*. New York: Ballantine Books, 1992.

Coates, Norma. "(R)evolution Now?: Rock and the Political Potential of Gender." *Sexing the Groove: Popular Music and Gender*. Ed. Sheila Whiteley. New York: Routledge, 1997. 50–64.

Duncombe, Stephen. *Notes from Underground: Zines and the Politics of Alternative Culture*. London: Verso, 1997.

Gottlieb, Joanne, and Gayle Wald. "Smells Like Teen Spirit: Riot Grrrls, Revolution and Women in Independent Rock." *Microphone Fiends: Youth Music and Youth Culture*. Eds. Andrew Ross, and Tricia Rose. New York: Routledge, 1994. 250–274.

Juno, Andrea. *Angry Women in Rock, Vol. One*. New York: Juno Books, 1996.

Nehring, Neil. *Popular Music, Gender, and Postmodernism: Anger Is an Energy*. Thousand Oaks, CA: Sage Publications, 1997.

Chapter 10

Out of the Indian Diaspora: Mass Media, Myths of Femininity, and the Negotiation of Adolescence between Two Cultures

Meenakshi Gigi Durham

I find I am constantly being encouraged to pluck out some one aspect of myself and present this as the meaningful whole, eclipsing or denying the other parts of self. But this is a destructive and fragmenting way to live. My fullest concentration of energy is available to me only when I integrate all the parts of who I am, openly, allowing for power from particular sources of my living to flow back and forth freely through all my different selves, without the restrictions of externally imposed definition.

—Audre Lorde, *Age, Race, Class, and Sex*

Growing up in two cultures, or coming from one to live in another, is like moving in two directions at once, or like being in two places at once. For those who haven't experienced it, it seems a simple matter of picking and choosing the best of both worlds, but for some of us, it's more painful than that.

—Voice over, Indu Krishnan, director of the film *Knowing Her Place*

I realized recently that when people question me about my origins (as they often do), I say I am from the mountains—as though I sprang full-fledged from a crevice of earth and rock rather than having been born in the usual way. Perhaps this mental block is a result of having lived all my life in a miasmic region between countries, between languages, between identities, and between media cultures; somewhere outside of the defining racial lines of black and white, which has led me on a lifelong quest to be, in some quintessential way, self-defining.

In the quotation above, it is clear that Audre Lorde knows all about externally imposed definitions: that ontology can be everything in the creation of meaning. My life has been lived as a process of deconstructing ethnic and gendered ontologies to try to reconstruct my own, particularly in adolescence. This was especially true of my dealings with mass media discourses and images throughout a girl-hood spent moving back and forth from Canada to India to the United States.

Negotiating this kind of resistance on the already contested terrain of adolescence brought me, as a young girl, face to face with myths and models of womanhood that shaped my entire concept of self. Reflecting on it, I want to offer some insights about growing up as a teenager caught between South Asian and North American media cultures in a way that I hope will illuminate this territory for others who have lived it or whose daughters will live it one day.

In this essay I focus on media culture and its role in adolescent girls' developing concepts of womanhood and woman-identity, particularly in the context of the South Asian diaspora. As Douglas Kellner points out, "Media culture . . . provides the materials out of which many people construct their sense of class, of ethnicity and race, of nation-ality, of sexuality, of 'us' and 'them.' . . . Media stories and images provide the symbols, myths, and resources which help constitute a common culture for the majority of individuals in many parts of the world today" (1).

In my experience, media myths are central to the interiorized con-stitution of womanhood. Mass-mediated myths of femininity in the United States and Canada are built primarily on a rhetoric of consum-erism, but they rely heavily on much older constructions of the femi-nine. I would not say that these myths are categorically negative or damaging; as Angela McRobbie has observed, girls are using mass media discourses on femininity as pathways to explore new permuta-tions of class, gender, and racial meanings, even as societal and cul-tural uncertainty over what it means to be a woman increases. In spite of this emancipatory potential, it is also clear that these media dis-courses are being generated and framed in the context of traditional cultural representations as well as the strictures of a capitalist economy; thus, the possibilities for interpretation are limited by the codes with which these discourses are inscribed. In the case of girls whose ethnic and racial identity is unclear because it does not conform to existing social definitions, the uncertainties are heightened, and the contradic-tions in discursive formulations of womanhood must be addressed and analyzed in ways that may not be as relevant for girls whose cul-tural identities are more stable.[1]

"The deeply ideological nature of imagery determines not only how other people think about us, but how we think about ourselves," writes Indian filmmaker Pratibha Parmar (as cited in hooks 5). Sometimes I am surprised and a little frightened by the extent to which I, as a prepubescent child, internalized mass-mediated myths of femininity. This realization underscores the urgency of critically interrogating the role of media myths in constituting concepts of womanhood.

The whole notion of "myth" conjures up a welter of powerful images and associations for me. Roland Barthes explored myth as a "signifying consciousness," a process of language and representation that works to normalize ideologies. As Myra Macdonald explains, "The Barthian model claims that the diverse and multifaceted qualities of reality are flattened into routine ways of thinking and talking. . . . By posing as 'natural' and 'common-sensical,' myths obscure their ideological role in helping to shore up systems of belief that sustain the power of the powerful" (1). Barthes and Macdonald both understand popular media to be instrumental in this normalizing process, playing a strong ideological role as they construct the topics and concepts that they present.

Particularly regarding the question of what it means to be "feminine," contemporary women take many of their cues from mediated constructions of ideal femininity. This process begins in childhood and continues throughout adolescence. This is not to imply that women and girls swallow media myths wholesale or unquestioningly, yet the normalizing power of these myths is incontestable. "American women today are a bundle of contradictions because much of the media imagery we grew up with was itself filled with mixed messages about what women should and should not do, what women could and could not be" (Douglas 9). Elizabeth Frazer's work with teenage girls reveals that they accept media versions of girls' lives as more legitimate than their own lived experiences. Lisa Duke's interviews with adolescent girls indicate that they base their norms of desirable female body image on media depictions. Susan Bordo talks about the grip of culture on the body, pointing out that "we are surrounded by homogenizing and normalizing images—images whose content is far from arbitrary, but is instead suffused with the dominance of gendered, racial, class, and other cultural iconography" (250). This supports Barthes's definition of myth as "giving an historical intention a natural justification" (142) as it "abolishes the complexity of human acts" (143).

Cognitively, intellectually, as a Ph.D.-toting college professor, I understand these conceptualizations. But when I think of myth, my mind's *eye* conjures up something wildly different: vividly colored images of the women of Indian legend—Sita, Savitri, Damayanti, Radha, Draupadi, and all of them are confused with the almond-eyed, pink-cheeked beauties of the Indian screen who represented them, literally and metaphorically, as I came of age in India, and whose looks and behavior epitomized ideal, unattainable Indian womanhood.

My family moved from Canada to India when I was on the verge of puberty. During my Canadian childhood, my father filled the spaces before bedtime with dramatic stories drawn from Indian folklore and legend. I contemplated his tales with bewilderment and detachment as I played with my Barbie dolls and listened to Monkees 45s on my pink plastic *I Dream of Jeannie* record player. In looking back, I realize that I had no way to picture the exotic and wondrous female characters that populated his narratives. The only Indian woman I had ever seen was my mother: small, smart, outspoken, funny, in no way to be confused with an *apsara*—the celestial nymph of Indian mythology. It was easy for me, by contrast, to believe in the no-less exotic and wondrous women of American and Canadian mass media. I grew up in Canada in the late 1960s and early 1970s, just before huge waves of Indian immigration hit the country. My family lived in a small town in British Columbia, in the foothills of the Rocky Mountains. For my entire childhood, we were the only dark-skinned people in the city, with the exception of the residents of the native Okanagan/Salish reservation outside of town, who were largely invisible. In the Canadian social stratum that accommodated my parents—highly educated, middle class, ultimately bourgeois—the world was blindingly white, save for us.

I do not recall any incidents of overt racism while I was growing up. I do, however, remember believing unquestioningly that I was ugly, and knowing with absolute certainty that I would never play "the princess" in our grade-school plays because of the way I looked. (Why I wanted to play the princess is another matter, but one that does not bear a great deal of examination here. All the little girls I knew dreamed of being princesses.) And we all understood that princesses looked like Barbie; princesses looked like Marcia Brady; princesses looked like my blonde, blue-eyed friends Connie and Lynne. Any girl who looked like me could not be pretty, was in fact the polar opposite of pretty, simply by reason of her coloring.

So discourses of the body are the first feminine media myths I remember being conscious of, and perhaps this is not unusual. Perhaps, in thinking back on the myths that shaped their concepts of self, all women could point to these same discourses. And perhaps for all women they were destabilizing, positioning virtually everyone as "other," outside of the perfect physical type. I only know that the ideal female form to me was always whiter than white, tall, pale-skinned, pale-haired, and pale-eyed, so that when I looked at my reflection in the mirror I saw something that was somehow not a woman at all, had no potential to be one.

Oddly, this view of the ideal feminine form did not much change when I moved to India, where fair skin, light eyes, large breasts, and long straight hair were still held up as hallmarks of great beauty. And at that point other angles on this mysterious notion of "femininity" began to make themselves felt: issues of dominance and submission, new and uncomfortable girl-roles that centered on being consummately nurturing and self-sacrificing, new and scary notions of sexual desire and desirability that were all wrapped around conventions of behavior and speech and dress on which I had a very poor grasp.

I already knew about sex when we moved to India—I had learned all about it from my salacious sixth-grade friend, Christine, who had college-age siblings.[2] I was also very confident about sexiness, which was, as far as I knew, an eminently admirable quality. This concept of "sex appeal" (a phrase I had acquired from Canadian TV commercials) involved trendy clothes—notably the miniskirts and tight tops of the period—and the other accouterments of feminine comeliness I had learned about from television, *Seventeen* magazine, and Archie comic books.

I was aghast to discover that in Indian mass media, sexiness—by these Western standards—was not only not admirable, it was actually reviled. In the process of arriving at adolescence, I had, like most Canadian girls growing up in the wake of the sexual revolution, internalized the message that self-fulfillment, power, and happiness rested on developing an active and potent heterosexuality by conforming to media standards for it. This was to be achieved, I knew, through the purchase of appropriate sex-appeal-enhancing products. Myra Macdonald describes how *Cosmopolitan* magazine in the 1970s stressed "the young woman's aspiration to shine in the game of (hetero)sexual play as an index of her ability to handle all interpersonal and work relations with self-confidence and panache, [relying] on a paradigm of independence based on economic self-sufficiency and individualism" (172). I absorbed this lesson easily. By the time I was 10, I understood completely the importance of developing my sex appeal according to these formulas in order to become a successful woman.

But in India, despite the beauty ideals vaunted in every ad and movie I saw, this kind of flagrant sexuality was, I learned, the hallmark of a very evil woman. Indian women were urged by advertisements to use "Fair and Lovely" skin lightening cream, bust developers, and henna to lighten their hair, but the goal of these efforts was to become good, chaste, and apparently asexual wives. This realization came to me partly through my viewing of Indian movies, where I began to discern the characteristics of a successful woman in my new cultural context. "Generally, the presentation of 'good' women in commercial Hindi films has been without variety," writes Shamita Das Dasgupta. "They are portrayed as long-suffering and submissive. The ideal woman in Hindi films has traditionally been a controlled, chaste, surrendering individual, not afraid of sacrifices for the good of her family. The 'bad' woman, on the other hand, has been depicted as westernized, individualistic, and sexually aggressive, ready to lead men to their ruin" (56).

Ajay Kumar identifies seven stereotypical role specifications for women that still persist in Indian mass media:

1. A woman's place is in the home,
2. The most important and valuable asset of a woman is physical beauty,
3. A woman's energies and intellect must be directed to finding the right man and keeping him,
4. Women are dependent, coy, and submissive, and they are masochistic in their dealings with the indignities, humiliations, and even physical violence inflicted on them,
5. The good woman is the traditional housewife, long-suffering, pious and submissive; the modern woman who asserts herself and her independence is undesirable and can never bring happiness to anybody nor find happiness herself,
6. Women are women's worst enemies,
7. The working woman is the undesirable exception who must be brought into the marriage fold and made to conform to social norms. (135)[3]

Tamil films and TV, to which I was exposed rather more than Hindi media, often contained dramatizations of tales from Indian mythology. The films echoed my father's old bedtime stories—of Sita, the wife of the god Rama, so pure that she walked through fire twice to prove her chastity to her husband and then asked the earth to swallow her so she didn't have to submit to the desires of the demon Ravana; of Savitri, who followed the God of Death into hell to plead for her husband's life. Rinki Bhattacharya writes of Indian cinema's "undying obsession with Indian mythology," noting that: "putting together a mythology on the screen was one of the simplest means of reaffirming myths about our social values. The engaging screen portrayals of epic characters like Ram and Sita or Nala and Damayanti were the best way to keep alive myths or re-establish the validity of these myths. Throughout the long history of Indian mainstream cinema we have seen new myths churned out of the old. Exemplary epic figures keep returning, reinforced under different, often deceptive garbs" (34–35).

Prabhati Mukherjee confirms that in India: "a loyal and chaste wife alone, having an abiding interest in her household affairs to the exclusion of all other outside interests, came to be the ideal in society. The emphasis was on a faithful and docile wife whose life centered round her family and home alone. This particular image of ideal women has been projected and their memory kept alive through different mass media" (50).

Adds Ajay Kumar, "Girls are socialized to be passive, submissive and docile because they grow up with such role models, which also define their lives as a preparation towards marriage and motherhood in almost total exclusion of any other aspect" (135).

The dawning recognition of my future social role in India, and the bewildering contradiction of my fairly entrenched Canadian beliefs, stirred a great deal of anger in me. My adolescence in India became marked by an extreme degree of resistance and rebellion—the kind of rebellion that is unheard of in Indian society, especially for girls. I refused to wear Indian clothes, interpreting saris and salwar-kameezes[4] as the social equivalent of prison garb. I cut my hair brutally short, jeeringly repudiating the beauty norm of long, flowing tresses. I spoke only English, steadfastly refusing to learn Tamil (a decision I've regretted ever since). I slouched to hide my budding breasts; I cast away my Indian name, Meenakshi, and would allow people to call me only "Gigi," a childhood nickname that I insisted be registered officially on my school records and then my passport. I purposely desexed myself, dressing androgynously in jeans and shorts and boys' shirts, keeping my hair cut extremely short, cultivating behaviors that were as different from all of the feminine myths I had learned as I could imagine.

This did not go over well in India.

In retrospect, as painful as it was at the time, I think my "androgynous phase"—which lasted for four or five years—was a significant first step in my growth as a feminist. I had never heard the word "patriarchy" and knew nothing of gender socialization or stereotyping, and I did not consciously recognize that the myths of femininity being presented to me were all centrally aimed at satisfying male standards for women's behavior, whether in Canada or in India. Yet I rejected and resisted them; they made me angry, though I had no way to articulate or understand that anger. And in rejecting and questioning, I was performing my own clumsy and uninformed critical interrogations of categories of race and sex and class and culture, for the first time aware of being on the outside looking in. Thus were the seeds of feminist activism planted.

There were negative aspects to this resistance, as well, however. My inchoate rage at repressive standards of behavior for Indian women caused me to savagely reject all things Indian, a position that remained more or less unchanged until I was well past adolescence and began to reconnect with my Indian cultural heritage. I was equally unsure about Western culture. My Canadian friends devoutly sent me magazines and posters recording the pop culture iconography of the '70s, but poring over photographs of Farrah Fawcett-Majors and Mary Tyler Moore frustrated me even further as I struggled with my quest for identity. Every standard of femininity I encountered seemed irreconcilably foreign to me, especially as I had no avenue for reaching any of them. Embedded in the rhetoric of consumerism, the American teen magazines I was reading exhorted me to buy Jordache jeans, Gee Your Hair Smells Terrific shampoo, and Bonne Belle flavored lip gloss to attract boys who looked like Sean Cassidy. None of these was anywhere in evidence in Ootacamund, India. At the same time, models with "wheat complexions" and dark-brown hair that fell to their knees hawked Sunsilk shampoo and Limca soda pop on local billboards and magazine pages. Most of these models were from North India and phenotypic rarities on the subcontinent, while others were in fact of mixed European and Indian parentage, which explained their very non-Indian looks, but I didn't know this at the time. Their looks, as well as their attitudes and behaviors, were unrelated to anything in my life.

It is important for me to note that my peers did not give any evidence of experiencing the same kind of dissonance and isolation from media archetypes. I attended a private, exclusive, and expensive girls' school, and then in my late teens an equally exclusive women's college. At both of these institutions, the majority of students were from affluent and orthodox Indian families. They expected to have arranged marriages (most of them, in fact, eventually did). The lives, loves, and stylings of Indian film stars and models were the subject of endless fascination and discussion among them. I am struck now as I remember the extent to which Western fashions and mores were coopted and adapted to the Indian environment by these girls: when Bo Derek, for example, sported cornrow braids, the Indian movie star Zeenat Aman promptly imitated the style, with the result that dozens of senior girls at my school appeared in classes wearing them. Platform shoes complemented the traditional salwar kameez outfits. The more daring among them donned halter blouses under their saris. But the underlying assumption was always that these fashion experiments were geared to one thing only: finding a place as a housewife and mother, acquiring perfection in the domestic role while having a career, "if my husband will allow it," as they said without rancor.

They talked of marriage, but not of romantic love or of sex. Aware that marriage was unquestionably their fate, and that it would be arranged by their parents in the Indian tradition, their discussions of men were pragmatic. "He should be quiet and fair-skinned." "I don't care if he is good looking or not, but he should have a good job." "If he wants to settle abroad, then he should be willing to come back to India every year to visit." Sex was not discussed; physical intimacy was talked about only in the most squeamish and ingenuous ways. "Wonder if my husband will want to kiss me before we are married. . . ." "What's it going to be like, touching a man *that way*?" No one knew.

The social expectation in India for upper-middle-class women was, and still is, virginity before marriage. It always surprises my Western friends when I talk about this, and about how faithfully Indian women adhere to this expectation. Very few girls I knew dated, and when they did it was an act of transgression, done secretly and rebelliously. But even in dating relationships, sex was off-limits. When I was in high school and college in India, most of my peers were terrified of even being suspected of sexual activity. This fear reached absurd proportions at times. I remember one of my friends telling me seriously, when I was seventeen or eighteen years old, "You know, Gigi, if you wear jeans all the time like you do, people will think you are not a virgin." In retrospect, understanding more about the way that Western culture is mythologized in India, I can see the curious logic of her inference; at the time, I was dumbstruck by the absurdity of the remark.

My teenage years were thus principally marked by complete cultural alienation. In many ways I felt Western, that is, Canadian; but I knew that that identity stamped me as a "bad woman" according to Indian mores. And I could not fully understand or accept the ways in which I felt Indian. There is no way to describe this feeling of existing in a total limbo. I began to feel like some sort of freak, disconnected from every evident social norm of femininity. In reading the existing literature on adolescence (for example, Pipher, Thompson), it seems that a certain percentage of teenage girls in the United States, at any rate, experience a similar isolation. In India, my experience seemed unique, at least among my peers. Now, with a growing South Asian diaspora in Great Britain and North America, these kinds of experiences may be more common. The actress and writer Meera Syal, born in India and raised in England, has said that belonging to the Indian diaspora feels as if every step she takes is a step away from her culture and into the abyss. "You always have to hide a part of yourself," she said in a recent interview with Suzie Mackenzie in *The Guardian*. Notes Mackenzie, "Duty and desire . . . have formed the basic tension of her life. Duty to her parents and to her culture. And desire 'to find out who I really am'" (T12). It took years for Syal to work things out, and visiting India as an adult actually helped her to eventually find some clarity about her identity—a way to define herself through difference, in both cultures.

This can be a tricky proposition, especially in adolescence, when "difference" is terrifying and abhorrent. Difference marked me so strongly that as a teenager I felt my only option was to cling to it and carry it to extremes of costuming and behavior, which in turn became even more isolating. Meera Syal's strategy during her English adolescence was to gain weight. Because she knew that "good" Indian girls could not have romantic involvements, fatness protected her from social criticism, gave her a reason and an excuse for conforming to the Indian standard of chastity. "[T]he physical body is closely intertwined and constituted by awareness, oppression, consciousness, the senses, and language" (Bhaskaran 196). As brown-skinned, dark-haired girls, our physical appearance catapulted us into the spider's web of racialized social discourses. We played out our pain, fear, and confusion on the surface of our bodies, which is a classic adolescent defense against control and erasure.

Writing about American teenage girls who cut themselves, Pipher argues: "Self-mutilation can be seen as a concrete interpretation of our culture's injunction to young women to carve themselves into culturally acceptable pieces. As a metaphorical statement, self-mutilation can be seen as an act of submission: 'I will do what the culture tells me to do'; an act of protest: 'I will go to even greater extremes than the culture asks me to'; a cry for help: 'Stop me from hurting myself in the ways that the culture directs me to' or an effort to regain control: 'I will hurt myself more than the culture can hurt me'" (158).

While the choices I made about my body were not as extreme as those of the girls in Pipher's study, cultural conflict unquestionably lay at the root of my decision to reconstruct myself physically in a way that felt safe but that, paradoxically, caused me further pain by separating me from my peers.

Kamala Visweswaran writes that she has always been haunted by "predicaments of the hyphen": "The increasing currency of such terms as 'Indo-American' or 'Indian-American,' even given the maturing of a generation seeking its voice, does not reassure me. Rather it signals for me the continual virulence of identity politics in the United States. . . . The Indian-American hyphen retains the imaginary of the nation-state, its mobile diaspora with increasing (if complicated) choices about whether to go or stay. It is a hyphen that signals the desire (and the ability) to be both 'here' and 'there'" (302). This dislocation and ambiguity takes on life-threatening dimensions for an adolescent. The power of these cross-currents is overwhelming and terrifying. India is rapidly becoming Westernized in certain superficial ways—now there are McDonald's and Domino's Pizza franchises in the larger cities, and *Baywatch* can be seen on television—but the mediated myths of femininity remain largely unchanged. Both Western and Eastern myths continue to define women through models of femininity based on relationships with men: in media texts generated in the West, the woman's role is hypersexual; in Indian media discourse, it is uxorial. Both mythical models carry strong overtones of subjugation and restriction. Now there are some feminist films and television in India, but they tend to relate the experiences of women and girls from generally low-income and low-status backgrounds. In the mainstream mass media of both North American and Indian cultures, the stereotypical representations of middle- and upper-class women continue to be hair-raisingly patriarchal and rigid, and representations of adolescent girls still focus on nubile appearance and vulnerability. With the increasingly close juxtaposition of Western and Eastern myths, the conflations, intersections,

and contradictions are becoming sharper and more evident. Given
that the mass media are a significant factor in adolescent girls' socialization, I cannot imagine anything but turmoil in the hearts of teenagers of the Indian diaspora, who are grappling with these texts in the
way that I did, trying to make sense of them in order to try to make
sense of their lives.

So the pivotal question for me is: How can a "multicultural" adolescent resolve multiple and contradictory media representations of womanhood in terms of finding her "true" self? I pose this question with
the full awareness that there may not be an answer at all. First of all,
of course, the notion of a "true" or "authentic" self is problematic,
especially for anyone caught in the sex-gender-race-ethnicity debates.
Setting those issues aside for the moment, it would seem that detach-
ing from cultural expectations, especially from the implicit impera-
tives of popular culture, would be an obvious step, but one that is
unrealistic, if not actually impossible, to ask of any teenage girl. There
is generally very little awareness of or research into the ways in which
media representations of race and gender affect adolescents of immigrant diasporas. I can offer insights almost solely on the basis of my
own experience. But it is clear to me that these issues need to be
interrogated, with a view to developing a new and radical politics of
identity that would give adolescents some way to understand themselves and to frame their experiences between cultures. One faint ray
of hope, to me, is the growing presence of the South Asian diaspora
in popular culture: writers and filmmakers are documenting their experiences through various mass media, and many of these efforts express women's perspectives. Films like *Mississippi Masala* and *Bhaji
on the Beach*, and books like *Our Feet Walk the Sky*, are unpacking
pieces of the diasporic experience, perhaps giving adolescents new
characters for changing myths even as they unravel some of the old
ones. And in the end, the challenge comes in the words of the Jamai-
can-English writer Andrea Levy: "If Englishness doesn't define me,
redefine Englishness" (Jaggi 31).

Redefining media culture would be my idea of a radical and effective intervention. To a certain degree, I am a product of the mass
media environment. Now it needs to be produced by me and other
women who are negotiating their lives between cultures. First theoretically and then in praxis, we need to begin to explore the notion of
a dialectic between the self and the media with a view to subverting its
colonizing power. Bhaskaran asks, "Even though I claim that my iden-

tity is constructed by multiple communities, why am I encouraged to think there is a crisis of my subjectivity, identity or authorship for my politics? How can there be a crisis over categories that were never intended for my subjecthood?" (199). She's right—we need to find ways of defining subjectivity that accommodate the immigrant diasporas of this changing world, that are based on process rather than on ontologies developed from a history of race- and gender-based oppressions. When these new subjectivities come to be understood by the producers of mass culture, we'll be on our way to an answer.

Notes

1. I suspect that girls whose sexual identities do not conform to normative ontologies go through similar deconstructive processes. I hope women who have had such experiences with media culture will write about them, as well.

2. I think in this respect I was extremely precocious compared with most Indian children: I remember the discussion of human reproduction as being part of my ninth-grade biology class in India, and even then the teacher refused to talk about how exactly the sperm reached the egg.

3. There are now several significant feminist filmmakers in India, but during my adolescent years feminist cinema was so obscure as to be invisible.

4. The salwar-kameez is the traditional North Indian woman's garb of a long tunic, baggy trousers and a veil-like scarf.

Works Cited

Barthes, Roland. *Mythologies*. Trans. Annette Lavers. New York: Hill and Wang, 1972.

Bhaskaran, Suparna. "Physical Subjectivity and the Risk of Essentialism." *Our Feet Walk the Sky: Women of the South Asian Diaspora*. Ed. The Women of South Asian Descent Collective. San Francisco: Aunt Lute Books, 1993. 191–202.

Bhattacharya, Rinki. "Portrayal of Women in Indian Cinema." *Indian Films Today: An Anthology of Articles on Indian Cinema*. New Delhi: Directorate of Film Festivals, 1985. 34–37.

Bordo, Susan. *Unbearable Weight: Feminism, Western Culture, and the Body*. Berkeley: University of California Press, 1993.

Dasgupta, Shamita Das. "Feminist Consciousness in Woman-Centered Hindi Films." *Our Feet Walk the Sky: Women of the South Asian Diaspora*. Ed. The Women of South Asian Descent Collective. San Francisco: Aunt Lute Books, 1993. 56–63.

Douglas, Susan J. *Where the Girls Are: Growing Up Female with the Mass Media*. New York: Times Books, 1994.

Duke, Lisa. "From *Seventeen* to *Sassy*: Teen Magazines and the Construction of the Model Girl. "Paper presented at the annual meeting of the Association for Education in Journalism and Mass Communication, Washington DC, 9–12 Aug. 1995.

Frazer, Elizabeth. "Teenage Girls Reading *Jackie*." *Media, Culture and Society* 9.4 (1987): 407–425.

hooks, bell. *Black Looks: Race and Representation*. Boston: South End Press, 1992.

Jaggi, Maya. "The New Brits on the Block." *The Guardian* 13 July 1996: 31.

Kellner, Douglas. *Media Culture: Cultural Studies, Identity and Politics between the Modern and the Postmodern*. London and New York: Routledge, 1995.

Kumar, Ajay. "Women and Media." *Women in India: Today and Tomorrow*. Ed. Mukta Mittal. New Delhi: Anmol Publications, 1995. 127–149.

Lorde, Audre. "Age, Race, Class and Sex: Women Redefining Difference." *Sister Outsider*. Freedom, CA: Crossing Press, 1984. 114–123.

Macdonald, Myra. *Representing Women: Myths of Femininity in the Popular Media*. London: Edward Arnold, 1995.

Mackenzie, Suzie. "Passage from India." *The Guardian* 6 April 1996: T12.

McRobbie, Angela. *Postmodernism and Popular Culture*. London and New York: Routledge, 1994.

Mukherjee, Prabhati. *Hindu Women: Normative Models*. Hyderabad, India: Orient Longman, 1978.

Pipher, Mary. *Reviving Ophelia: Saving the Selves of Adolescent Girls*. New York: Ballantine, 1994.

Thompson, Sharon. *Going All the Way: Teenage Girls' Tales of Sex, Romance, and Pregnancy*. New York: Hill and Wang, 1995.

Visweswaran, Kamala. "Predicaments of the Hyphen." *Our Feet Walk the Sky: Women of the South Asian Diaspora*. Ed. The Women of South Asian Descent Collective. San Francisco: Aunt Lute Books, 1993. 301–312.

Chapter 11

The Body of Evidence: Dangerous Intersections between Development and Culture in the Lives of Adolescent Girls

Mary K. Bentley

As I was walking through a major department store in our local mall I was stopped dead in my tracks by a mannequin in front of me. I'm sure many of you have had the experience of being "snuck up on" by a mannequin, but the reason for my fear was not its placement, its wild hair, or strange dress, it was the mannequin itself. It (it was a she) looked sick, emaciated, as if it could hardly stand under the burden of its own weight. I stood there gawking at this shocking image, with disbelief and concern about the message it conveyed, when I heard two young women commenting on the dress worn by this mannequin. Their conversation, with this form looming above them, went something like this:

GIRL #1:   I love that dress.
GIRL #2:   Me too, but I would have to lose forty pounds to wear it.
GIRL #1:   You! Look at my gut, I am a huge hog. I should never eat.
GIRL #2:   You know Jenn, in fourth period, she didn't eat for two days and her stomach was totally flat.

As I peered around the display, I saw two girls about twelve or thirteen years old strolling toward the cosmetic department, clutching plastic bags and drinking Diet (in large letters) Cokes. Neither one of them was overweight. They looked like healthy middle school girls. This scene bothered me so much that I decided to go back to the store with a measuring tape and actually take the measurements of this form.

When I attempted this, I was stopped by a sales clerk who wished to direct me to the rack where I could find the dress on display. I tried to explain the situation to her, but she got very uncomfortable and called the manager. After explaining to three different people that I was contributing to a book on adolescent girls and I was interested in knowing the proportions of the mannequins they used in their displays, I was finally told that I could not disturb the display and was referred to the corporate office. I called the corporate office. After some additional explanation, I was given the phone number of a man who is in charge of dressing displays. A brief phone conversation with him led to a visit.

He was a wealth of information and gave me a fascinating account of the historical evolution of the mannequin. He explained that mannequins have gone through many incarnations over the past thirty years. He was very animated in his descriptions of mannequins that had exaggerated body parts, like cinched waists and large hips and breasts in the 1950s, mannequins that were actual body casts of models complete with genitalia in the 1970s, and the advent of the girlish flat-busted form of the 1980s. The mannequins he currently uses for displays are generally very thin. He explained: "The waif-like heroin addict is the look that dominates most of the young women's displays." He further added that in some of the displays they now "add a substantial breast to the form, the Pamela Anderson kind of thing, for more provocative displays."

He was in the process of dressing two mannequins and agreed to measure them for me. The first was 5'8" tall. Her measurements were 30" bust (she had no pads on, a la Pamela Anderson), 23" waist, and 32" hips. The second was 6 ft. tall with a 32" bust, 23" waist, and 31" hips. They both had 18" thighs and upper arms of less than ten inches. When I asked how the proportions of the mannequins were determined, he replied: "They were made so the clothes fit right and look the way they are supposed to." Perhaps even more disturbing were his projections about the future evolution of the female form in displays. He replied by saying that display dressers were going toward a complete abstraction of the forms to display clothing. He cited designers who were "just using two sticks" or "abstract metal cross-like forms." At that point we both just looked at each other, mouths open, and said, "Wow," at the same time.

A mannequin is by definition a life-sized model of the human body, used to fit or display clothes. If the forms he measured were real bodies, there would be very little life in them. The average woman in the

United States is a size 14. According to international sizing charts, this means she has a 38–39" bust, 29–31" waist, and 39–40" hips, more than 6 inches larger than this mannequin (32–23–31). Strange as it seems, the girls were right. They *would* have to lose forty pounds.

Learning about Being Female

> Young women are engaged with questions of "being female"; that is, who will control, and to what extent they control, their own bodies.
> —Michelle Fine, *Disruptive Voices*

Girls are constantly barraged by images of women from a wide array of cultural sources. From these many sources girls begin to understand the implications of power, prestige, wealth, and male attention that are bestowed upon women who are culturally defined as "attractive." Consequently, their value is measured by physical attraction.

In an extensive study looking at how adolescent boys and girls rate their self-worth, Stephanie Harter concluded that physical appearance is the most important domain contributing to children's and young adolescents' sense of self-worth, outpacing social acceptance, scholastic and athletic competence, and behavioral conduct. This seemed to be particularly true for girls (Harter 227). So where does an adolescent girl get the idea that how she looks determines her worth?

A primary source of attractiveness messages for girls can be found in widely read magazines targeted to this population, such as *Seventeen* and *YM*. Numerous studies have documented the fact that these magazines focus primarily on beauty and fashion (Duffy and Gotcher, Peirce), weight loss and physical attractiveness (Guillen and Barr), physical self-improvement (Evans, Rutberg, Sather and Turner), and the link between being physically beautiful and sexually attractive to males (Durham).

In addition, there is evidence that one of the strongest, most pervasive sources of such messages is television, specifically commercials. Television commercials strongly reinforce the importance of appearance and attractiveness. In the mid-1980s, Chris Downs and Sheila Harrison examined 4,294 network television commercials and found that 1 out of 3.8 featured an attractiveness-based message (17). They estimated that children and adult viewers were, at that time, exposed to an average of 14 of these messages each day. They proposed several reasons why television advertising acts as a primary disseminator of attractiveness stereotypes. Perhaps the most significant of these is that attractiveness messages are not critiqued by the viewer. In fact, the authors claim that it is television that makes this attractiveness norm "real," particularly for children and adolescents, since they most often believe that what they see on TV is "the real world." These researchers concluded: "Overall then there are compelling reasons to suspect that television acts as a salient source of 'attractiveness oriented socialization'" (14).

More recently the effect of television advertising on body image distortion in young women was examined. Phillip Myers and Frank Biocca found that watching as little as thirty minutes of television programing and advertising had an effect on how women evaluated their bodies. "There may be some cumulative effect of all these messages. It is reasonable to imagine that each of these body image messages is just one strike on a chisel sculpting the ideal body inside a young woman's mind" (111).

Like the mannequins in the mall, models who embody the ideal female form also have an effect on the ways in which girls learn to evaluate their attractiveness, and hence their worth, in the culture. Mary Martin and Patricia Kennedy asked girls in grades eight and twelve to answer questions about their physical attractiveness, the way they rated themselves, and their overall self-esteem. They found that as girls get older they tend to compare themselves with fashion models more often. This comparison was even more pronounced for girls with lower scores on measures of self-perceptions of physical attractiveness and/or self-esteem. Remarkably, the researchers found "even one-time exposure to highly attractive advertising models raises comparison standards for physical attractiveness in 8th and 12th graders" (527).

According to Myra and David Sadker: "As girls move into adolescence, being popular with boys becomes overwhelmingly important. It is the key to social success because the boys measure the girls' physical attractiveness. They (girls) look to males for esteem, hoping to see approval and affirmation in their eyes" (85). In this difficult time they learn that the labels of popular and pretty are handed out by the boys and reinforced by both the girls and the boys. It is these labels that will, to a large extent, determine who will be successful. So girls learn to self-monitor their food intake, their exercise, and the appearance of their bodies as a necessary measure to achieve social, economic, and relational success.

In fact, obese girls and women often suffer a myriad of cultural/social sanctions for their unacceptable physical appearance. Numerous studies have demonstrated that obese women are most likely to suffer from job discrimination and a hostile work environment, are less popular, and less successful with dating and marriage opportunities (Margolin and White, Wooley and Wooley cited in Fredrickson and Roberts 177–179). For obese females there is little or no consideration for the genetic/metabolic indicators that are major etiological factors in obesity. The culture condemns them as "women who have let themselves go," who are "lazy," "inactive," and, most importantly unattractive, hence of little value (Fredrickson and Roberts 179). This phenomenon plays out differently for women than it does for men. "For women, positive self-concept hinges on perceived physical attractiveness, whereas for men, it hinges on perceived physical effectiveness" (Lerner, Orlos, and Knapp cited in Fredrickson and Roberts 179).

We must remember, however, that cultural ideals of attractiveness are subject to dramatic changes. What was considered attractive and desirable in one decade may change dramatically in the next. Marilyn Monroe was considered the ideal of feminine beauty in the 1950s and was a size 12 in her movies only through constant dieting. For most of her life she was a size 16 (Nadelson). In contemporary culture the yardstick by which girls self-monitor is an extraordinarily thin, unhealthy, and in most cases unobtainable ideal, like the mannequin. But this cultural ideal is so pervasive that it becomes each individual girl's responsibility to "make herself right." In this regard there is an expectation that a girl "should" reduce her size and change the appearance of her body through the restriction of food intake or dieting. Part of being the "perfect girl" is being a thin girl, and that means taking control of her unruly body and appetites. The problem is that when girls are learning this female responsibility, they are also experiencing profound changes—that is to say they are developing a woman's body: "[S]ensing something amiss at adolescence, they sought the answer in their individual biology. Their bodies were changing, becoming curvy and fuller, taking on the shape of a woman. They [girls] were changing, in a way over which they had no control—they did not know whether they would be small breasted and large hipped or whether their bodies would eventually end up as the teenagers in *Seventeen*" (Orbach 168).

Growing into Girls: Development

> Like the tightening of a corset, adolescence closes around these precocious, authoritative girls. They begin to restrict their interests, confine their talents, pull back on their dreams.
>
> —Sadker and Sadker, *Failing at Fairness*

In elementary grades girls possess a strong sense of themselves, of what they can be and who they can become. They exist side by side with boys, inviting new challenges, eager to try anything, interacting with the world, physical, vital. For many girls, this freedom is short-lived as they begin to understand what it means to be female in a world that objectifies and devalues the feminine.

Girls often learn to censor themselves and present the "nice girl," the "perfect girl" to those from whom they need approval. This means abandoning aspects of their former selves, the bravado and zest for life, leaving behind all their knowledge about self and the world learned through this way of being. As their bodies change, so do their identities. For girls, adolescence is not only a time of changing body shapes, but a time they are mandated by the culture to change their identities, the essence of who they are and how they take in the world. Girls must transform themselves into the role of the feminine in our culture, which means being nice, sweet, pretty, and thin. These are the things that we have come to know as "feminine." These are also the characteristics that make it difficult for girls to be agents on their own behalf as they perpetuate objectification and passivity.

There is also significant evidence that as girls enter adolescence they experience a marked drop in self-esteem (Sadker and Sadker 77–78). If, as the aforementioned research points out, physical attractiveness is the yardstick by which girls will be measured, then it follows that their self-worth would diminish as their bodies grow out of control and away from this very thin cultural standard. Self-esteem is not only a vital sign of mental health, it is also a connection to academic achievement and a direct link to career goals and hope for the future (Sadker and Sadker 78–79). Learning to be female in our culture not only diminishes a girl's potential, it also, and rather suddenly, reduces her worth in the larger culture. She is reminded through constant body and behavioral monitoring whether or not she is meeting the perfect girl standard. It is this very standard that pushes her away from authentic relationships, which are critical to healthy growth and development, and into relationships where she learns to play the role of nice girl.

In their book *Failing at Fairness*, Sadker and Sadker asked middle schoolers this question: "Suppose you woke up tomorrow and found you were a member of the opposite sex? How would your life be different?" (83–85). Many of the girls (42 percent) came up with very good things about being male, like having more respect and more money and being less worried about what other people think. Boys, however, were often repulsed by the notion of being female. Only 23 percent of them could come up with any benefits, and 16 percent came up with desperate fantasies about how to get out of the female form, mostly involving suicide. "I would kill myself right away by setting myself on fire so no one knew." "I'd wet the bed, then I would throw-up. I'd probably go crazy and kill myself." After reading hundreds of boys' essays, the researchers were "shocked at the degree of contempt expressed by so many" (Sadker and Sadker 85).

Taking Control?

Given this playing field, where boys are so repulsed by the notion of being female, it is difficult to determine how a young girl could successfully negotiate her changing world. What would control over her body, perhaps one of the only sources of control available to her, mean? For most girls dieting becomes a way of life. Approximately 50 percent of adolescent and young women are dieting at anyone time, while half of these individuals are at or below normal weight (Centers for Disease Control). Despite many of the media-generated claims to the contrary, dieting simply does not change a girl's morphology, or body type. In fact, dieting in normal weight individuals can have detrimental psychological and physiological effects, with weight fluctuation, not permanent weight loss, as the most prevalent result. According to the Centers for Disease Control, "one third to two thirds of the weight lost during dieting is regained within one year, and almost all is regained within five years" (2811).

While girls may believe that dieting will increase their sense of power, self-esteem, success, and control, diets, and the weight fluctuation that is most often the end result, do just the opposite. Weight fluctuation has been strongly associated with negative psychological effects in normal weight and obese individuals (Foreyt). So if a girl diets and the diet fails to change her body into the ideal one, she may have an even further diminished sense of worth.

One of the most widely cited surveys on body image was conducted in 1972 and 1985 by *Psychology Today*. In 1997 they again asked their readers to respond to more than five pages of items related to how they see, feel, and are influenced by their bodies (Garner). The first 4,000 respondents were included in the analysis. Most were white (87 percent), female (86 percent), college graduates (62 percent), and heterosexual (93 percent). Women seemed to be more dissatisfied with their bodies than ever before with 89 percent wanting to lose fifteen pounds or more. Among young women ages 13–19, 62 percent claimed they were dissatisfied with their weight. When asked about the origins of this discontent, most women (58 percent) claimed it was their personal feeling about weight, 44 percent, claimed it was from being teased by others, and 23 percent claimed they had been influenced by movie or TV celebrities. In the extremes of weight management, 23 percent of women reported vomiting and 50 percent reported cigarette smoking. Fifteen percent claimed they would sacrifice more than five years of their lives to be thin, while 24 percent were willing to sacrifice three or more years of their lives. "We can confidently conclude that a significant minority of you believe life is not worth living if you are not thin" (Garner 30).

Strategies for Control?

[A]lthough young women today enjoy greater freedom and more options than their counterparts of a century ago, they are also under more pressure, and at greater risk, because of a unique combination of biological and cultural forces that have made the adolescent female body into a template for much of the social change of the twentieth century.

—Joan Brumberg, *The Body Project*

With 62 percent of the young women responding that they are dissatisfied with their weight (Garner), and an overwhelming number of girls who consider themselves overweight or anorexic/bulimic, it becomes clear that they are responding to some kind of cultural demand. The experience of girls as they move into adolescence can be seen as a kind of cultural mirror, reflecting back strategies for coping with the increasingly loud messages they are receiving about who the culture demands they should be. There appear to be three strategies young girls use to take control of their lives and hence their bodies: dieting, overeating, and anger. The first two have led to an increase in young girls with eating disorders, the third to young girls being rebellious.

The first strategy is best described by Hilde Bruch in her book *The Golden Cage: The Enigma of Anorexia Nervosa*. Although this book is more than twenty years old, it continues to be a relevant source for describing this disorder. Here she describes what the extreme end of self-imposed restriction means to the girls who live with it and the way it gives them a sense of control. "[N]ot to give in to any bodily demand becomes the highest virtue. Most vigorously denied is the need for food. However painful the hunger, to tolerate it for one more hour, to postpone even the smallest amount, becomes a sign of victory" (62). She further describes that this detachment from internal body signals also applies to body fatigue: "Hunger is not the only bodily demand that is denied: not giving in to fatigue rates equally high. Swimming one more lap, running one more mile, doing ever more excruciating calisthenics, everything becomes a symbol of victory over the body" (63).

Louisa Perimenis describes this extreme control in terms of what it means about the cultural context of being female: "Anorexia nervosa is an expression of the construction of gender in American society; it is both a ritual of self-effacement and a ritual of empowerment for women and girls par excellence. In a visceral way it allows women and girls to experience (and display) what it means to be inferior—hence, unentitled members of society—through the physical pain of constant hunger" (49).

In *The Body Project*, Joan Brumberg suggests this obsession with the body has become so culturally indoctrinated that it is used as a proxy to measure mental health. "The increase in anorexia nervosa and bulimia in the last thirty years suggests that in some cases the body becomes an obsession, leading to recalcitrant eating behaviors that can also result in death. But even among girls who never develop full-blown eating disorders, the body is so central to definitions of the self that psychologists sometimes use numerical scores of 'body esteem' and 'body dissatisfaction' to evaluate a girl's mental health" (xxiv).

A second strategy for resolving these cultural dilemmas is practiced by girls who compulsively overeat. Anorexics share with compulsive overeaters a conscious desire to control their world. Overeating may be a way to avoid being sexually objectified. It is a way to take yourself out of competition with other girls and to be left alone by boys. This makes authentic relationships, with both boys and girls, more likely. These girls are safer, easier to be real with. They can also be seen as a reminder that they will not be controlled. They will eat what they want and wear it, literally. "The crucial difference for anorexics and for overweight women is that the kind of attention they do attract is of a different nature, outside the status of a sex object. Broadly this means men will dismiss her and other women will relax in her presence" (Orbach 174).

A third strategy, particularly among those who also experience discrimination and oppression in addition to those imposed by gender, is that of anger. These girls act out their anger both physically and verbally with an "in your face" attitude. In more than six years of listening to the stories of adolescent girls in detention centers and juvenile facilities in both New Mexico and New York, I have heard very clearly and very loudly these voices of resistance. These girls are not "nice." They are not "sweet." They are "bad girls," rejecting the feminine by acting out their anger and assuming the role of the male—being one of the guys. In a chapter co-written with Pat McPherson, Michelle Fine wonderfully describes this strategy, gleaned from conversations with four self-defined "bad girls":

> The behavior, clothing and values associated with such identification with boys and sports suggests both a flight from femininity they collectively described as "wearing pink," "being prissy," "being Barbie," and "reinforcing guys all the time,"—and an association of masculinity with fairness (vs. cattiness), honesty (vs. backstabbing), strength (vs. prissiness, a vulnerability whether feigned or real), initiative (vs. deference or reactionary comments), and integrity (vs. the self-doubt and conflicting loyalties dividing girls). The four's risk-taking behaviors—driving fast, sneaking out at night—reinforced identities as "one of the guys." Such are the bad girls. (Fine 196–197)

This strategy of rejecting the feminine by being "one of the guys" may also be evidenced in the numbers of girls who are committing violent crimes. Take notice of the growing numbers of girls in corrections and detention facilities, just like the boys.

Offering Alternatives

The question becomes: In a culture that trains adolescent girls to be quiet, nice, thin, and invisible to the point of incarceration or anorexia, what supports are necessary to help them negotiate this developmental period and come out intact? That is, how can we help them come through adolescence with a clearer sense of who they are and what forces have shaped them? We need to cultivate strategies that offer alternatives to playing the role of the "perfect girl," who is primarily concerned with how attractive she is. Alternative means to achieving cultural success and opportunities for relationships need to be established and maintained within institutional structures so girls have a wider array of options available from which to learn who they are and what they could become during this important developmental period.

A Critical Lens
First, girls need to learn how to identify and critique cultural messages. Identification is the first essential step. The mannequin, for

example, is a clear cultural message that contributes to an unrealistic ideal. The act of taking the measurements, of critically assessing how unrealistic this form is, is healthy and self-affirming. Acts such as these help girls to understand the magnitude of the conspiracy afloat. The translation of the message from the unconscious mind to a conscious realization of the effect these images have is an essential skill for girls. This skill needs to be taught in all manner of ways, in public (schools, community groups) as well as private (family, relational) spaces. All youth need to learn to critique the messages that inundate them by measuring these messages against their lived experiences, not the "real" as depicted by television, advertisements, magazines, and mannequins. This kind of vigilance gives girls a tool, a way to sift through the images and messages, and make meaning of them in a conscious way. This is an active process of taking in the world that allows girls a chance to be agents on their own behalf, so that the objectification girls experience in their daily lives does not lodge so firmly in their collective brains. Girls need to understand that the option to critique and reject some of these images is as strong a possibility as the options of dieting, anorexia, obesity, violence, and diminished sense of self. Susan Faludi, in her book *Backlash*, writes about the cultural backlash against women saying: "It [the backlash] is most powerful when it goes private, when it lodges inside a woman's mind and turns her vision inward, until she imagines the pressure is all in her head, until she begins to enforce the backlash too, on herself" (xxii).

Safe Spaces

Second, girls need safe spaces. Girls need a chance to experience their bodies and their voices in spaces where they will not be held to the cultural restrictions of the "feminine." They need places where they can run, play, and explore, without self-censoring, silencing, and monitoring. This may mean having girls-only spaces, or spaces where girls can interact with women who are committed to letting girls be rather than insisting they conform to the cultural stereotype.

These spaces will have to be outside of the traditional spaces where girls interact with the larger culture. School is one of the most dangerous places for girls to be authentic. It is where the rules for being a girl are most strongly enforced. Instead, athletics, organized clubs, and outdoor trips where girls are measured by what they can do provide spaces where girls can excel on their own terms. Girls need opportunities where they can see what their changing bodies can do. They need spaces where they can know what they know and try new identities without self-censoring. Without safe spaces, girls will not be fully able to discover who they are and who they would like to become.

Voice Lessons

Third, girls need models of women and of other girls who have had the courage to speak up, to use their voices on their own behalf, with positive, self-affirming results. This requires women to challenge the silence in their own psyches and become examples of courage. Girls need to see women in their daily lives who summon the courage to speak and who insist on taking up space, in both public and private spaces. They need to know the consequences of surrendering their voices and taking on the voice of the "perfect girl." They need to understand that depression and suicide, as well as anorexia, unintended pregnancies, smoking, HIV, and a whole host of other dangerous situations are all consequences of "lost voice." Perhaps it is best said by the very courageous Audre Lorde: "My silence has not protected me. Your silence will not protect you. . . . In the case of silence, each of us draws the face of her own fear—fear of contempt, fear of censure, of some judgment, of recognition, of challenge, of annihilation. But most of all I think, we fear for the very visibility without which we cannot truly live" (Lorde 20–21).

Reflecting on a series of dinnertime conversations with a group of four girls from a variety of racial and socioeconomic backgrounds, Michelle Fine and Pat MacPherson (Fine 185) comment: "They (the girls) are often reminded of their bodies as a public site (gone right or wrong), commented on and monitored by others—male and female. But as often, they reminded us, they forcefully reclaim their bodies by talking back and by talking feminist. 'It'd be harder not to talk,' Sophie thinks. 'It'd be harder to sit and swallow what people are saying.'"

Voice is not without consequence. Detention centers and juvenile facilities are full of girls who speak out in anger. Many of these girls refused to be invisible, refused to be mute. These girls underscore the need not only for safe space but also for guidance, like "voice lessons." It is critical to have the opportunity to practice, to learn when it is safe, when there is support, and when there is not. There is no question that as the world becomes an increasingly unsafe place, there are times when it is not in the best interest of an individual girl to resist those who are unjust. Voice lessons involve learning a variety of ways to use tone, pitch, and volume. So that girls won't be taken out of the discourse by falling mute from a diminished sense of self, being locked up from acting out, or disappearing altogether from anorexia, it is critical for girls to learn and practice the full range of voice possibilities as strategies to stay intact, as a path for nurturing self, and increasing opportunities.

When writing a speech for a feminist gathering, Audre Lorde was contemplating her fear of using her voice, of her move from silence: "And of course I am afraid, because the translation of silence into language and action is an act of self-revelation, and that always seems fraught with danger. But my daughter when I told her of my topic and my difficulty with it, said, 'Tell them about how you're never really a whole person if you remain silent, because there is always that one little piece inside you that wants to be spoken out, and if you keep ignoring it, it gets madder and madder, and hotter and hotter, and if you don't speak it out one day it will just up and punch you in the mouth from the inside'" (8).

We as women (mothers, aunts, sisters, daughters, friends), and all those who want girls to learn to honor and respect themselves, those of us who know the lost potential in our own lives, need to better understand the dilemmas that girls navigate each day and help them develop strategies within and around them. Perhaps this way fewer of us will be punched in the mouth, from the outside or the inside. Perhaps then we can better navigate these <u>dangerous intersections</u>.

Works Cited

Bruch, Hilde. *The Golden Cage: The Enigma of Anorexia Nervosa.* Cambridge: Harvard University Press, 1978.

Brumberg, Joan Jacobs. *The Body Project: An Intimate History of American Girls.* New York: Random House, 1997.

Centers for Disease Control. "Leads from the Morbidity and Mortality Weekly Report." *Journal of the American Medical Association* 266 (1991): 2811–2812.

Downs, Chris, and Sheila K. Harrison. "Embarrassing Age Spots or Just Plain Ugly? Physical Attractiveness Stereotyping as an Instrument of Sexism on American Television Commercials." *Sex Roles* 13 (1985): 9–19.

Duffy, Margaret, and J. Micheal Gotcher. "Crucial Advice on How to Get the Guy: The Rhetorical Vision of Power and Seduction in the Teen Magazine *YM*." *Journal of Communication Inquiry* 20 (1996): 32–48.

Durham, Meenakshi G. "Dilemmas of Desire: Representation of Adolescent Sexuality in Two Teen Magazines." *Youth and Society* 29 (1998): 369–389.

Evans, Ellis D., Judith Rutberg, Carmela Sather, and Charli Turner. "Content Analysis of Contemporary Teen Magazines for Adolescent Females." *Youth and Society* 23 (1991): 99–120.

Faludi, Susan. *Backlash: The Undeclared War against Women.* New York: Doubleday Books, 1991.

Fine, Michelle. *Disruptive Voices: The Possibilities of Feminist Research.* Ann Arbor: University of Michigan Press, 1992.

Foreyt, James. "Psychological Correlates of Weight Fluctuation." *International Journal of Eating Disorders* 17 (1995): 263–275.

Fredrickson, Barbara, and Tomi-Ann Roberts. "Objectification Theory: Toward Understanding Women's Lived Experiences and Mental Health Risks." *Psychology of Women Quarterly* 21 (1997): 173–206.

Garner, David. "The 1997 Body Image Survey Results: An In-Depth Look at How We See Ourselves." *Psychology Today* Feb. 1997: 30–44, 75–84.

Guillen, Eileen O., and Susan I. Barr. "Nutrition, Dieting, and Fitness Messages in a Magazine for Adolescent Women, 1970–1990." *Journal of Adolescent Health* 15 (1994): 464–472.

Harter, Stephanie. "The Determinants and Mediational Role of Global Self-Worth in Children." *Contemporary Issues in Developmental Psychology.* Ed. Nancy Eisenberg. New York: John Wiley and Sons, 1987. 18–72.

Lorde, Audre. *Sister Outsider: Essays and Speeches*. Trumansburg, NY: Crossing Press, 1984.

Martin, Mary C., and Patricia Kennedy. "Advertising and Social Comparison: Consequences for Female Preadolescents and Adolescents." *Psychology and Marketing* 10 (1993): 513–530.

Myers, Phillip N., and Frank Biocca. "The Elastic Body Image: The Effect of Television Advertising and Programming on Body Image Distortions in Young Women." *Journal of Communication* 42 (1992): 108–136.

Nadelson, Robert. "Marilyn Monroe: Was She Really a Size 16?" *Style Magazine* Sept. 1995: 88–91.

Orbach, Susie. *Fat Is a Feminist Issue*. New York: Berkeley Books, 1978.

Peirce, Kate. "A Feminist Theoretical Perspective on the Socialization of Teenage Girls through *Seventeen* Magazine." *Sex Roles* 23 (1990): 491–500.

Perimenis, Louisa. "The Ritual of Anorexia Nervosa in Cultural Context." *Journal of American Culture* 14 (1991): 49–59.

Sadker, Myra, and David Sadker. *Failing at Fairness: How Our Schools Cheat Girls*. New York: Touchstone/Simon and Schuster, 1994.

Contributors

Amy Aidman is a Research Associate at the ERIC Clearinghouse on Elementary and Early Childhood Education. Her areas of interest include mass media and children, media literacy, and the social impact of communications technologies. She has lectured and taught courses on these topics in the U.S. and Israel.

Mary K. Bentley is an Assistant Professor in the Department of Health Promotion and Human Movement at Ithaca College where she teaches courses in wellness, community health, family health and human sexuality. She has published articles in the *Journal of Health Education* and contributed book chapters on HIV education, and critical pedagogy. She is currently completing a video documentary from filmed interactions with youth in detention facilities titled "Ya Know What I'm Saying?"

Amy Bowles-Reyer received her M.A. in African American Studies at Yale University (1992) and her Ph.D. in American Studies at George Washington University (1998). She currently is working on revising and publishing her dissertation, "Our Secret Garden: How Judy Blume Sexually Educated a Generation," and on formulating her next book about the revolutionary power of female sexuality. She lives in Bethesda, MD with her husband, Adam, and son, Elias.

Rhiannon S. Bettivia attends Central High School in Champaign, Illinois where she is enrolled in tenth grade. In addition to this chapter she has co-authored two others with Angharad N. Valdivia. She also plays the clarinet, saxophone, and piano, paints, and listens to music in her spare time.

Meenakshi Gigi Durham is an Assistant Professor in the Department of Journalism at the University of Texas at Austin. Her research interests involve critical studies of gender, race and ethnicity in mass media. She is currently at work on an ethnographic project focusing on adolescent girls' use of mass media in peer group interactions. Her article "Dilemmas of Desire: Representations of Adolescent Sexuality in Two Teen Magazines" appears in a recent issue of *Youth and Society*. In addition, her work has appeared in *Communication Theory*, the *Journal of Communication Inquiry*, and other scholarly journals.

Zillah Eisenstein is the mother of Sarah Eisenstein Stumbar and Professor of Politics at Ithaca College. Her most recent books are *The Color of Gender* (University of California Press, 1994), *HATREDS: Sexualized and Racialized Conflicts in the 21st Century* (Routledge, 1996), and *Global Obscenities* (New York University Press, 1998).

Carol Jennings manages the Professional Production Unit of the Roy H. Park School of Communications at Ithaca College where she also teaches in the Department of Cinema and Photography. She is a filmmaker whose short films and documentaries have screened at festivals in Oberhausen, Poitiers, Madrid, Rome, Montreal, Los Angeles, Boston, New York and on Showtime Network.

Sharon R. Mazzarella is Associate Professor in the Department of Television and Radio at Ithaca College where she teaches courses in youth culture, media effects and research methods. Her research focuses on youth culture and mass media. She has published articles in *Popular Music and Society*, the *Journal of Broadcasting & Electronic Media*, and *Communication Research*, and currently is writing a book on media framing of "Generation X."

Debra Merskin is an Assistant Professor at the University of Oregon, School of Journalism & Communication. She has a professional background in advertising and her research involves how women and minorities use, and are represented in, mass media. In 1997 she received the Marshall Award for Innovative Teaching. Her publications include a chapter in *Dressing in Feathers* (S. Elizabeth Bird, ed.) called "What Does One Look Like?" In addition, her published work can be found in *Journalism & Mass Communication Quarterly*, the *Journal of Communication Inquiry*, and *Journalism Educator*.

Norma Pecora is an Assistant Professor at Ohio University, School of Telecommunications. Her teaching and research interests are in the area of children and popular culture, issues of gender, media research and theory, and media economics. Her most recent work is a book titled, *The Business of Children's Entertainment* (Guilford Press, 1997).

Caitlin Rakow is a sixth grader in the Grand Forks, North Dakota public school system. She likes the movie *Titanic* but does not like piano lessons or Barbies. She has a two-year-old brother who is benefiting from her approach to gender.

Lana Rakow is a Professor of Communication at the University of North Dakota, and has served in several administrative capacities at the University of North Dakota and the University of Wisconsin-Parkside. She is the author and editor of three books and numerous book chapters and journal articles on gender and communication and on curriculum and administrative reform. Her book, *Gender on Line: Women, the Telephone, and Community Live* (University of Illinois Press, 1992) was awarded the 1993 Book of the Year by the Organization for the Study of Communication, Language and Gender. She was the 1997 Spotlight Scholar of the National Communication Association's Feminist and Women Studies Division.

Sarah Eisenstein Stumbar is thirteen years old and a student at Ithaca High School, Ithaca, New York. She was a delegate to the First National Girl's Conference at the United Nations in 1997. She is the author of several short stories about girls across the globe which are published in *Stone Soup* and *Skipping Stones*. She also has compiled an annotated bibliography of more than 100 books about children in hiding during World War II.

Angharad N. Valdivia is a Research Associate Professor at the Institute of Communications Research, University of Illinois. Her main areas of interest are gender, popular culture, and Latin America or US Latina/Latino Studies. She is the editor of *Feminism, Multiculturalism and the Media: Global Diversities* (Sage, 1995) and of the forthcoming Culture and Communication section of the *Global Women's Encyclopedia*. She has just finished a book titled *Gendered Identities and Media Culture: Essays in Multiculturalism* (University of

Arizona Press, forthcoming) and published in numerous journals including the *Journal of Communication*, the *Journal of International Communication*, *Camera Obscura*, the *Journal of Inclusive Education*, and *Cultural Studies Review*.

AC Adolescent
Cultures,
SS School &
Society

General Editors: Joseph & Linda DeVitis

As schools struggle to redefine and restructure themselves, they need to be cognizant of the new realities of adolescents. Thus, this series of monographs and textbooks is committed to depicting the variety of adolescent cultures that exist in today's post-industrial societies. It is intended to be a primarily qualitative research, practice, and policy series devoted to contextual interpretation and analysis that encompasses a broad range of interdisciplinary critique. In addition, this series will seek to provide a pragmatic, pro-active response to the current backlash of conservatism that continues to dominate political discourse, practice, and policy. This series seeks to address issues of curriculum theory and practice; multicultural education; aggression and violence; the media and arts; school dropouts; homeless and runaway youth; alienated youth; at-risk adolescent populations; family structures and parental involvement; and race, ethnicity, class, and gender studies.

Send proposals and manuscripts to the General Editors at:

Joseph & Linda DeVitis
Binghamton University
Dept. of Education & Human Development
Binghamton, NY 13902

To order other books in this series, please contact our Customer Service Department at:

(800) 770-LANG (within the U.S.)
(212) 647-7706 (outside the U.S.)
(212) 647-7707 FAX

or browse online by series at:

WWW.PETERLANG.COM